PSYCHO–CYBERNETICS 2000

bobbe sommer, ph.d.
with mark falstein

with forewords by

david barone, ph.d.
president, MAXWELL MALTZ psycho-cybernetics foundation, and

anna harabin maltz

Prentice-Hall International (UK) Limited, *London*
Prentice-Hall of Australia, Pty. Limited, *Sydney*
Prentice-Hall of Canada, Inc., *Toronto*
Prentice-Hall Hispanoamericana, S.A., *Mexico*
Prentice-Hall of India Private Limited, *New Delhi*
Prentice-Hall of Japan, Inc., *Tokyo*
Simon & Schuster Asia Pte. Ltd., *Singapore*
Editora Prentice-Hall do Brasil, Ltda., *Rio de Janeiro*

© 1993 *by*

Maxwell Maltz
Psycho-Cybernetics Foundation, Inc.

10 9 8 7 6 5 4 3

Library of Congress Cataloging-in-Publication Data

Sommer, Bobbe L.
  Psycho-cybernetics 2000 / by Bobbe Sommer with Mark Falstein.
    p.   cm.
  Includes bibliographical references and index.
  ISBN 0-13-735895-4   ISBN 0-13-735903-9 (book and cassette)
  1. Success—Psychological aspects. I. Falstein, Mark. II. Title.
  BF637.S8S644 1993
  185'.1—dc20   93-4255
                                                 CIP

ISBN 0-13-735895-4

ISBN 0-13-735903-9 PKG

PRENTICE HALL
Career and Personal Development
Englewood Cliffs, NJ 07632

Simon & Schuster, A Paramount Communications Company

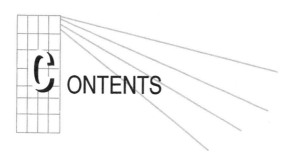

CONTENTS

CONTENTS

CONTENTS

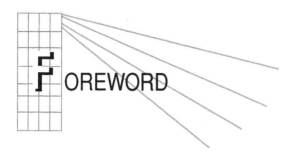

FOREWORD

David Barone, Ph.D.
Associate Professor of Psychology, Nova University
President, Maxwell Maltz Psycho-Cybernetics Foundation

It is a pleasure to introduce *Psycho-Cybernetics 2000*. The Maltz Foundation is responsible for overseeing the legacy of Dr. Maxwell Maltz, and we are confident that this book will contribute to that legacy. Although Dr. Maltz was not a psychologist or psychotherapist by training, he cared deeply about his patients' recovery in his practice as a plastic surgeon. At a time when mental-health professionals were wed to the Freudian model which downgraded people's control over their lives, Dr. Maltz put together some of the best formulations ever on how people can improve themselves. Today professionals have moved in the direction Dr. Maltz advocated: self-image, self-realization, biofeedback, positive self-talk, and imaginative exercises are central to how we think about psychological improvement, whether self- or therapist-directed. As a professional research psychologist, I can assure you that the ideas and techniques you will be reading about are consistent with current professional theory and practice.

Updating Dr. Maltz's message is Dr. Bobbe Sommer. She has dealt with issues of self-improvement in depth with her psychotherapy clients and more generically with her thousands of workshop participants. She knows what people's concerns are, and (like Dr. Maltz) she's a great communicator. The cases she offers from her psychotherapy practice should speak cogently to a wide range of readers' concerns. The exercises she provides should be as effective for her readers as they have been with her clients and audiences.

This project has other essential participants. Mark Falstein is a gifted writer, and his efforts to make this book as readable as it is can be found on every page. We had to pull him away from working on his novel, but our gain should result in only a temporary delay to literature. It was our good fortune to work under the editorial direction of Ellen Schneid Coleman, Senior Editor at Simon & Schuster. Thanks to her guidance, this project was launched and has stayed on target with clear language and a presentation to sustain readers' interest.

Finally, I would like to pay tribute to Anna Harabin Maltz, who made it all possible by donating the rights to her late husband's works to start the Maltz Foundation. She read the manuscript of *Psycho-Cybernetics 2000* with great joy, enthusiastically contributing a Foreword, which follows. Sadly, Mrs. Maltz died on March 16, 1993. Her long and full life ended secure in the knowledge that she had successfully passed the torch from Dr. Maltz to the Foundation and that the Psycho-Cybernetics message would live on.

The final part of the project rests with you, the reader. As you read this book, if you are connecting with us and Dr. Maltz and the shared human project of self-realization, and if you put its exercises and lessons into practice in your life, then our message will be accomplished. May you be one of millions of a new generation entering a new century with Psycho-Cybernetics as an inspiration and guide. Happy reading, conscientious exercising, and more successful living!

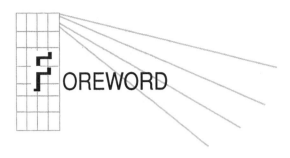

FOREWORD

Anna Harabin Maltz

In 1960, Dr. Maltz introduced his great concept of Psycho-Cybernetics to the world. Since then over 30 million people have purchased the book, with possibly twice that number reading it.

As a plastic surgeon he was most interested in helping people give themselves emotional facelifts. His powerful message touched their lives like a magic scalpel. He gave people a road map to take them from darkness to light. From despair into happiness. From hopelessness to zestfulness.

He dreamed that his message would live on long after him. And it has. It has because his concepts of goal achievement and personal fulfillment are timeless—as truth always is.

Because of his dream, I am delighted to introduce this new work, *Psycho-Cybernetics 2000*.

It is my sincere hope that this book will help you to have renewed vision, confidence, and energy as you turn your face to the future.

ACKNOWLEDGMENTS

Grateful acknowledgment is offered for use of the following material:

Concepts introduced in *Not Another Diet Book*, By Bobbe Sommer. Copyright © 1987 by Hunter House, Inc., Publishers. Used by permission of the publisher.

Excerpt from *Revolution From Within: A Book of Self-Esteem*. Copyright © 1992 by Gloria Steinem. By courtesy of the publisher, Little, Brown & Company.

Concepts introduced in *The Unfair Advantage*. Copyright © 1986 by Tom Miller. By permission of the author.

Excerpt from *The Sky's The Limit*. Copyright © 1980 by Wayne W. Dyer. Reprinted by permission of Simon & Schuster, Inc.

Excerpts and paraphrases from *The Right-Brain Experience*, by Marilee Zdenek. Copyright © 1983 by Marilee Zdenek. By permission of the publisher, McGraw-Hill, Inc.

Excerpt from *Honoring the Self*, by Nathaniel Branden. Copyright © 1988 by Nathaniel Branden. Used by permission of Dell Books, a division of Bantam Doubleday Dell Publishing Group, Inc.

Excerpt from *Superlearning* by Sheila Ostrander, Nancy Ostrander & L. Schroeder. Copyright © 1979 by Sheila Ostrander, Nancy Ostrander & Lynn Schroeder. Used by permission of Dell

Books, a division of Bantam Doubleday Dell Publishing Group, Inc.

Excerpt from *The Twenty Minute Break,* by Ernest Rossi with David Nimmons. Copyright © 1991. Jeremy P. Tarcher, Inc., Los Angeles, CA. By permission of St. Martin's Press, Inc.

"Six On-the-Job Stress Reducers" from *Whole Brain Thinking* by Jacqueline Wonder and Priscilla Donovan. Copyright © 1984 by Jacqueline Wonder and Priscilla Donovan. By permission of William Morrow & Company, Inc.

Excerpt from *Metamedicine,* by Vida C. Baron. Copyright © 1990 by Vida C. Baron. By permission of Barez Publishing, Inc.

Excerpt from *See You At The Top,* by Zig Ziglar. Copyright © 1974 by Zig Ziglar. By permission of Pelican Publishing Company.

Excerpt from *They Shoot Managers, Don't They?* by Terry L. Paulson. Copyright © 1988 by Lee Canter & Associates, Inc. By permission of the publisher.

Excerpt from *Self-Esteem: Paradoxes and Innovations in Clinical Theory and Practice,* by Richard Bendar, M. Gawain Wells, and Scott R. Peterson. Copyright © 1989 by the American Psychological Association. By permission of the publisher.

Excerpt from *Learned Optimism,* by Martin E. P. Seligman. Copyright © 1990 by Martin E. P. Seligman. By courtesy of the publisher, Random House, Inc.

Excerpt from *Megatrends 2000* by John Naisbitt and Patricia Aburdene. Copyright © 1990 by Megatrends Ltd. By permission of William Morrow & Company, Inc.

All attributions to Maxwell Maltz, M.D., F.I.C.S., are from *Psycho-Cybernetics,* © 1960 by Prentice Hall, Inc.

Mandala designed and executed by Clement Designs, San Francisco, California

HOW THIS BOOK CAN TRANSFORM YOUR LIFE

Psycho-Cybernetics, Dr. Maxwell Maltz's celebrated program for personal fulfillment through self-image enhancement, has been the cornerstone of my work as a psychotherapist and lecturer for more than 20 years. In my classes and seminars, and in my clinical practice and international speaking tours, I am frequently quoting Dr. Maltz and referring to his landmark theories. Did I say quoting? I meant proselytizing. *These ideas work.* It is your self-image that sets the limits for what you can and cannot achieve—"the area of the possible," as Maltz called it. By expanding your self-image, you expand the limits of your talents and capabilities. It's that simple. Millions of people have used the program Maltz set forth in his best-seller, *Psycho-Cybernetics* (Prentice Hall, 1960) to turn disappointment and failure into happiness and success.

Tinkering with the work of a legend is a heady experience. It's not every disciple who gets the chance to build on the work of the master. I was flattered and delighted when the Maxwell Maltz Psycho-Cybernetics Foundation asked me to spearhead their update of Maltz's program for today's readers. Flattered because their request certified me as an expert in the field of self-image psychology in general and on Dr. Maltz's contributions in particular. Delighted because I was being offered the chance to reinterpret Maltz's ideas to a new generation—to guide you in taking control of your life without the need for expensive "self-actualization" seminars or psychotherapy.

This book is your seminar. *You* are your own therapist. By applying this simple, pragmatic program, you can empower yourself to

- Deprogram yourself from self-doubt and negative self-evaluations
- Expand the scope of your personal and professional goals
- Increase your earning potential
- Achieve a happier, healthier love life
- Overcome procrastination, excessive inhibition and irrational fears
- Become more assertive in personal and work-related situations
- Build into your personality the elements that lead to success
- Create an ideal job for yourself
- Overcome your resistance to change
- Reduce the level of stress in your life
- Transform your dreams into action plans for self-fulfillment
- Effectively challenge such habits as smoking, eating disorders and aggressive behavior
- Cast off the scars of old emotional wounds

. . . in general, to become a person who *acts* instead of one who just reacts—to live your life according to your own plan.

⊞ How Psycho-Cybernetics Transformed My Life

I was introduced to Psycho-Cybernetics as a graduate student. A friend of mine offered me a ticket to a lecture Dr. Maltz was giving in Los Angeles. At first I was hesitant. I had heard of Maxwell Maltz, but I knew little of his ideas. I had a vague notion that he was one of those self-appointed prophets who claimed to have solved the problems of the universe, and I'd heard enough false prophets by then to be wary of yet another. On the other hand, a free ticket was a free ticket. And as a result of that lecture, my life was transformed.

This is not an empty cliché or an exaggeration. My life was not merely "changed." I experienced a fundamental shift in its direction and purpose. Listening to Dr. Maltz, I realized for the first time that I had made few real choices about my life. Most of what I had thought had been "my" choices had actually been made by others—"for my own good," to be sure, but they had not been mine. I can remember sitting in that auditorium feeling that the time had come to take control of my own life. I found myself asking questions like: What did I want from life? What was I willing to give in return? What did I want the focus of my life to be? How had my childhood impacted my life as an adult? What were my goals? How effectively was I using my imagination and creativity?

I bought a copy of *Psycho-Cybernetics*. From the first pages, what impressed me about Maxwell Maltz was that the man made *sense*. I was working on a degree in psychology; I was evaluating theories of the personality by the truckload. This was the 1960s. There were all kinds of gurus out there, every one of them eager to teach us how to realize our "human potential." We could go to Esalen for a touchy-feely encounter group with Billy Schutz. We could scream at an empty chair under the guidance of Fritz Perls. We could take a trip on LSD with Timothy Leary. In contrast to these exotic pathways to self-awareness, here was Maxwell Maltz with his common-sense approach.

Dr. Maltz became my mentor, and I became his ardent disciple. I still have my old dog-eared copy of *Psycho-Cybernetics*. I memorized entire passages. I remember sitting on the patio of my home and writing down goals that summer while my children were playing. Other people began to notice my transformation. Friends remarked that I was not only more determined than before but more relaxed and at ease with myself and with others as well. My husband commented that I seemed more patient with our three young sons; "I haven't seen you lose your famous temper in weeks," he said. These were areas of personal development that I had worked on diligently for months without success. I had repeatedly applied willpower ("I will not lose my temper") and positive thinking ("I am a calm, patient person"), only to let frustration and anger get the better of me every time. Now, increment by increment, Maltz's exercises and affirmations were taking effect—and almost without effort on my part. As if by magic, I was growing into my own life's goals. There were no fireworks, only a steadily increasing flow of positive feelings about myself and the direction of my life. Psycho-Cybernetics was leading me to restructure my life, as it has millions of others. It felt wonderful to know that I was at last taking control of my life.

⊞ *Psycho-Cybernetics 2000:* Not a Revision but a Revitalization

So, I hear you asking, if the original idea was so good, why are you tinkering with it? It's a valid question. To paraphrase Henry Ford's famous aphorism, if it ain't broke, why are you fixing it?

In fact, I'm not. Before I even switched on my word processor, I realized that what was required was not a revision of *Psycho-Cybernetics* but a revitalization. Instead of modifying Dr. Maltz's theories, I would bring them forward into the future. Instead of taking a historical approach to the program he introduced, I would have to take a teleological approach.

Teleology is a prominent concept in Psycho-Cybernetics. The word implies purpose, design, goal-centeredness. Dr. Maltz used it to describe the way the human mind works. By focusing on a goal to be achieved, we respond to feedback by making course corrections, always targeting on the goal.

Goal-centeredness is also the concept behind this revitalization of Dr. Maltz's theories. We'll consider the skills and qualities that will fuel success and happiness in the coming years, revitalizing Maltz's ideas with new input to meet the challenge of life in the year 2000 and beyond. By doing so we add vigor to his original program without altering any of the concepts that made it such a potent force.

Psycho-Cybernetics was published in 1960. The ideas set forth in the book were developed by Dr. Maltz in the 1940s and 1950s. Although they are still valid today, their frame of reference is of another era. Think of just a few of the changes that have taken place since then:

New information, new insights. For starters, according to Richard Wurman in *Information Anxiety,* humankind has accumulated more new information since 1960 than in the previous 5,000 years. This new information allows us to approach Maltz's program with a far deeper level of understanding than was possible in 1960. *Psycho-Cybernetics 2000* incorporates recent breakthroughs in psychology, information technology, the physiology of the brain and other sciences to more precisely focus the process of transforming your self-image.

The sexes. Or, consider the status of women. *Psycho-Cybernetics* is filled with quotes from business executives, athletes and other role models of the 1950s; and virtually every one of them is male. The case studies Maltz chose to illustrate his ideas also involved men almost exclusively. The few references to women nearly all cast them in the role of housewife and mother. This is not an indictment of Maxwell Maltz as "sexist" (nor for that matter a belittlement of homemaking), it is only an indication that his times were not ours. More than two-thirds of the new jobs created in the United States over the past two decades have been filled by women. In 1960 it was rare to find women in leadership roles. As we approach the millenium, it is becoming increasingly more common, and to anyone born since 1960, there is nothing remarkable about it. Many women today are having to meet two mandates at once; to be an effective professional and an effective wife and mother, a double whammy that can put unbearable strain on a woman's image of herself. These changes and others require an updated approach to Psycho-Cybernetics, one that reflects the goals and concerns of both sexes in today's world.

"So how's the family?" While Maltz recognized that the self-image is largely formed in early childhood, no one in 1960 had

ever heard of "dysfunctional families" or "the inner child." It would be unjustifiable today to consider your self-image without paying considerable attention to the early influence of family and peers. This is *not* to imply that "everything is Mother's fault"—or Father's, or Big Brother's. Psycho-Cybernetics is not about assigning blame for the past; it's about building a plan for the future. But as I, myself, discovered, feelings of inadequacy and unfulfillment are often the result of subconsciously following a plan that someone else scripted for you years ago. *Psycho-Cybernetics 2000* will guide you in recognizing how your family of origin conditioned your present self-image and your goals, the more easily to challenge their limitations and formulate your own plan for success.

The workplace. Then there is the economic environment to consider. New technologies, new corporate cultures, the maturing of the "baby boomers," multinationalization, the obsolescence of certain careers and the emergence of new ones are all delivering hammer blows to the self-concept of workers in offices, workshops, factories, and boardrooms (not to mention unemployment lines). On the plus side, these changes have made available a cornucopia of new opportunities to anyone whose self-image is healthy enough to accommodate them. In this book I'll show you ways to preserve and enhance your self-image as you meet the challenge of these changes, and I'll present new models for success that reflect the workplace of today and tomorrow.

Psycho-Cybernetics 2000 considers these issues and many others in showing you how to reshape yourself for success. You'll learn how people very much like yourself have successfully used the ideas and techniques of Psycho-Cybernetics. (All the case studies presented in this book represent real individuals or composites; names and other particulars have been changed.) These examples illustrate how *you* can find solutions to specific problems, among them:

- How to overcome habits of shyness and self-consciousness that may be keeping you from achieving a loving relationship.
- How to develop feelings of competence and confidence about learning new job skills.

- How to be assertive with an abusive family member or coworker.
- How to avoid feeling fearful in situations that pose no actual threat.
- How to maintain your "ideal weight" and get off the binge-diet cycle.
- How to cope successfully with severe emotional blows.
- How to develop more effective parenting skills.
- How to determine what personal and career goals are right for you.
- How to develop and stay with an action plan for achieving your goals.
- How to avoid becoming discouraged while pursuing your goals.
- How to manage your time more efficiently.
- How to anticipate and prepare for career changes.
- How to upgrade mutual understanding in interpersonal relationships.
- How to develop the courage to take risks.
- How to accept yourself nonjudgmentally.
- How to cope with new responsibilities without feeling overwhelmed.
- How to recognize and correct aggressive behavior.
- How to break the hold of self-destructive feelings of resentment.
- How to respond constructively to negative criticism.
- How to keep negative thoughts from eroding your self-esteem.

How to *Use* This Book Instead of Just Reading It

Like Maltz's own books, *Psycho-Cybernetics 2000* has been designed not only to be read but to be experienced. As you read each chapter, activate your imagination. Review the key points highlighted in the *Targeting on Ideas* section at the end of each chapter. Jot down your summation of points particularly pertinent to you under *Set Your Own Targets*. Fill in the checklists and questionnaires you'll find throughout the book and use your answers as guideposts as you work your way through the Psycho-Cybernetics program.

Six Weeks to a New Self-Image

Above all, practice the techniques and exercises. They are easy to do, but they must be done regularly if they are going to work. Don't let yourself become discouraged if nothing happens right away. A negative self-image is nothing but a bad habit, and my experience has taught me that it takes about six weeks to break an old habit. (Six weeks is just an average—some habits may take you 10 days or less to break, while others may take as long as several months.) During this time don't be surprised if you feel a little "unnatural," a little self-conscious as you begin to change your self-image. Don't try to measure changes, rationalize what you're doing, or ask yourself, "Is this really working?" Just follow the advice I give in my seminars, "Fake it till you make it." At first you may only be "acting as if " you were feeling good about yourself. Give it six weeks and you'll feel that a miracle has taken place.

Try something right now: Clasp your hands together with the fingers interlaced. Which thumb rests on top, the left or the right? Whichever it is doesn't matter. The point is that it was an *unconscious* act; a habit. Chances are, whenever you clasp your hands and interlace your fingers the same thumb is always on top. Now reclasp your hands the other way, so that the other thumb is resting on top. How does it feel? Uncomfortable, right? Because you made it a *conscious* act. You thought about it before you did it. Yet if you were to practice clasping your hands this way for a few weeks, it would feel just as natural as the other way. I'm talking about something this simple when I ask you to reserve judgment for six weeks.

Those of you who have read Maxwell Maltz's books and have been influenced by the principles of Psycho-Cybernetics will already be convinced of the effectiveness of these ideas and methods. For you this book will be a postgraduate seminar, a refresher course, a facelift for your self-image as you prepare to enter the twenty-first century. Enhancing your self-image is a process that can continue throughout your lifetime.

As for the millions of young people who may never have heard of Maxwell Maltz because his books came on the scene before they did, or who may have dismissed his ideas because they seemed "dated," this book can be your key to a fulfilling life. It is to this new generation that I dedicate *Psycho-Cybernetics 2000*. It is to you that I offer the challenge of opening yourself to your own imagination and inner qualities. You are indeed the future, and it is my pleasure to be able to awaken you to these opportunities.

—**Bobbe Sommer, Ph.D., 1993**

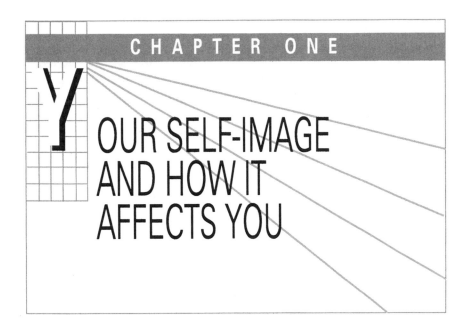

CHAPTER ONE

YOUR SELF-IMAGE AND HOW IT AFFECTS YOU

The significance of the self-image has been around for more than a decade. Yet there has been little written about it. Curiously enough, this is not because "self-image psychology" has not worked, but because it has worked so amazingly well. As one of my colleagues expressed it, "I am reluctant to publish my findings...because if I presented some of my case histories and described the rather amazing and spectacular improvements in personality, I would be accused of exaggerating, or trying to start a cult, or both."

—*Maxwell Maltz*, Psycho-Cybernetics *(1960)*

Self-esteem is the likeliest candidate for a *social vaccine,* something that empowers us to live responsibly and that inoculates us against the lure of crime, violence, substance abuse, teen pregnancy, child abuse, chronic welfare dependency, and educational failure. The lack of self-esteem is central to most personal and social ills plaguing our state and nation as we approach the end of the twentieth century.

—*California Task Force to Promote Self-Esteem and Personal and Social Responsibility,*
Toward A State Of Esteem *(1990)*

1

Consider the case of a man I'll call John: 28 years old, unmarried, lonely and unhappy, eager to meet a woman with whom he could have a satisfying and lasting relationship. John was always attending singles parties, structured outings and other such events hoping to meet the elusive "Ms. Right." But when he thought about actually talking to a woman at one of these functions, he was terrified. He believed that every woman in the world was going to reject him. Each time he thought about introducing himself, he would think something like, "Wow, there's a really beautiful woman over there. I'd sure like to meet her. But she's so good looking, she probably won't give me the time of day. In fact, I'm sure she's not going to like me. If I try to talk to her, she'll reject me and I'll only feel worse. I'll be better off if I just stay here and drink my beer and leave well enough alone."

John had had such negative experiences in the past—ever since junior high school, where he was labeled a "geek," a "nerd," or whatever such cruel term was then current to describe the socially awkward. The breakup of a relationship six years before had reinforced this image of himself. On those rare occasions when he actually worked up enough self-confidence to approach a woman, sure enough, he would fail.

Or, consider the case of a woman I'll call Laura: 42 years old, divorced, two children. Laura was convinced that she was stupid—despite a master's degree, near-professional competence as a violinist, and fluency in four languages. As a young child she was slighted by her parents in favor of an older sister and younger brother. Their talents were encouraged while hers were ignored or dismissed. Her father addressed her so frequently as "Laura, damn it" that as a toddler she thought it was her name—her best friend was "Mary Ann"; she was "Laura Dammit." All through school she explained away her good grades by saying, "Oh well, I studied hard." She dropped out of graduate school after being reprimanded by a professor for neglecting her work in her degree area—sociology—to take more language courses. Since then she has had a series of low-end office jobs, always backing away from anything more challenging or failing whenever her boss gave her increased responsibilities. Recently she has found even the office jobs harder to come by. They all require computer skills, and Laura "knows" she is too stupid to learn to use a high-tech machine.

Self-Image: The Key to Your Personality

Every one of us always acts, feels, and behaves in a way that is consistent with our self-image—regardless of the reality of that image.

It is very important to understand this. Neither John's feeling that no woman could find him attractive nor Laura's conviction that she was stupid had anything to do with reality. They were entirely the product of the images they carried of themselves. Everyone has read stories about people suffering from anorexia nervosa—people who have become so convinced they are overweight that they starve themselves into emaciation. So it was with John. So it was with Laura.

So it may be with you.

"Whether we realize it or not," Maltz wrote, "each of us carries...a mental blueprint or picture of ourselves. It may be vague and ill-defined to our conscious gaze. In fact, it may not be consciously recognizable at all. But it is there, complete down to the last detail. This self-image is our own conception of the 'sort of person I am.' It has been built up from our own *beliefs* about ourselves. But most of these beliefs . . . have been formed from our past experiences, our successes and our failures . . . and the way people have reacted to us . . . . Once an idea or belief about ourselves goes into this picture it becomes "true," as far as we personally are concerned. We do not question its validity, but proceed to act upon it *just as if it were true."*

We all know how easy it is to identify with our disappointments and failures. Maltz called it the *destructive instinct.* Instead of telling ourselves, "I failed to get that job I wanted," we conclude, "I'm a failure." Instead of thinking, "That relationship just didn't work out," we say to ourselves, "Who would want me?" Every one of us is familiar with the inner voice that tells us, "I'm not good enough." As a result of such negative self-reinforcement, we become trapped behind walls of fear, anxiety, guilt, self-condemnation and self-hate. We have no idea how we got there (other than "I'm no good") and no clue as to how to tunnel our way out.

So at the outset, please take a moment to internalize this thought: *It doesn't have to be that way.*

It is our self-image that prescribes our limits. And achieving a positive self-image—the *life instinct,* rather than the destructive instinct—is within the capability of every man, woman, and child.

Psycho-Cybernetics: Your Mind and Its Automatic Guidance System

Maxwell Maltz was not a psychologist by training. He was a medical doctor, a plastic surgeon. During his years of practice, he had noticed that most patients he treated for severe facial disfigurement exhibited profound personality changes within weeks after their operation. Their growing self-esteem and self-confidence seemed to reflect their new outward appearance. It was as though changing the face had reconstructed the psyche as well. But in some cases surgery failed to effect any such changes. The patient continued to feel "inadequate," "inferior", or "ugly." In a few cases, the patient would look in a mirror and insist that the surgery had made no change whatever.

This observation convinced Maltz that it was not the surgery itself that caused the personality changes. Rather, the facial reconstruction sometimes brought about the renewal of some inner quality as well. He concluded that this inner quality was the self-image. If plastic surgery changed a person's mental and spiritual self-concept, the personality was changed as well. If there was no change in the self-image, the patient continued to feel ugly and inadequate.

The idea that the self-image is the key to our psychology had been around since the 1930s. But no one had ever answered the question of *how* the self-image creates personality. Maltz found an answer in the science of cybernetics. This word was coined in 1948 by Dr. Norbert Wiener, a mathematician and computer scientist. It comes from a Greek word meaning a ship's steersman and refers to the operation of an automatic guidance system, or *servomechanism*. Maltz determined that the human brain and nervous system function as a kind of servomechanism, a goal-seeking device like those used to guide airplanes on automatic pilot. This is why he called his central idea *Psycho-Cybernetics*: the science of cybernetics as applied to the human mind. The self-image, Maltz maintained, is the key element that determines whether our internal guidance system functions for success or for failure. It defines the size and scope of the targets our goal-seeking device has to shoot for—"the area of the possible."

You Have the Power to Create Change

The power of this idea lies in the notion that *each of us is capable of taking control of our self-image and programming our automatic guidance system for success*. When Maltz first proposed this revolutionary idea, the psychology "establishment" had two fundamental and opposing ways of regarding personality. On the one hand, there were the psychoanalysts who maintained that personality was formed in the unconscious mind and could not be addressed by conscious effort. On the other were the behaviorists, who asserted that the unconscious was irrelevant and that only observable behavior could be addressed. Both approaches disempowered the individual, relegating personality to something determined by biology or culture. On the left, Oedipus and his mother. On the right, rats in mazes.

Self-image psychology filled a great deal of the space left vacant by the other two systems. To the behaviorists' contention that only observable behavior was relevant, Maltz responded that all behavior—all actions, all feelings, all human capabilities—was defined by the self-image. *No real behavioral changes could take place unless the self-image was changed*. To the analyst who spent five years exploring a patient's hang-ups from all angles, Maltz countered that the *causes* of a negative self-image didn't matter. *Anyone could start a new and self-fulfilling life by changing his self-image*.

Maltz presented this idea in a clear and personally reassuring way. His simple, step-by-step "how-to" model for creating and maintaining a new self-image went something like this:

- Understand the role imagination plays in self-perception
- Use your imagination to create images of success
- Identify, confront and cast off false beliefs that provide negative targets for your internal guidance system
- Decondition yourself from stressful emotional responses that prevent your internal guidance system from working effectively
- Set specific goals of success for your internal guidance system
- Cultivate specific aspects of personality that lead to success
- Use your negative experiences as feedback to correct your course toward your goal
- Remove the emotional scars that inhibit your personality
- Deflect assaults on your self-esteem by responding appropriately and creatively to emotional pressures
- Build feelings of success into your personality

Self-Image: The Key to a Better Life

The idea that self-image is the key to human personality and behavior may have been a radical one in Maltz's day, but no longer. Building an adequate self-image is recognized today as a necessary strategy in the empowerment of individuals and a promising step toward the correction of social ills. Government and private institutions across the United States and around the world have acknowledged the role of individual self-esteem in the major concerns of our time. In 1986 the state of California appointed a committee of psychologists, medical doctors, educators, child-development specialists, and other professionals—"the California Task Force to Promote Self-Esteem and Personal and Social Responsibility"—to create a new approach to problem solving, "a work plan and a call to action." The definition of self-esteem they adopted as the basis of their report—"Appreciating my own worth and importance and having the character to be accountable for myself and to act responsibly toward others"—was essentially the same as the one Maltz had proposed 30 years before.

In an address to his people on New Year's Day, 1990, Czechoslovakian president Vaclav Havel equated national and personal insecurity with political repression. "Only a person or a nation self-confident in the best sense of the word," he said, "is capable of listening to the voice of others and accepting them as equal to oneself. Let us try to introduce self-confidence into the life of our community and into the conduct of nations."

The business community too has accepted the idea. The modern corporate environment has undergone a dramatic shift away from management-for-control. Instead, the emphasis is on a style of leadership tailored to bring out the best in people by furthering their self-esteem. Business leaders have come increasingly to recognize that while capital and technology are important resources, it is people that make or break a company.

In *The One-Minute Manager* Ken Blanchard and Spencer Johnson urged executives to "catch people in the act of doing something right."

In *They Shoot Managers, Don't They?* Terry Paulson pointed out that, "The winner is the man or woman who does not personalize poor results. Such a person can be disappointed without feeling like a failure."

Even social activists, who once saw political and economic action as the only solutions to such problems as poverty, racism, drug abuse, and domestic violence, have recognized that individual self-esteem can go a long way toward addressing those ills, or at least toward neutralizing their effects. The Reverend Jesse Jackson began his rise to national prominence by urging young African Americans to internalize the mantra, "I am somebody." If that isn't self-image psychology, what is?

Publisher and women's-rights advocate Gloria Steinem prefaced her best seller, *Revolution From Within: A Book Of Self-Esteem* with the assertion, "[E]ven I, who had spent...years working on external barriers to women's equality, had to admit there were internal ones too."

Jaime Escalante, the Los Angeles teacher whose inspirational true story was told in the 1985 movie *Stand And Deliver*, found that the low self-esteem of his Mexican-American students was their greatest barrier to mastering college-level mathematics. Once they were convinced that they *could do it*, these ghetto teenagers who'd been "tracked for failure" achieved spectacular success.

A Michigan woman who survived an abusive childhood, teenage pregnancy, drug addiction, and an oppressive marriage remarked to me, "It didn't matter that my rage was perfectly justified; it didn't get me anywhere until I was willing to confront and overcome my own feeling of self-worthlessness." This woman, a school dropout at the age of 16, was earning a Ph.D. in microbiology at 45.

We all know how elusive a feeling of self-worth and importance can be. All too often we focus on our failures and disappointments and tend to forget or disregard our successes. John's experiences with women had "proven" to him that his image of himself as "nerd" was correct. Picture him at a singles dance, awkward and anxious and shy, for all purposes wearing a sign that says, "Reject me!" Laura had "reaffirmed" to herself time and again that she just didn't have the smarts for any job that paid more than $19,000 a year. Imagine the way she would react if her boss suggested she take a word-processing course. After all, she has objective "proof" that she is just too dumb to learn any such thing.

We always act in a way that is consistent with our self-image. We may try to change our behavior through "willpower," "positive thinking," or "affirmations" ("I will approach that woman with self-confidence." "I will get a better job." "I am a non-smoker."), but such efforts will work *only* if we change our concept of ourselves. In later chapters we'll explore the reasons why "positive thinking" and "willpower" are pitfalls. For now it is important to understand that they are guaranteed to fail, leading us to further disappointment and frustration, unless the self-image is fundamentally changed.

But you can change your self-image. And by doing so, you can change your behavior and your feelings. It may even seem to you that you're developing new talents and abilities (which of course were really there all along). Many of my clients have used the same terms to describe the moment when they understood that the key to a better life was in their own hands: "It was like clouds parting and the sun breaking forth." In time you will find yourself, as Laura did, saying to yourself in wonder, "It doesn't have to be this way!"

Psycho-Cybernetics is a program for developing a self-image you can live with, one in which you can feel secure, one that you can be proud to express to others, one that leads to self-confidence and success.

You can develop a self-image that will enable you to "add more living to your life," no matter how old you may happen to be.

You can develop a realistic self-image that will empower you to live your life effectively in the coming century.

Six Steps to Success: What You'll Find in This Book

Maxwell Maltz developed Psycho-Cybernetics largely through observation and intuition. Starting from the premise that the self-image is the key to a better life, he explored a number of interrelated concepts that described the way our self-image is formed and how it contributes to our success and well-being. Thirty years later his intuitive conclusions have been validated and strengthened by solid scientific evidence. In chapters to come we will consider each of Maltz's concepts to see how you can build a new, positive and realistic self-image—one consistent with the person you are and the person you want to be.

1. Program Yourself for Success

Central to Psycho-Cybernetics is Maltz's idea of the human brain as an automatic guidance system. This human servomechanism can be either a success mechanism or a failure mechanism. It all depends on the targets our thinking mind establishes for it and on the way it responds to its own errors. If your servomechanism is "homed in" on targets of success and if it responds to feedback by correcting its course, the result is success. If it has no goal to seek or if it fails to respond correctively to feedback, the result is failure.

And that's where your self-image comes in. It is your self-image that sets the limits of what your servomechanism can aim for. John's self-image, for example, presented a target that said REJECTION. Laura's presented a target that said I'M STUPID. There was no possibility for their internal guidance systems to reach any other outcome. They were programmed for failure.

Psycho-Cybernetics 2000 will update Maltz's analogy in the light of current scientific understanding. In chapter 2 you'll discover how your subconscious mind, which contains all your fundamental assumptions about yourself, is programmed by your conscious, thinking mind. You'll find a simple five-step procedure by which you can *re*program the way you think about yourself by consciously casting out negative data and replacing it with new information that will keep your automatic mechanism locked on target for success.

2. Imagine Your Way to Success

People always feel, act and behave according to what they *imagine* to be true about themselves and their circumstances. This is because the subconscious mind can't tell the difference between a real experience and one that is vividly imagined. Through your creative imagination you can create images of success that by incorporation into your self-image can be turned into actual success.

Creative imagination, as Maltz used the term, is separate and distinct from what we think of as artistic creativity. It is a capacity we all possess, the ability to create images in our minds. By realizing that our actions, feelings and behavior are a result of what we *imagine* to be true, we can change these actions, feelings, and behavior by changing our mental pictures.

Maltz contended that the false and negative beliefs about ourselves that are reinforced as we exercise our "destructive instinct" constitute a form of hypnosis. He spoke of using the "creative mechanism" and "theater of the imagination" to "dehypnotize yourself from false beliefs." This concept, and the exercises he created in support of it, are today better understood. Scientific evidence, deriving from what is popularly known as *split-brain research,* has given us sound physiological reasons why they work. In chapters 3 and 4, you'll learn simple and effective techniques for accessing the right side of your brain to create new images of yourself that will lead to new attitudes and patterns of action. You'll learn how to focus on desired changes instead of dwelling on past mistakes. You'll find questionnaires that will guide you in identifying the false beliefs that have limited your goals, and in *acknowledging* their falseness. And you'll learn how to use your imagination to replace those beliefs with "new memories" that will form the bedrock of a positive self-image.

3. Relax and Turn Stress into Success

Relaxation is the key to activating our creative imagination, the only state in which our servomechanism can work properly. Yet most of us have no idea how to relax. We are conditioned to respond to events in our lives in ways that lead to increased stress. By learning to relax, to decondition ourselves from these responses, we can reduce the level of stress in our lives. In chapter 5, you'll be introduced to a variety of exercises that aid in relaxation. You'll learn how these techniques can promote better health, creative thinking, insightful problem solving, and the learning of new skills—including the skill of enhancing your self-image.

In 1960 tranquilizer drugs had just come into widespread use as a means of reducing stress. Maltz pointed out that tranquilizers work by reducing or eliminating our responses to negative feedback. As an alternative he proposed a series of stress-reducing mental exercises he called "do-it-yourself tranquilizers." In chapter 6 you'll find a five-step procedure for responding to stressful situations in a way that defuses stress and leaves your self-esteem intact. We'll use Maltz's concept of drug-free tranquilizers as a starting point for an exploration of the true stress factors in your life. (What you think is "stressing you out" may not actually be the root cause!) You'll learn how to use visualization to reduce stress and how to avoid mistaking imaginary problems for real ones. And you'll learn simple techniques to prevent your automatic mechanism from overheating by responding with calmness and confidence to the "difficult" situations that occur in your life.

4. Set Goals: A Prerequisite to Success

Maltz likened a human being to a bicycle: we maintain our balance only while we are moving forward toward something. Trying to maintain balance while sitting in one place makes us feel shaky and, ultimately, we fall.

Enhancing your self-image is not an end in itself. It is a necessary prerequisite for establishing goals of success. A poor self-image can keep us from setting goals or discourage us from pursuing them. If we have no worthwhile personal goals, it is easy to conclude that life itself is not worthwhile. It is only by establishing specific and attainable goals that we turn our servomechanism into a success mechanism.

In chapter 7 you'll see how your belief system may limit your goals. You'll be guided through simple procedures and questionnaires for reviewing goals that you have worked toward in the past, for realistically assessing your skills, and for determining the goals that are most appropriate to your desires and abilities. You'll find a five-step plan for *setting* goals that are realistic and attainable and a seven-point action plan for effectively *working toward* your goals. In chapter 8 you'll learn techniques that will maximize your success as you pursue your goals—procedures for overcoming procrastination, for monitoring your progress, for motivating and disciplining yourself; and other strategies for keeping your automatic mechanism on target for success.

5. Use Negative Feedback to Point You Toward Success

Once you have established goals, your internal guidance system kicks in. But again, it is your self-image that determines whether or not you remain locked on target. In chapter 9 we'll review the components of the Psycho-Cybernetics program, present two case studies illustrating how they function together, and answer some residual questions about them.

People whose self-image is positive find it easy to develop and nurture what Dr. Maltz called the *success-type personality*. When such people receive negative feedback—signals that they have gone off course—the servomechanism responds by making a course correction, helping to "guide us down the road to creative accomplishment." But to people with poor self-images, such negative feedback serves only to confirm their sense of inadequacy.

Dr. Maltz used the letters of the word SUCCESS as an acronym to illustrate the components of the success-type personality. He used a similar acronym to describe what he called the *failure mechanism*—the negative feedback that serves as a warning signal that a course correction is necessary:

S-ense of direction	**F**-rustration
U-nderstanding	**A**-ggressiveness
C-ourage	**I**-nsecurity
C-harity	**L**-oneliness
E-steem	**U**-ncertainty
S-elf-confidence	**R**-esentment
S-elf acceptance	**E**-mptiness

In chapter 10 we'll look at each of Maltz's seven elements of success in a contemporary and future-focused context as interpreted by the California task force and other specialists on self-esteem. You'll learn what skills contribute to a sense of direction with regard to your career and personal life, what "charity" means in the context of personal success, and so on. Then we'll explore a set of key principles and techniques that will guide you in *acquiring* each element—tips for cultivating the interpersonal respect that leads to understanding, for developing the courage to take risks; procedures for enhancing all the factors in your life that will shape your personality for success.

As for the negative feelings and attitudes that can lead to failure, everyone experiences them on occasion. The important thing is to recognize them as warning signals and take corrective action. In chapter 11 you'll learn how to recognize the elements of failure and to respond to them positively and appropriately. You'll find a self-test that will guide you in assessing your frustration level and correcting your course, a chart to aid you in determining whether your problem-solving stance with other people is assertive (positive) or aggressive (negative), and other such strategies for keeping your internal guidance system on target for success.

6. Disinhibit Your Personality and Fuel Success

Maltz maintained that what we call "personality" is the outward manifestation of our self-image. Thus everyone's real personality is a "good personality," a sign that the individual has "freed...the creative potential within him." Conversely, Maltz equated a "poor personality" with an inhibited personality. He maintained that excessive shyness, self-consciousness, hostility and other symptoms of inhibition resulted from too much negative feedback.

Think of John and his fear of rejection. When negative feedback becomes excessive, or when our servomechanism becomes too sensitive to it, the result is not a course correction but total inhibition of response. Our servomechanism overcorrects, performing an exaggerated series of lateral zig-zags until progress toward the target ceases altogether.

Maltz called the inhibiting factors in our lives "emotional scar tissue" and the techniques for overcoming them "a face-lift for your personality." He outlined a series of exercises by which you can "practice disinihibition" and thus unlock your real personality. In chapter 12 we'll take a look at the emotional wounds that can inhibit your personality. We'll review and supplement Maltz's techniques for removing the "emotional scars" caused by negative feedback in the past and for preventing new ones from forming as you remain focused on the future. You'll learn how the images you hold of your body affect your personality and how you can assess and challenge a negative body image. You'll learn how to take positive action to remove the stumbling blocks that may be preventing you from forming close personal relationships. You'll learn the single most powerful strategy for overcoming the feelings of resentment that may be inhibiting your personality. And you'll learn five techniques for immunizing yourself against future emotional wounds.

Maintaining self-esteem is a lifelong process, one which may require an occasional "booster shot." In chapter 13, we'll show you how to ensure that the changes you effect through Psycho-Cybernetics will continue throughout your life. You'll learn how to access the feelings that lead to a positive self-image and to deflect the feelings that can erode your self-esteem. And you'll learn how to apply the ideas in this book as you go on through life to maximize your chances for lasting self-fulfillment.

Become the Person You Want to Be

Take some time to review these six steps. Consider the data you've been using in your self-program.

- Have you programmed yourself for failure rather than success?
- Does your mental image of yourself, your thoughts, attitudes, and interpretations—the "memory" of your internal guidance system—describe you in negative terms?
- Do anxiety and stress prevent you from making the effort to reprogram yourself in a positive way?
- Do you hold back from setting goals for yourself, or are your goals limited by discouraging feelings about your abilities?
- Does negative feedback stop you from pursuing your goals instead of guiding you toward correcting your course?
- Do you feel that such negative feedback has led an to inhibition of your personality?

If your answer to any of these questions is "yes," consider how a new self-image can help you to become the person you want to be.

What Does Success Mean to You?

In using this book it is important always to remember that "success" is an entirely subjective concept. To some people it is equated with money and material possessions. To others, it means a fulfilling family life and personal relationships. To still others, it's measured by accomplishments of the heart, mind, body, or spirit—writing poetry or playing the drums, building a treehouse or customizing a car, playing a better game of bridge, running a marathon, doing volunteer work, or completing *War and Peace*. Your long-term goals for success may also be different from your short-term goals. While you may wish 10 years from now to be settled into a new and more exciting career, it may be more meaningful for you right now to gain your boss's recognition for a skill you're cultivating on your present job. As you use this book, always remember to measure success by your own standards— not "the Joneses'" or your mother's, or anyone else's.

You have the right to feel good about yourself. In fact, you owe it to yourself to focus on your positive qualities. The principles of Psycho-Cybernetics, updated and revitalized by current perspectives, can be your key to building a new self-image, your program for "getting more living out of life." You can learn to use the automatic guidance system within you as a success mechanism rather than as a failure mechanism.

It's as easy as getting started.

Targeting on Ideas

- You always act, feel and behave in a way that is consistent with your self-image—regardless of the reality of that image.
- You can achieve a positive self-image—one that will empower you to set and achieve goals of personal happiness and professional success—by diligently practicing a few simple techniques.

SET
YOUR OWN
TARGETS

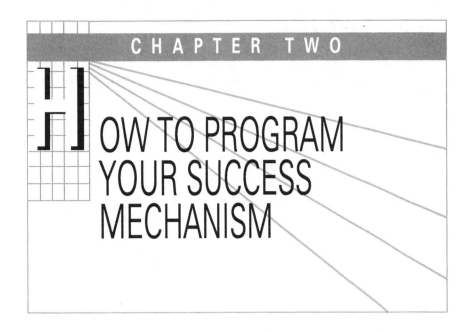

CHAPTER TWO

HOW TO PROGRAM YOUR SUCCESS MECHANISM

[The] creative mechanism within you is impersonal. It will work automatically and impersonally to achieve goals of success and happiness, or unhappiness and failure, depending on the goals which you yourself set for it.

—*Maxwell Maltz,* Psycho-Cybernetics *(1960)*

When we are deprived of the ability to stretch our boundaries and capabilities, we can exist in an almost hibernating state, semi-alive, with all but our survivalist abilities on hold, and a feeling of being cold and alone, cut off from nature and the universe. But when our talents are required and rewarded, we can stretch our abilities, use the energy of self-esteem to activate the unique mix of universal human traits we each possess, and uncover a microcosm of the universe within ourselves.

—*Gloria Steinem,* Revolution From Within: A Book Of Self-Esteem *(1992)*

When my son Rob was 15, I was teaching him to drive. I was coaching him during a spin around our neighborhood one day, and I noticed that he was steering awfully near the curb. "Watch the curb; you're very close over here," I said. He paid little attention, and I repeated my point a bit more forcefully: "Rob, you've got to watch that curb; you really are close!" He nodded, but still there was no change in his driving. "Rob," I said emphatically, "you've got to watch that curb!" A moment later I felt the grinding of the hubcap as Rob crunched the car against the curb. "Rob," I said (as only a parent can say), "what in the world are you doing?"

He looked me in the eye, scowled (as only a teenager can scowl), and said, "I'm *watching* the *curb*, Mom!"

The point? Success is instinctive, but sometimes we block the instinct. We all possess a built-in guidance system that moves us toward the things we think about. If we watch limits instead of destinations, we bump up against those limits. If our self-perception is so negative that we allow ourselves no destination at all, we wander all over the road. Eventually we crunch up against a curb and despair about why we never seem to get anywhere.

But if we have specific, realistic, images of success to guide us, and if we stay focused on these images, we needn't worry about curbs. We may wander outside our lane from time to time, but our built-in guidance system keeps us on course. It automatically corrects our steering and keeps us moving forward toward success and happiness.

This chapter is about your built-in guidance system and how you can learn to control it. We'll take a close look at:

- how your internal guidance system works, and the role of your self-image in programming it.
- a five-step procedure for breaking old habits that keep you crunching up against curbs and installing new habits that will lead to happiness and success.
- how real people in today's world have upgraded their internal guidance system to earn job promotions, develop new skills, overcome self-consciousness and cure chronic worry.

⊞ Correcting Your Programming: Tap Your Success Instinct

Let's start with Maxwell Maltz's central idea of the human brain as a servomechanism. Driving a car is a perfect example. Your brain is constantly comparing the car's position to the position you want it to be in. If you stray too far out of your lane, your eye sends a signal to your brain. The brain compares the desired position of the car to its actual position. Then it signals your arms to put the car back on course by using the steering wheel.

This, in essence, is how a servomechanism works. In a guided missile, for example, the desired position is determined by a computerized map, the actual position by radar. The missile has no brain, but it does possess an electronic device that continually corrects its course, keeping the difference between the two positions as close to zero as possible.

Let's get back in your car. Do you think about any of those things when you're driving? Of course not. They're all subconscious acts—except perhaps when another driver honks his horn at you and makes an obscene gesture. But think back to when you were first learning to drive. You thought about everything you did. Watching your position, steering, accelerating, braking—they were all conscious acts. Sometimes you overcorrected. Sometimes, most likely, you crunched up against a curb. But eventually your thinking mind programmed your subconscious mind to function automatically behind the wheel of a car.

Maltz maintained that all living creatures possess such a built-in goal-striving mechanism, a *success instinct* that guides them toward goals of nourishment, defense, and reproduction. But in human beings the success instinct helps us achieve emotional and spiritual satisfaction as well as mere physical survival. It operates as a *creative mechanism*, guiding us toward fulfillment of the many goals that make us human and contribute to a rich and satisfying life.

But being human, we may also program our creative mechanism with bad data that can sabotage our success. And the main factor that determines our programming and the data it can accept, once again, is our self-image.

In conceptualizing Psycho-Cybernetics, Maltz's leaned heavily on the ideas of scientists involved in the development of the earliest computers. If you're old enough to remember the 1950s, you know that it was popular then to speak of the computer as an "electronic brain." Today computer science tends to emphasize the differences between human and machine intelligence rather than their similarities, but such terms as "programming," "input," and "data" are still useful in understanding how your servomechanism works. In fact, with computers so familiar to us today, the concept is more readily understandable. When you get a phone bill for $3,725 instead of $37.25, you might call up the phone company and scream, "Hey, your computer is trying to rob me!" But you know that the error lies not with the machine but with the data that was entered into it. And if the computer's programming—its "software"—contains errors, it may to fail to function correctly no matter what information is put into it.

So it is with our creative mechanism. It always operates according to the way our self-image has programmed it. Program it with images of success, and it operates as a success mechanism. Program it with negative images and limitations, and it operates as a failure mechanism.

But like any servomechanism, its programming can be changed.

How to Change Habits of Failure into Habits of Success

Our self-image begins with others' opinions about us. Our awareness of these opinions forms our earliest sense of self—our servomechanism's basic program. We then "confirm" this program by acting in accordance with it. Let's take a look at four individuals and see how their self-image programmed their creative mechanism with "bugs" that kept it from functioning as a success mechanism.

Brad was a sturdy, athletic child whose "learning curve" didn't keep up with his physical growth and coordination. He was repeatedly told that he was "not too bright" and grew to accept this notion as a fact. Later, when he was trying to establish himself in the business world, every time he was up for a promotion he found himself acutely ill. He was never able to keep an appointment for a performance review. It was as though he *could not hear* that he had a bright, promising future. As far as Brad's self-image was concerned, his future had been left on the football field.

Tina never had any problem believing she was bright. She had an IQ of 150 and was a successful attorney. When she was a very young child, she seemed always to be stumbling and bumping into things. Her parents used to joke about it, saying that Tina had "two left feet." This image stayed with her throughout her adolescence, when she convinced herself that she could never learn to dance. Later, when she met the man of her dreams, she was devastated to learn that he loved to dance. She kept making excuses not to go dancing with him. She even considered breaking off their relationship rather than reveal to him the shameful "fact" that she had two left feet.

Greg was a systems analyst whose early-childhood difficulty in relating to his peers had left him with poor social skills. He heard the phrase "Shut up, Greg" so often that he freqently was afraid to open his mouth. He functioned splendidly whenever he was alone with his computer. But when he had to interface with human beings, he became nervous and ill at ease. Because of this awkwardness with people, he was unable to appreciate his successes as a systems analyst. At home he would fret over his inability to carry on a conversation without feeling self-conscious. He found that alcohol temporarily lifted his spirits, and he soon developed a serious drinking problem.

Emily had always had outstanding "people skills." She was upbeat and outgoing and thought she would be a natural in real-estate sales. She completed a home-study course and passed the real-estate exam on her first attempt. But every time a prospective buyer asked her about interest rates or other mortgage data, she became paralyzed. Emily was the only girl in a family of four brothers. Her father was a CPA, and all her brothers were math whizzes. Emily was no worse than average in math, but by comparison with her family she felt "dumb." Her father had always consoled her by telling her that girls weren't expected to do well with numbers. "And besides," as her brothers had kindly put it, "you're always so cheerful, so good with people. Why do we need another math genius in the family?"

You Really Can Create Change

In each of these cases, a poor self-image caused the individual's servomechanism to operate as a failure mechanism. Brad's and Tina's self-image had them so convinced that they were failures that they were unable to visualize themselves as successful. Greg and Emily had established realistic goals of success, but they kept bumping up against "curbs" imposed by their self-image.

But in each case the self-image had nothing to do with reality. It was something that had been *learned*. Anything that has been learned can be reevaluated and challenged. Anything that has been challenged can be "relearned" with new data to replace the old.

Please memorize those last two sentences. A negative self-image can be erased, like a tape recording, and replaced with a new, positive self-image. You acquired your self-image through subconscious habit. It's not *easy* to change such a habit...but it is *simple*. It just takes repeated practice. Remember when I asked you to interlace your fingers and then reverse the procedure so that the other thumb was on top? One way felt comfortable because it was a habit; an unconscious act. The other felt awkward because it was unfamiliar; it required conscious awareness. But do you really think you'd find it impossible to get used to? If you consciously practiced doing it that way, it would become an unconscious habit fully as much as the way you're now used to doing it.

Changing the programming of your internal guidance sytem is no more complicated than that.

The CRAFT of Reprogramming: Five Steps to a New Self-Image

How can you take control of your creative mechanism and reprogram it as a success mechanism? Change comes about through *awareness* of a negative self-image, by *challenging* the bad habits that support this image, and by *creating* a new, positive self-image that allows you to set and achieve worthwhile goals. Let's use Emily as an example and go through the five steps she followed. It's easy to remember these steps if you think of reprogramming your automatic mechanism as a CRAFT:

1. **C**-ancel
2. **R**-eplace
3. **A**-ffirm
4. **F**-ocus
5. **T**-rain

Later, we'll talk about how and why these five steps work. For now, try to reserve judgment about them. Just see how Emily used them and think about how they might apply to you.

1. Cancel old, negative data. Emily went about her business as usual. But any time she found herself thinking, "I just don't have a head for numbers," she said the word "cancel!" out loud. This made her conscious of her negative beliefs and formed in her the habit of challenging these beliefs. It also made her rather interesting to be around while walking through the supermarket. But it was important for her to do this every time she was consciously aware of such negative self-thoughts.

It was also important for Emily (and for you) to actually *say* "cancel" (or "stop") instead of just thinking it. By hearing yourself speak the thought, you complete what psycholinguists call the *language loop*. It's a double reinforcement: *your* ears hear *your* voice giving the order. It makes your focus clearer. Have you ever noticed that when you mutter to yourself, "Okay, now *where* did I put those keys?" it actually seems to help you find them? The same principle is at work here. By repeatedly *hearing* her own voice CANCEL her negative program, Emily moved toward actual CANCELlation of her old self-image.

2. Replace it with new, positive data. Once Emily was conscious of her old habit, she replaced the old program "I'm dumb at math" with a new one: "I'm very good at my job, and the 'numbers' aspect is part of it." She repeated this new data several times each day. Every time the old program popped up, immediately after saying "cancel" she would reaffirm the new program to herself.

3. Affirm your new image to yourself. Emily made affirmation cards on which she wrote out the statement defining her new, positive self-image. She placed one card on her desk at work and taped the other to her bathroom mirror at home where she would see them every day. By doing so, she reminded herself to reinforce her new self-image on a repeated basis.

It is important here to remember what Maltz had to say about affirmations: used alone they will not change habits. *Only if the self-image is in a process of change will they begin to take effect.* Affirmations help to point you back on course when feedback from your old, negative self-image makes you concentrate on the curb instead of your destination. But unless you *have* a destination, *affirm*-ation will turn quickly to *frustr*-ation.

4. Focus on an image of a successful you. Every day Emily allowed herself 10 minutes to sit by herself, relax, and picture herself answering clients' questions about interest rates and other mathematically related topics. This is the process Maltz called "mental pictures" or "entering the theater of the imagination." I call it "focusing your daydreams" or "reflective relearning." By vividly imagining success, Emily caused her subconscious mind to respond as though she had actually been successful.

This is not a metaphysical process. The brain works in pictures. Visualization is crucial to reprogramming your servomechanism, and relaxation is crucial to visualization. This book devotes several chapters, with appropriate exercises and techniques, to the roles that imagination and relaxation play in bringing about changes in your self-image. For now, don't worry too much about the *specifics* of how to achieve them. Just be aware of their importance.

5. Train yourself for lasting change. Meanwhile, Emily "acted as if" she were already operating under her new program: she reviewed the math she needed to answer questions from prospective home buyers and practiced using it whenever the opportunity came up. A new self-image was not magically going to put this information into her head. *But it did allow her to see herself as capable of learning it.* Under her old programming, she couldn't even consider the idea. Meanwhile she took repeated opportunities to tell herself "I'm mastering the mathematics of the real-estate business." She made a lot of phone calls during her work day, and she made a point of repeating this statement to herself every time she picked up the phone. These reinforcements served as an insurance policy for her new attitude and behavior. They continually reminded her that she was in the process of change.

⊞ Your Two Minds—And How to Change Them

Perhaps the CRAFT process seems *too* simple. All I can tell you, once again, is to give it time to work. It can work for you if you practice it daily for six weeks, in coordination with other simple techniques you'll be reading about in this book. To understand how and why these five steps work, let's take a closer look at your servomechanism and how *it* works. It's useful to consider your goal-seeking mechanism as a function of your subconscious mind and your conscious mind operating together under a few basic "rules":

THE TWO PRINCIPLES OF THE SUBCONSCIOUS MIND

The **agreement principle:** *The subconscious mind always says "yes" to everything the conscious mind tells it.*

The **compliance principle:** *The subconscious mind always moves in the direction in which the conscious mind points it.*

The agreement principle describes the way your self-image was formed. Your subconscious mind is a hopeless "yes-man." It accepts every conscious thought you have as 100 percent gospel truth. Each time you consciously absorb the thought, "I am severely lacking in intelligence (sex appeal, social skills, coordination, financial sense, musical talent—*whatever*)," your subconscious mind replies, "Amen." When Emily's conscious mind said, "I can't do math," her subconscious mind said, "You're right." When Brad's conscious mind said, "You're just a dumb jock; you'll never get anywhere in a job that requires thinking," his subconscious mind responded, "Duh, yeah, if you say so." When Tina's conscious mind told her "You have two left feet," her subconscious mind replied, "Oops!"

Are you beginning to see how negative input programs us to fail?

The compliance principle is illustrated by Rob and his student-driving experience. Once your subconscious mind has accepted the way the conscious mind is trying to move it, it moves in that direction every time. If you watch the curb, you move toward the curb. Emily could realistically tell herself, "I *had* that sale; that couple liked the house; they liked *me*. I just got flustered when they started asking about bank rates and balloon payments." Instead, her programming pointed her away from success in any field that involved using numbers. "I'm dumb in math," her self-image told her. "I'll never succeed in this business because I can never understand those things...." *Crunch!* Greg might be justified in thinking, "I blew that talk with the boss because I was self-conscious, but I really am good at my job." Instead, his thoughts moved his subconscious mind toward the limit imposed by his self-image: "My social skills are the pits; I'll never be successful at anything that requires me to interact with people...." *Crunch!*

The conscious mind sets the vision. The subconscious mind's role is *pro*-vision. It provides the support system to enact the conscious mind's decisions. The subconscious mind can't make a decision. It can't take a joke. It can't tell the difference between a real experience and one vividly imagined. It can't tell whether the data the conscious mind sends it is fact or nonsense. It merely agrees and moves toward the image consistent with that data. It seeks out any target we set for it or no target at all. It can work for us or against us, depending on how we program it.

Or, as the computer people say, "Garbage in, garbage out."

How to Create Your New Program

To understand how you can unlearn the old data and replace it with new, positive data, let's now take a look at how the conscious mind works.

THE TWO PRINCIPLES OF THE CONSCIOUS MIND

The **selection principle:** *The conscious mind looks at options and makes purposeful choices among them.*

The **elimination principle:** *Once the conscious mind has made its selection, all other possible options are eliminated for that given moment.*

When you look over a menu in a restaurant, you make conscious choices: fish over veal, baked potato over fries, white wine over red. Once you choose, you effectively eliminate the rest of the menu from your dinner plans. If this sounds trivial and arbitrary, so are our self-image choices. When the conscious mind sets a goal, it eliminates all alternatives. Once Brad's conscious mind had selected "I'm dumb," it eliminated the option, "I deserve that promotion." Once Tina's conscious mind had opted for "I have two left feet," it eliminated "I can learn to dance." Once Greg's conscious mind chose "I can't relate to people," it eliminated "I can do this job."

But the conscious mind also can say, "Waiter, I've decided to change my order. I *hate* fish."

By "changing your order," you exercise the selection and elimination principles again. By choosing to tell his subconscious mind "I can do this job," Brad eliminated for that moment the option that said, "I am dumb." By *repeated* selection of the positive option *every time the choice came up*, he effectively eliminated the negative option on a permanent basis. He changed his self-image. He provided a new program for his servomechanism.

By choosing an image of herself that said "I can learn to dance," Tina eliminated the one that said "I am clumsy." Of course it took a little help from Arthur Murray and a lot of practice on the dance floor (the "T" of CRAFT). But all the lessons in the world could not have helped her if she hadn't *chosen* a new image for herself and made it a habit.

In his book *The Unfair Advantage*, psychologist Tom Miller compares our two minds with a horse and rider. Anyone who has had any experience with horses will appreciate this analogy. Even if you've had nothing to do with horses since that dreadful summer at Camp Arapaho, stick with me awhile.

It's easy to train a horse to follow a path. Every day you ride it out along the same route: one mile south, turn left, one-half mile east, turn right, one-half mile, stop; return. After a while the horse gets it. Boy, does it get it. Once a horse has become used to following a route, it is maddening to try to get it to follow another. If it habitually turns right at a particular spot, it is almost impossible to get it to turn left, even if you threaten it with the glue factory. By this time does it matter whether the rider is John Wayne, Dale Evans, Geronimo, or Princess Anne? No. The horse will carry *any* rider along the same trail, day after day.

The subconscious mind is the horse; the conscious mind is the rider. The horse follows the agreement and compliance principles. It is the rider's job to teach it a new path by the selection and elimination principles.

Of course it's simple for the rider to teach the horse a new route. Once again: it's *simple*—but it isn't *easy*. It takes care and repeated application. If the horse is used to turning left, it isn't going to turn right unless you pull the reins *hard* at the proper place and do it the same way day after day. Anything the horse perceives as different it automatically treats as wrong. The rider (your conscious mind) is a slave to the horse (your subconscious mind) until you provide a new route for it to follow.

And that brings us back to the CRAFT process. Once again the steps are:

1. **Cancel** old, negative data
2. **Replace** it with new, positive data
3. **Affirm** your new self-image
4. **Focus** on an image of success
5. **Train** yourself in your new attitudes and behavior

Each time you say "cancel" and replace your old negative data with new positive data, your rider makes a firm tug on your horse's reins: "Not that way, *this* way." Your conscious mind makes a *selection* ("I'm very good at my job and the numbers are just part of my job"). By doing so, it *eliminates* the old, negative option ("I can't do math") that you've always chosen to make. Your subconscious mind—the horse—automatically *agrees* with what your conscious mind tells it. By repeated affirmation, the horse *complies* with the new path. It moves in the direction defined by your new program. By visualizing yourself as successful, you direct your horse toward something positive and rewarding. By "acting as if" the skill were already incorporated into your concept of yourself, you train the horse to recognize the new path as the only path.

What path would you like your horse to follow? You may not have any problem accepting yourself as intelligent, graceful on the dance floor, "good with people" or capable of learning new job skills. But you can use CRAFT to challenge *any* negative habits and replace them with new, positive habits.

Have you consigned yourself to a marginal life because you're feel that you're "just no good at handling money"? You can train your horse to follow a path toward financial success by changing this image of yourself.

Do sexual inhibitions make you feel incapable of a fulfilling romantic relationship? You can consciously reprogram yourself in a new image, one that allows you to feel confident and caring with your partner and to achieve a healthy and satisfying sex life.

Do you punish yourself for just "taking what crumbs are offered you" instead of "going after what you want"? CRAFT can help you replace that passive self-image with a new program that will lead to positive, assertive behavior.

Once again, the process takes repetition and time—about six weeks for most people. But if you follow the five steps on a regular daily basis, *you will succeed in reprogramming your servomechanism for success*. It's all a matter of consciously establishing a new image of yourself and training your subconscious mind to move in the direction of that image. And once you've completed your reprogramming, you have the power to achieve any positive and realistic goal that's consistent with your new program.

Let Feedback Help You Move Forward

Remember, Emily had to actually use the mathematics of the real estate business as part of her reprogramming process. Similarly, Brad had to show up for his performance reviews, Tina needed to dance and Greg had to seek out interactions with people. Their new self-image enabled them to accept that they could do these things. Once they got started, feedback from their environment provided further affirmation that helped keep them on course.

When Maltz first proposed that the human brain worked this way, all he had to go by to support his view were his observations and intuition. The notion that a person could consciously bring about changes in unconscious processes was scoffed at by science. In the 1960s and 1970s this idea was confirmed through research on a psychological treatment known as biofeedback. Through this method people learn to control such physical processes as body temperature, heartbeat, and blood pressure that are normally considered involuntary. The person is connected to a machine and asked to visualize, for example, her hands being warmed over a gentle fire. When the temperature of her hands actually rises, the machine gives a signal. Without such feedback the person would not be able to detect such a change. The knowledge of her success serves as an affirmation that the process is working.

No machine can give you feedback on your progress of reprogramming your servomechanism. But then, you don't need one. You can get the feedback from the people around you and from the changes you feel within yourself.

Experience Your Self-Confidence Growing

Remember John, the shy and inhibited young man you met in the last chapter? The guy who was certain no woman would ever find him attractive or interesting? Through a conscious reprogramming of his internal guidance system via the CRAFT process, he was able to change this image of himself and place himself on the road to the success he wanted.

John recognized that he had programmed himself with "sense and nonsense." Yes, it made sense that a pretty woman at a singles event was going to have a choice of partners and might reject him. But to be convinced that she was certain to reject him was nonsense—bad data programmed by his self-image.

John started with Step 1. Each time he found himself thinking, "No woman would want me," or, of a specific woman, "She's going to reject me," he said "cancel." Then he followed immediately with Step 2. He replaced the negative statement with, "She may or may not reject me; I'll never know unless I try. Everyone gets rejected sometimes." For the first few weeks John didn't approach *anyone* at singles events. He just sat there, aware of what his mind was telling him, while he practiced steps 1 and 2. He told himself, "She may like me; she may not. I really don't know until I've tried, but I don't have to try today." Meanwhile, John moved ahead with steps 3 and 4: He affirmed to himself daily with written statements that he was not automatically going to be rejected, and he created mental images of successful encounters.

John moved on to step 5 only after he had practiced the first four steps for several weeks. He went up to a woman, introduced himself, said, "I just wanted you to know I think you're very attractive"—and went back and sat down. In this way, he began training himself to approach a situation that scared him while he reprogrammed his servomechanism. Meanwhile he practiced the four steps every day. Only after he had followed this procedure four or five times did he take the big fifth step: to make contact; to ask a woman to dance, to buy her a drink, to initiate a conversation. The positive feedback he received from these encounters indicated to John that the process was working. He soon was dating again after having been alone for six years.

By selecting an image of himself that said, "No woman would ever find me interesting," John's conscious mind had eliminated the possibility of any woman finding him interesting. His subconscious mind could move only in the direction his conscious mind dictated—toward rejection. But once he began consciously to choose a new image of himself every time he was presented with the option, his subconscious mind began to move toward that image. His rider retrained his horse to follow a new path. He reprogrammed his servomechanism.

You May Only Think You're Depressed

A woman I'll call Sandra used CRAFT to rid herself of a severe case of depression. Sandra was 35; she was married with two children. She was an endless worrier who felt that she had no control over events and always expected the worst. Constantly thinking that her world was about to collapse left her feeling depressed most of the time. Sandra hated her job as a commercial artist and was actively seeking a new one. Her credentials and experience should have qualified her for a well-paying position. But every time she went on a job interview, she would tell herself, "I know I'm not going to make it. I'm going to flunk the personality test." Her depression was taking its toll on her family and on her work. Worst of all, she knew she was a "realist": everything *was* as bad as she envisioned it, so how could she be anything *but* depressed?

As you might have guessed, it was not events that were causing Sandra's depression but her unrealistic "realist" image of herself. When she began to explore the process by which she had come to such a negative view of the world, she thought of the grandmother who had raised her. This woman had believed in "Murphy's Law" as firmly as others believe in the Ten Commandments. You remember Murphy's Law: "Everything that can possibly go wrong *will* go wrong." And so Sandra found herself a victim of the subconscious mind's two principles. Every time her grandmother said something like "Don't count your chickens before they hatch," Sandra's subconscious mind said, "That's right." She had learned through constant repetition to expect the worst.

By expecting that the long arm of Murphy's law was about to grab her in a chokehold, Sandra eliminated the possibility of anything good ever happening. When we are programmed to agree with everything negative, we screen out all positive input. I call this the knock-on-wood syndrome. Have you ever noticed that when people "knock on wood," it's never to dispel a negative statement? We do it to drive out the evil spirits that are lurking around, waiting to prevent something *good* from happening: "Boy, I really think the boss liked my proposal—knock on wood." Sandra was one of many people who suffer from depression because they have been conditioned to regard as "realistic" an internal program that expects the bad and qualifies the good.

In order to approach her depression through her servomechanism, Sandra needed a new vision, a new target on which her subconscious mind could focus. She made a point of listenening to her internal dialogue. Whenever she caught herself expecting the negative, she was to say aloud—you guessed it—"cancel." She was to replace the old, negative data with new, positive data. She sat quietly for 10 minutes each day, relaxed and visualized herself as a positive person. Note that she did not try to become Pollyanna, to replace Murphy's Law with its opposite. She visualized herself seeing and experience positive, life-affirming events around her only to give her subconscious mind further provisions with which to work.

Meanwhile, as Sandra practiced these steps daily and repeatedly, she "acted as if" she were positive—as if she were positively joyous. She awoke every day and say, "Okay, I'm going to make this a FUN day." Even though her subconscious mind didn't believe it at first, her conscious mind was giving it time and new ways to absorb the new data. Her rider was forcing her horse to turn in a new direction.

Within a month Sandra began to feel significantly better. Her co-workers asked her if she was "on" something. And she was—on a new image of herself as an upbeat, positive person. And of course, her subconscious mind agreed and complied with her conscious instructions. A few months later she found a new and exciting career position with a publishing company.

Remember, you don't need a therapist to effect such changes. CRAFT is designed for you to use on your own. You may not expect everything in your world to go wrong, but chances are there's some false assumption that's negatively impacting your self-image. Using these five steps, you can consciously expel old, negative data from your subconscious mind and replace it with new, positive data that will empower you to develop an awareness of your competence and worthiness. You'll unlock abilities and talents you didn't know you had. It's simply a matter of changing your programming.

Be Aware of the Curbs; Focus on the Destination

Your new self-image will come about only through repeated practice. You may be a tempted to start in right away on daily application of the CRAFT process, but hold off for just a little while. You won't reprogram your servomechanism through haste or impatience. There's no point in retraining a horse until you know exactly where you want it to go. In the next several chapters, you'll learn skills that will help you to:

- visualize yourself as the person you want to be
- select positive new data for your reprogramming
- access the part of your brain that will best help you in using your powers of imagination and visualization
- identify your negative programming and be aware of its falseness
- use relaxation to optimize the efficiency of your creative mechanism
- select goals for your success mechanism to achieve
- be sensitive to positive feedback that reassures you that you're on course toward your goals
- make the best use of negative feedback to correct errors in your course as you move toward your goals

Meanwhile, prepare for your transformation by thoroughly familiarizing yourself with the process. Reread this chapter from time to time as you work your way through the book. Review the CRAFT steps. Pay attention to the two principles of your conscious mind, the two principles of your subconscious mind, and the way they work together to form your automatic guidance system. Keep your mind open to examples of how the human servomechanism works in your experiences and in those of people you're close to. As you become aware of your own automatic creative mechanism, try the following exercises:

1. Make a list. Make two lists. Jot down aspects of yourself that you see as positive and aspects that you see as negative. Be aware of your negative programming that keeps you "watching the curb" instead of focusing on a destination. Be aware of positive aspects of your self-image that can serve as a foundation for reprogramming your servomechanism.

2. Every time you find yourself saying or thinking something negative about yourself, write down the thought. Become aware of the "bad data" you'd like to cancel. For each item that comes to you, write down an item of positive data you'd like to replace it with.

3. Visualize your horse and rider. Be aware of the path your horse follows and of how it developed the habit of following that path. Think about the new path you'd like to train your horse to follow.

4. Instead of viewing a mistake or setback as evidence of personal inadequacy, consider it as an event—one of many events, positive and negative, that make up your life. Be as aware of the positive events as you are of the negative ones. Each time you find yourself dwelling on a negative event, visualize yourself keeping calm and staying on top of the situation—*acting on,* not *reacting to* the event. Keep it in perspective. Think of how unimportant the event is in the "big picture." Don't let your concern over the event become anxiety about your life. Do what you can to deal with it effectively while remembering that not every event in life will be positive.

Remember, a servomechanism works by making errors and responding to them. Any path to success is defined by mistakes and corrections. Don't dwell on your mistakes—but don't be afraid of them either. Trust your own servomechanism to do its job. After a time, your subconscious mind will forget the errors of the past and learn to follow the new path you have created for it.

Targeting on Ideas

- Your built-in guidance system moves you toward the things you think about. If you watch limits instead of destinations, you bump up against those limits every time.
- The main factor that determines the programming of your internal guidance system is your self-image.
- Use the CRAFT process to reevaluate, challenge and replace old habits of attitude and behavior.

**SET
YOUR OWN
TARGETS**

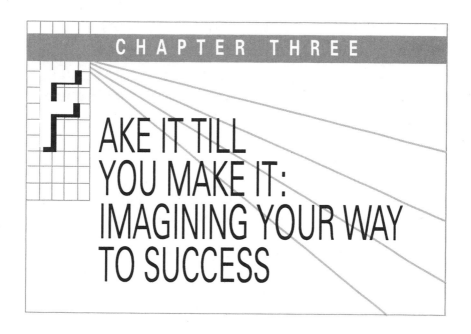

CHAPTER THREE

FAKE IT TILL YOU MAKE IT: IMAGINING YOUR WAY TO SUCCESS

Realizing that our actions, feelings, and behavior are the result of our own images and beliefs gives us the lever that psychology has always needed for changing personality.

—*Maxwell Maltz*, Psycho-Cybernetics *(1960)*

You are responsible for the thoughts you have in your head at any given time. You have the capacity to think whatever you choose, and virtually all your self-defeating attitudes and behaviors originate in the way you choose to think.

—*Wayne Dyer, Ph.D.*, The Sky's The Limit *(1980)*

Geoff was a rugged, handsome young man who bore a resemblance to the actor and playwright Sam Shepherd. Six feet one inch tall, 26 years old, he was many women's ideal of masculine beauty. Yet Geoff had never had a satisfying sexual relationship with a woman. No, he wasn't gay; he'd always been attracted to women, and they to him. What Geoff had was an image of himself as "sexually inadequate."

Geoff's mother had become pregnant at 17 and hastily married his father. He was an abusive alcoholic, and when she divorced him four years later she had taken Geoff and his younger sister to another city. She could not speak of her ex-husband without expressing disgust for male sexuality as "the cause of all my troubles." When Geoff reached puberty she began to focus her contempt on his own emerging sexuality. She ridiculed his adolescent urges and shamed him when she found a copy of *Playboy* hidden under his mattress. On a later occasion, when she caught him masturbating, she took his bedroom door off its hinges.

At 18 Geoff had his first erotic encounter with a young woman he met at college. He became so anxious and embarrassed that he could not sustain an erection, and though his partner was patient he was not able to achieve penetration. A few subsequent experiences (with women who were not so patient) only deepened his "performance anxiety" and his sense of "not being a man." Now he had met a woman who seemed to care for him, but he was sure she wouldn't stick around once she became aware of the permanence of his "problem." Geoff was convinced that he was impotent. His self-image with regard to sexuality had become so bound up with shame and humiliation that he couldn't even *imagine* himself as a "normal," functioning male.

The word *imagination* is related to the word *image:* "that which is seen." Our self-image is bound up intimately with our imagination. It is based 100 percent on what we imagine to be true. "You act and feel," Maltz wrote, "not according to what things are really like but according to the image your mind holds of what they are like. You have certain mental images of yourself, your world, and the people around you, and you behave as though the images were the truth, the reality, rather than the things they represent."

It's easy to underestimate the role imagination plays in shaping your perceptions. Though you're usually unaware of it, your imagination is constantly active. Think of the last time you awakened from a dream that seemed so real it took a while to convince yourself it was "only a dream." Think of times you were cruising along in your car so involved in daydreams that you missed your turnoff. Whenever you're "lost in thought," your imagination is hard at work.

Now, which of your two minds is engaged when you're asleep or daydreaming? Your subconscious mind, of course. Whenever it's in control, these dreaming states "just happen." Geoff's impotence was no more substantial than a dream. It was based entirely on images that he agreed and complied with. To recall Tom Miller's apt metaphor, Geoff's horse had been trained to view itself as a gelding.

Suppose however that Geoff could *consciously* engage his imagination to create a new image of himself? How might such "active daydreaming" affect his success?

How might it affect yours?

This chapter is about your creative imagination and how you can use it to build a more positive concept of yourself. You'll learn:

- how your behavior is conditioned by what you *imagine* to be true, and how you can change your behavior by focusing your imagination.

- how successful people use mental imaging to create positive conditions for their successes in business, sports and the arts.

- how you can use *reflective relearning* to replace expectations of failure, feelings of inadequacy and self-restricting fears with appropriate images of success.

"Believing Is Seeing": How Your Imagination Can Guide You Toward Success

The subconscious mind can't tell the difference between a real experience and one that is vividly imagined. It agrees with every suggestion the conscious mind gives it. It accepts all your mental images as literally true and initiates the process of actualizing them, whether the images are creative or destructive. Everyone is familiar with the old saw, "seeing is believing." To your subconscious mind, just the opposite is true: "believing is seeing"!

Your imagination makes your subconscious mind *see* what your conscious mind *believes*. Imagine that a friend who's just moved to a newly fashionable part of town has invited you to dinner. When you arrived the closest parking space you could find was on a side street four blocks away. Now it's late, and you're remembering that there are worse horrors in the big city than parking. The lighting is poor, the streets are empty, and the warehouses-turned-artists'-lofts on either side are like the towers of the villain's castle in an old Vincent Price movie. Suddenly you think you hear footsteps. You turn quickly and look. There's nobody there. It was only your imagination, you tell yourself. You continue walking. There they are again—footsteps right behind you.

What's happening to your body—your heart, your hands, your blood pressure, your breathing? Does it matter whether there's really someone following you? Of course not; these physiological preparations for fight or flight are entirely a product of your subconscious mind. They were programmed into the species before we were human. They're going to happen whether you're being stalked by a saber-toothed cat, a mugger, or the echo of your own footsteps.

You break into a run. The footsteps stay right with you. Adrenalin surges through your body. You run as though your life depended on it—maybe it does! You're only a block from your car; you can make it.

"Hey, will you slow down?" a familiar voice calls. With relief you turn and see your friend panting toward you, waving your favorite hat. "You forgot this. I had no idea you were in such good shape. Hey, who did you think I was, the Boston Strangler?"

What happens to your pounding heart, sweating palms, and Olympic speed? Everything quickly returns to equilibrium. By the time you get to your car, your behavior has made a complete U-turn. It was your beliefs, not reality, that triggered your body's responses. Your feelings, actions and behavior responded to what you *believed* to be true.

Now, how do suppose this fact applies to your success mechanism? Right: if your self-image leads your rider to believe that you're incapable of success, then regardless of reality, your horse can only respond as though the image were true. But if your self-image tells you that you *are* capable of success—if your rider vividly imagines that you've *already achieved* success—then your horse will respond with the self-confidence that comes from *actual* success.

Your Imagination Can Change Your Beliefs

Another example: you're in the market for a new car and have narrowed your selection down to two models. Call them Car A and Car B. Both have similar features at comparable prices. It's six of one versus a half-dozen of the other. Finally you decide on Car A. You go to the dealer, sign the contract and drive away in your new car.

Now, remember the selection and elimination principles? As soon as you're out on the street you begin telling yourself how smart you were to have selected Car A and eliminated Car B. This thought is now in your conscious mind. So you're driving home, thinking about how you're going to show off the new car to your friends. As you look at other vehicles, what do you see? Right—many cars like yours. And what do you tell yourself? "Boy, was I smart to buy this car. Look at all those other smart people. No wonder there are so many Car A's out here—they're the greatest!"

See how your perception has changed in the direction of your beliefs? You justify your choice by telling yourself what a great decision you've made. You ease the tension of the decision-making process by glorying in your choice and knocking the opposition. What do you tell yourself when you see Car B on the street? "Boy, am I glad I didn't buy *that* car. Funny, I never noticed how boxy it is. And that grille? Bor-ring! Glad I did the smart thing and bought Car A." And this only happens for a few days. After that you don't even notice Car B. What pops out of the environment is what you choose to see. Suddenly there are Car A's everywhere.

But suppose a poor self-image causes you to doubt your decisions. Suppose from the moment you sign the contract your conscious mind invalidates the selection process. Even before you leave the dealership you're telling yourself, "Gee, maybe I should have chosen Car B." Suddenly the streets seem to be full of happy, sexy Car B drivers. What you see reinforces your conviction that you've made the wrong choice. Once again: your perception of what is real is entirely a function of what you *imagine* to be real.

⊞ Reflective Relearning: Four Keys to Creating New Attitudes and Behavior

Take a moment to consider the four facts these examples demonstrate about your imagination:

- Anything you imagine to be true is accepted *as* true by your subconscious mind.
- An *imagined* experience is perceived and acted on by your subconscious mind exactly the same as a *real* experience.
- Your behavior follows what you *believe* to be true.
- Your behavior *changes* in the direction of your beliefs.

Beliefs are powerful. They create communities, order our lives, and define our capabilites. But your imagination is even more powerful, because it can *change* your beliefs.

Maltz cited numerous case studies that demonstrated how the mind accepts imagined experiences as equivalent to actual experiences. In his most dramatic example, he described an experiment in which groups of equally skilled basketball players practiced shooting free throws for 20 days, one group on the court, the other only in their minds. Those who used "mental practice" showed the same improvement in their skills as those who practiced in the gym.

"Realizing that our actions, feelings and behavior are the result of our own images and beliefs," Maltz wrote, "gives us...an opportunity to 'practice' new traits and attitudes, which we otherwise could not do.... If we picture ourselves performing in a certain manner, it is nearly the same as the actual performance. Mental practice helps to make perfect."

What Maltz called "mental practice" is what I call *reflective relearning*. It's the process of using your creative imagination to select positive images for yourself and eliminate the false, destructive, images your subconscious mind may be acting on *as if they were true*.

Remember, every idea that you have learned can be reevaluated and challenged. Every idea that has been reevaluated can be relearned with new data to replace the old. When you focus your imagination on the way you wish to be, your conscious mind directs your subconscious mind to accept these new images. And since your subconscious mind will agree and comply with the images your conscious mind creates, "acting as if" it were true will in effect *make* it true.

How Successful People Use Imagination to Program Their Success

Barbara and Ruth own a successful baby-clothes business. During most of their working hours they are busy handling details of design, manufacture, marketing, distribution, accounting and other aspects of small-business management. But every morning from 10:15 to 10:45, the two partners take time out for an activity they have pursued ever since they started their company.

During the first 10 minutes of this period, Barbara and Ruth share their visions of where they want their business to go. There is no predetermined structure to these discussions, and the topic may change from day to day. If on Monday they focus on increasing their market share, on Tuesday they may be concerned with cost efficiency, new product ideas, or employee relations.

Then for the next 10 minutes Barbara and Ruth let their creative imagination take over. They lower the blinds, shut off the phones, close their eyes, sit quietly and make themselves comfortable while they *visualize* a successful achievement of their goal. To approximate actual experience, they make their visualizations as detailed as possible. They allow themselves to see the finished product down to the last seam. They feel the texture of the fabric. They picture themselves in their community's leading department store, viewing the prominent display of their product and logo and the press of customers. Then during the last 10 minutes, the two partners discuss in detail their experiences in what Maltz called "the theater of the imagination."

It is this process of visualization to which Barbara and Ruth attribute their success. When they were first starting out, neither of them had any experience designing clothes, let alone running a business. Yes, they brainstormed; they compared, combined and synthesized their design sketches; they showed their designs to expectant mothers in obstetricians' offices to get their input; they took their revised concepts to department stores and hounded buyers and assistant buyers. But they give the credit for their success to their creative imagination. By spending time each day *visualizing* themselves as successful businesswomen, they guided their subconscious minds to accept the *image* of themselves as successful businesswomen.

In their daily sessions Barbara and Ruth followed three guidelines:

- They chose the same time every day for their mental picturing.
- They made sure that there would be no interruptions.
- They accepted all positive images as valid and helpful.

We'll take a closer look at these guidelines toward the end of this chapter. For now, though, understand that visualization—the F or focus step of the CRAFT process—is what enables your subconscious mind to provide a pathway to your conscious mind. Remember: if the conscious mind selects a vividly realized image and eliminates conflicting images, the subconscious mind will provide movement toward that image.

In an interview following the allied victory in the Persian Gulf War, General Norman Schwarzkopf described how he played out his battle plans in his mind before committing troops to combat.

Gymnastics champion Mary Lou Retton has described how she rehearsed her routines in her mind, visualizing every step, every leap, every turn, every placement of her hands before putting her body through actual performance.

Body-building champion and film star Arnold Schwarzenegger has said that lifting weights is only a physical follow-through to visualization: "As long as the mind can envision the fact that you can do something, you can.... I visualized myself being there already—having achieved the goal already."

Concert pianist Juliet McComas often practices in her head when readying a piece for performance. "Once I've memorized a piece, I can play it in my mind without touching a piano," she maintains. "If I visualize the keyboard, I can practice in an airport or at my kitchen table. It's just as useful as actual practice."

Interior and landscape designer Cleo Baldon maintains that, "In my field the importance of visualization is enormous.... I did a men's store, and before it was finished, I saw it—not in a dream state—but in a very relaxed state, I saw it. As though I had been there and seen it. As though I remembered it."

Of course none of these successful people achieved their goals through imagination *alone*. Picturing an end result only broadens and deepens the range of targets your automatic creative mechanism can shoot for. It's still up to you to do the work.

How to Release the Power of Your Imagination

Visualizing positive results can point your subconscious mind toward provision of these results. But the opposite is true as well. Remember, your subconscious mind can't take a joke. To your automatic mechanism a destructive image can be as equally valid a goal as a creative one. Of course you don't consciously think of negative images as "goals"—*but they are*. They can reinforce a poor self-image and keep you stuck in unhappy, self-destructive patterns. What you *want* to be is often in bitter conflict with what you *picture* yourself as being—which brings us back to Geoff and his "performance anxiety."

Geoff's conscious mind had been unable to select any positive images of male sexuality. His subconscious mind, the perfect yes-man, agreed and complied with the notion that to be a sexual male was "shameful and disgusting." It moved toward impotence as the only alternative. Because of his first negative experiences, Geoff's rider had selected a second negative image, "I'm not capable of sexual intercourse." Every time he was conscious of that image (almost every time he was with a woman in a potentially intimate situation), all other possibilities were eliminated. And so his horse had come to accept this image as the truth, the whole truth and nothing but the truth.

Geoff could see that there was no point in blaming his mother, his father or anyone else for the negative images that guided his automatic mechanism. The only way he was going to achieve a healthy, normal sex life was to *change* those images. Geoff set out to train his horse to follow a different path through the five-step CRAFT process. Every time had negative thoughts about his sexuality, he said *"Cancel!"* Then he *replaced* his old data with the thought, "Sex is a natural, normal part of life and I am a natural, normal human being." He *affirmed* this concept many times daily to ensure continual reinforcement.

Changing his self-image to accept these new data was a job for Geoff's creative imagination. He set aside 15 minutes every day, seven days a week, for *focusing* on the image of himself as he wished to be. During that time he found a quiet spot where he could be alone, away from any distractions, and entered the theater of his imagination. It was important for Geoff to develop *his own* positive images of male sexuality—not his mother's, *Playboy's*, Dr. Ruth Westheimer's or anyone else's. He closed his eyes and visualized himself in vivid detail as a confident, sexually active male, enjoying a full range of experiences with the woman in his life without shame or anxiety.

By creating new "mental pictures" and refusing to accept his old self-image as valid, Geoff brought his imagination under control of his conscious mind. He *trained* himself in his new self-image by reminding himself several times a day that he was in the process of replacing his old programming. He "acted as if" he had already stopped thinking negatively about his sexuality and worrying about performance anxiety.

By "faking it" while he grew into his new self-image, Geoff *changed his mind* at the subconscious level. He used reflective relearning to create a new image of himself, reprogramming his automatic creative mechanism to move toward a goal of healthy sexuality. Of course it helped Geoff to have a loving and understanding partner (who later became his wife). But it was the images created by his imagination that made his goal achievable.

Your own creative imagination is every bit as good as Geoff's. By putting it under control of your conscious mind, you can erase an old, negative program and replace it with a new, positive program—whether your program relates to sexuality, becoming a more effective salesperson, controlling your temper, disciplining your children or painting pictures. If you "fake it till you make it," your subconscious mind will eventually get the picture. You'll find yourself with a brand-new custom-designed self-image.

Why Reflective Relearning Works: Never Let Your Right Brain Know What Your Left Brain Is Thinking

"'Creative imagination' is not something reserved for the poets, the philosophers, the inventors," Maltz told us. "For imagination sets the goal 'picture' which our automatic mechanism works on. We act, or fail to act, not because of 'will' as is so commonly believed, but because of imagination."

Can you imagine Geoff trying to "will away" his impotence? Why is imagination effective in bringing about changes in attitudes and behavior while "willpower" isn't? What's really going on "inside our heads" when we engage in reflective relearning? The answers lie in the differences in function between the two halves of the human brain.

The idea that the left and right hemispheres of the brain control different functions of the mind and body has been around since 1836. Physicians noticed that patients suffering speech loss due to head injuries all had suffered damage to the same side of the brain—the left side. Such observations led them to conclude that verbal expression was controlled by the left side of the brain and to speculate that non-verbal perception might be controlled by the right. This theory was later confirmed by extensive neuropsychological testing. Additionally, observations of stroke patients indicated that each half of the brain controlled movement and sensation on the opposite side of the body.

It was not until the 1960s, however, when neuropsychologist Roger W. Sperry began the split-brain experiments that would win him the Nobel prize, that the deeper significance of our dual-functioning brains began to be understood. Communication between the two halves of the brain is controlled principally by a bundle of nerve fibers called the corpus callosum. Sperry and his students studied patients in whom this nerve bundle had been surgically cut in an attempt to control epileptic seizures. In these people the two brain hemispheres functioned independently of one another. Sperry found that *each half of the brain has its own conscious thought processes and its own memories.* In 97 percent of us the left brain controls the ability to produce and understand speech; the right brain enables us to form, store, and respond to sensory data such as we use when we put on our clothes, find our way to a known location or recognize a face. When a word was flashed to a split-brain subject's right hemisphere, she was unable to speak the word. The "verbal" left brain had not seen the word; the "visual" right brain knew what it was but could not speak it. When a subject's right brain was shown a picture of an apple, he could not name the object; but when his left hand (controlled by the right brain) was then given several unseen objects to choose from, he identified the apple.

Split-brain research has been trivialized in the popular media and its findings often misapplied, but a few generalizations about it are useful. When you are thinking linearly, critically, or evaluatively (such as when you read an editorial or calculate your income tax), you are using the left side of your brain. When you are thinking holistically, spatially, or imaginatively (such as when you're aroused sexually or when you hear footsteps on a dark street), it's the right side that's at work. The left brain is logical, sequential, and analytical; the right brain is intuitive, simultaneous, and synthetic. The left brain comprehends an object by its name; the right brain by the way it looks or feels. It has not been fully established what causes these differences in function, but it seems clear that the abilities of both cerebral hemispheres are necessary for a full human existence.

Avoiding the "Willpower" Trap

Now, what does all this have to do with your self-image? The answer, as you might already have guessed, lies in the word *image*. If you're perceiving yourself in images, which half of your brain is in charge? If you said "right," give yourself a pat on the back. If you try to address your self-image through the verbal, logical left side of the brain, it's not going to work. *That's not the left brain's job.* When you enter "the theater of the imagination," you're engaging your right brain and telling your left brain to take a back seat. You're decelerating the part of your brain that says, "If you'll only do things this way..." and allowing the part that thinks in pictures to take over.

No part of the brain has ever been identified with "the mind." Yet it's convenient to think of the left brain as generally working in tandem with the conscious mind, while the right brain tends to partner up with the subconscious mind. That's why "willpower" so often becomes "won't power." Willpower and "positive thinking" have never changed anyone's behavior. If the way you act and think is intimately bound up with your self-*image*, you're not going to change it by attacking the problem with the part of your brain that deals in *words*. Trying to change your behavior through your left brain traps you in an a cycle of frustration and despair. Geoff could tell himself with irrefutable logic that there was nothing shameful about sex and nothing physiologically wrong with him. "You're a man," his left brain could tell him. "Women perceive you as masculine, and that's nothing to be ashamed of." But in his right brain Geoff *saw* himself as "not-a-man," and all the logic in the world was not going to change that image. His right brain could not process that sort of information. He was like Sperry's split-brain patient who was unable to come up with the name for the image he saw on the screen. Only by engaging his imagination was Geoff able to address the part of his brain that controlled his self-image.

⊞ Turn Stumbling Blocks into Stepping Stones

With an understanding of how the two halves of your brain operate together, you can see how reflective relearning works. When you engage your imagination, you allow your subconscious, right-brain thoughts (images) to enter your left brain's conscious awareness. By creating a mental picture of the way you wish to be, you eliminate the stumbling blocks placed in your consciousness by your old, destructive self-image. With repeated practice, your subconscious mind provides agreement and movement toward the new images. After about six weeks these right-brain thoughts are fully brought to consciousness, and your left brain comes to act in accordance with them. Your feelings and actions have changed to become consistent with your new self-image. Take a look at some creative ways people have used the process to change their feelings, capablities, and actions. Assess how you might use it to transform a self-denying relationship with a spouse, friend, relative, or co-worker into to an assertive one based on mutual respect, overcome fears that keep you bound to self-limiting behavior, cast off feelings of inferiority that keep you from pursuing your ideal career, and discover hidden talents and capabilities that will aid you in achieving it.

How Mental Imaging Overcame an Abusive Relationship

For Stephanie the constant stream of negative criticism began shortly after her marriage to Bill at the age of 22. He was a demanding person who prided himself on being a "perfectionist," a "can-do problem solver." What he could do very effectively was berate his wife. She was "slow": she took too long to do everything. She was "socially inept": Bill's job required frequent get-togethers with colleagues and their spouses, and after every such occasion Bill would criticize her behavior. To hear him tell it she hardly opened her mouth, and when she did she invariably came out with something awkward and inane. She was slightly overweight, which to Bill meant "fat." He would comment, "You eat like a bird—a scavenger. You'll eat anything that's dead." As if these private rebukes weren't enough, after a while he began to belittle her in front of others.

Even before her wedding two of Stephanie's friends remarked on Bill's sarcastic abuse. She dismissed their concern, assuring them it was "just his sense of humor." After their marriage it dawned on her that Bill's humor wasn't so funny. When she protested, he ridiculed her: she was "supersensitive"; she was "unable to take a joke." Because she feared confrontation Stephanie learned to "let it slide," as she later put it.

Ever notice how the expressions we use tend to reflect reality? Things never slide up—they always slide DOWN. After three years of marriage, Stephanie was passively living out her husband's expectations. Without thinking consciously about it, she had come to accept his image of her. The self-portrait in her right brain was of a woman who was slow, socially awkward, and overweight. She found herself virtually paralyzed when in the company of others. It was as though she were wearing a T-shirt that said SOCIAL KLUTZ.

It was only after her friends sat her down for a heart-to-heart talk that Stephanie began to challenge Bill's mandates. They pointed out concrete examples of how she had changed. In college she'd been quiet and reserved, but while she never was the life of the party she'd led an active social life and had a good many friends. Everyone remembered her contributions to the journalism club and the school yearbook. Stephanie thought about how much she had enjoyed journalism. After her graduation she'd worked at improving her writing skills, hoping to contribute articles to magazines. She realized she hadn't written anything in two years. She also realized why. Bill was always finding errors in her manuscripts and ridiculing her efforts.

Stephanie got out her yearbook and reacquainted herself with her accomplishments. She could specifically remember many times in the past when she had been successful and confident. Her abilities had not changed, Stephanie realized, only her image of herself. "Slow and inept" was behavior she had *learned* through images imprinted on her right brain. It could be challenged, reevaluated and replaced with a more positive and realistic image of herself.

For the next six weeks Stephanie said "Cancel!" every time she caught herself reaffirming Bill's negative data about her, replacing it at once with the statement, "That's *his* opinion of me— *not mine!*" She affirmed to herself, "I'm quite comfortable with my personality and with my body." She spent 15 minutes each day in the theater of her imagination focusing on her past and future successes. She consciously showed her right brain how she had functioned with her friends before she met Bill. She let her right brain *see* herself working on the school yearbook, *feel* her satisfaction, *imagine* in detail the articles she planned to write.

Meanwhile, she considered herself "in training" to recapture her old-new self-image. In social situations she "acted as if" she was already operating under her new self-image, no matter how uncomfortable or "un-her" it seemed. When Bill made a sarcastic remark, she turned it into a neutral statement. If he commented about her weight, she said, "I know my weight is an issue for you, but it isn't for me. I'm very comfortable with my body." (This is a technique psychologists call the *broken record*. You restate the negative comment in a non-negative way, coupling it with the message you want the other person to hear, and you repeat it the same way every time.) She began to write again. When Bill asked to read her manuscripts, she politely but firmly refused, telling him "I'll only share my writing with people who accept my ideas."

Gradually her automatic mechanism, her conscious and subconscious minds working as a team, moved toward this new, confident image of herself. Success bred success, and Stephanie soon found that she was able to stand up for herself. When at a party her husband remarked, "You ought to just take that chocolate cake and apply it to your hips, that's where it's going anyway,"

Stephanie turned to him and said, "Bill, I've never liked your making comments like that in front of our friends. I know you think I'm overweight, but I really feel uncomfortable when you talk about it in front of other people."

Bill stopped in mid-chortle. To Stephanie's amazement, he even apologized on the way home. By changing her behavior, she had begun to change his as well.

How Mental Imaging Can Dissolve Your Fears

For several years Helen had experienced a growing fear that her house would burn down if she left it. She had only been outdoors four times in the last six months, each time at her husband's insistence and each time on foot. Her agoraphobia—fear of being out in open spaces—had made her too nervous to drive a car.

I met Helen when her husband brought her to my office. When I talked with her, I discovered that she had secretly harbored these inordinate fears throughout the 26 years of her marriage. But it had only been since the younger of her two daughters moved out six months earlier that her phobia had become acute. Clearly the belief that her house would burn down was only the tip of the iceberg. There were deeply seated issues that were only likely to be resolved through psychotherapy. But to overcome her fear of leaving her house and driving her car, Helen didn't need therapy. All she needed was to approach the problem Psycho-Cybernetically.

Helen chose one goal to aim for: to get in her car and drive to the supermarket five minutes away, then turn around and come home. She could rely on her conscious mind to eliminate thoughts of her house burning down by saying "Cancel!" when she needed to and by immediately affirming to herself, "All is well at home; I'm only driving to the store and back."

For several weeks Helen spent 20 minutes each day sitting quietly in her home and doing a relaxation exercise to engage her right brain. In her relaxed state she visualized herself getting dressed, walking into the garage and getting into her car, all the while seeing herself as calm and confident. In her imagination she saw herself start the car and slowly back it down the driveway. She visualized every detail of the trip to the supermarket—the stop sign by the school, the Shell station, the park with its playground and soccer field. She visualized herself pulling into the parking lot at the store, turning off the engine and sitting calmly in her car for a few moments; then she applied the same detail to the trip home. Helen repeated this exercise seven days a week, 20 minutes a day. Any time she had an interfering thought about her house burning down, she said "Cancel!" and reaffirmed that all was well.

After six weeks of reflective relearning, Helen rode to the store—as a passenger. A friend drove her car while she sat beside her with her eyes closed, visualizing the trip in her imagination. She repeated the exercise with her friend for three consecutive days.

On the third day, after her return from the store her friend got out of the car and Helen transferred herself to the driver's seat. While her friend sat and waited for her on the front porch, Helen drove to the store and returned with a triumphant smile in her eyes. When she called me that evening, she said, "Would you believe seventeen 'CANCELS' for the round trip?"

Within weeks Helen was successfully driving anywhere she chose. Yes, she still used CANCEL, reminding herself to *fake* it until her automatic mechanism could *make* the conquest of her fears a reality for her. By this time Helen needed no further proof that changing her mental pictures would lead to changes in her feelings and behavior. Her understanding made it easier for her to challenge her deeper, long-held fears that had precipitated her phobia.

How Mental Imaging Can Save Your Job in a Changing World

During a break in a seminar I was giving on "Making the most of your best through creative imagination," Carlos came up to me and introduced himself. He had signed up for the seminar, he explained, because he was afraid that he was about to lose his job.

Carlos was a court reporter who long ago had mastered the use of the transcript machine the job required. Recently he had heard that the machines were about to be made compatible with a new computer system the county was installing. All court reporters would have to learn to use it. "I just froze when I heard this," Carlos said. "I didn't think I was smart enough to learn to use a computer." Carlos was an immigrant from Central America and was still not entirely comfortable with English. He thought of himself as "slow" and "not as good as most people" when it came to learning new things.

But the seminar, Carlos told me, had led him to understand that this perception was a false image. It had been stamped on his right brain by his experiences as a newcomer adjusting to an unfamiliar culture and reinforced by his self-consciousness about his lack of formal education. His logical left brain told him that he *had* in fact learned English as a second language; he had mastered the hundreds of unwritten rules required for finding his way in his adopted country; he had learned to use the transcript machine. What he needed to do, he now realized, was to eliminate the old data from his subconscious mind that told him he was a slow learner. He needed to affirm to himself repeatedly that he was capable of learning the computer system. He needed to take time each day to access his right brain and to visualize himself as having mastered his new job skills.

Three months later I received a note from Carlos. He had completed the retraining process and was effectively using the new system. He had used the CRAFT process to replace his old feeling of being not-smart-enough with a new image of himself as confident and competent. He affirmed that he was "as least as smart as fifty percent of the people who had to make the switch-over."

Significantly Carlos made the commitment to spend 15 minutes each day exercising his creative imagination. In his daily visualizations he focused on one specific goal: he saw himself reading and mastering the manuals for the new computer system. (A speed-reading class helped facilitate his actual learning.) He also visualized himself as Rocky running up the steps, "training to be a winner." By visualizing himself as successful, Carlos was able to make his subconscious mind agree and comply with the notion that he *was* successful.

And, ultimately, he was.

Developing a Fake-It-Till-You-Make-It Attitude

For most people the hardest aspect of reflective relearning is convincing the left brain that it's going to work. The left brain is too logical to accept on faith that simply imagining successful results is going to move you toward them. It's often too impatient to wait for the cumulative effects of "mental practice" and "acting as-if" to take effect. Some people give up right from the get-go because they can't keep their left brains from wandering all over the place.

That's why I urge you, over and over again, to (all together, now): fake it till you make it. Building a new self-image doesn't happen overnight. The process is cumulative. It takes daily effort for about six weeks. Remember that nothing worthwhile happens overnight. Even getting born took nine months. Just keep your conscious attention focused on your new self-image and keep on behaving as though you've already achieved it.

Three Guidelines for Creating New Images

In the meantime, observe these guidelines to facilitate your re-learning:

1. Choose the same time each day for your mental picturing. *What* time you choose doesn't matter. Make it a time when you're least likely to be disturbed by internal or external pressures. Some people prefer the morning when they're fresh, others prefer the evening when they're not distracted by work. The important thing is to do it for 15 minutes *every* day, seven days a week, for six weeks. A consistent time of day is important because it helps make the exercise of your imagination a regular habit. Only through daily, repetitive mental practice will your new images be accepted by your right brain.

2. Make sure there will be no interruptions. If you're like most people, finding a private, quiet place to do your mental imaging is more difficult than finding 15 minutes. It is important that this be *your* time, uninterrupted by the demands of work, family or the telephone. If you can't find a time when you'll be alone in the house, hang up a DO NOT DISTURB sign and give your family firm instructions that it is to be honored. Make sure they know you are not available to receive visitors or phone calls. Better yet, unplug the phone. Some people sit in their car in the parking lot at work during their coffee break. Others drive to a park and find a favorite tree to sit under. When I began the process myself after my first encounter with Dr. Maltz, I used a walk-in closet. It was dark and cozy, and the hanging clothes muffled any uproar created by my three young sons.

3. Accept all positive images as valid and helpful. As your right brain is bringing up those lovely visual images, your left brain is going to try to yank the program back to logic. There you are picturing yourself in Paris, strolling along the Seine embankment. The Eiffel Tower is rising to your left, you're about to bite into a steaming croissant, and your left brain is assuming the role of Jiminy Cricket: "Hey, c'mon, who are you kidding? Paris? You don't even speak French!" The theater of the imagination is the right brain's space, and it's essential not to let the left brain intrude. That's how you end up hitting curbs. Tell Jiminy Cricket, "Hey, I have to remain open to all possibilities," and keep on letting your right brain do its job.

Change "What If?" into "So, What If?"

Don't be discouraged if you encounter setbacks. Often these "setbacks" are nothing more than worry over what *might* happen: "What if my husband says something at the barbecue that makes me feel so awkward I just close up like a clam?" "What if all my self-doubt comes rushing back in at the job interview?" "What if the boss doesn't like my presentation?"

What if...? What if...? What if...? The thing to do every time you catch yourself playing the what-if game is to add the word *so* to the formula. Ask yourself "So, what if...?"

Catch the shift in emphasis? By adding the word *so*, you become master of the situation. Say out loud, "So, what if he laughs at me?" "So, what if she leaves me?" Then add two more words: "Next time." Tell yourself, "Okay, so, what if I do blow it? It's not the end of the world. Next time, I'll..."

Of course when you first start making this shift, your conscious mind may still believe it *is* the end of the world. By now you should be familiar enough with the principles of Psycho-Cybernetics to know that this doesn't matter. The subconscious mind agrees with everything the conscious mind tells it. At first you may be feeling "Oh my God!" rather than "So, what if," but repetition will change your belief and lead you to behave in a manner consistent with your new belief. By changing "What if?" to "So, what if" and adding "Next time," *every time*, you shift your subconscious mind away from anxiety and toward control.

Turn Your Mistakes into Steps on the Road to Success

Then there are the times you do make mistakes—and make no mistake about it, you will. The important thing is to regard your mistakes not as indications of failure but as steps on the road to success.

Imagine for a moment that you're a visitor to Earth fresh off a flying saucer. On your planet there are no walls. The first day on Earth you walk right into one. Does it make you feel stupid? Of course not. You've never met a wall before. "Ah," you tell yourself, gingerly rubbing your antennae, "that must be why they have these things called *doors*. Next time I'll know better."

Most of us Earthlings don't operate that way. Instead of learning from our mistakes, we tend to let them intimidate us. Instead of looking for the door, we remember the times we walked into the wall. Indeed, we're constantly replaying the old mental tapes that show us walking into walls. In psychology we call these tape loops *ruminations.* "That was dumb," we tell ourselves. "I can't believe I did that. I walk into that same wall every time. Oh, brother, *am I stupid!*"

Now, if your subconscious mind is forever telling you, "Last time you hit the WALL; watch out for the WALL; don't be stupid and run into that WALL again," where is your internal guidance system going to direct you? Correct—smack into the wall. Remember, a servomechanism works by responding to feedback and making course changes. Instead of punishing yourself for your mistakes, acknowledge them as guideposts toward growth and change. Follow this procedure:

- Listen for your ruminations.
- Say "CANCEL!" and stop the tape when you find yourself replaying your past mistakes.
- Tell yourself, "Okay, I made a mistake. It's no big deal. Everyone makes mistakes."
- Consider how you would handle the situation differently if you had it to do over again.
- Visualize yourself handling the situation as you would have liked to.
- Remember to change "What if...?" into "So, what if...? and add "Next time..."

Your Right Brain at Play: Six Ways to Turn on Your Creative Imagination

1. *Take "time out" for yourself.* Get out your appointment calendar and decide on the best time for your daily 15 minutes in the theater of the imagination. Mark off the time as yours. Honor your appointment with yourself just as you would with a business associate, client, or friend.

2. *Make sure you'll be undisturbed during your appointed time.* Remove all distractions. Unplug the phone; turn off the TV and stereo. Advise your family, housemates and colleagues that you need to be completely alone for fifteen minutes. Hang up a "Do Not Disturb" sign.

3. *Make yourself as relaxed and comfortable as possible.* (In later chapters we'll be discussing techniques for relaxation and focusing). Wear loose-fitting clothing. Sit in a cool spot to avoid drifting into sleep.

4. *Make your imagining as detailed as possible.* You formed your present self-image by interpreting and evaluating personal experiences. Try to let your imagined experiences be as vivid as your real ones. Remember, your subconscious mind won't know the difference. Pay attention to details of sight, sound and smell to make your imagined environment approximate a real one. If you're imagining a confrontation with an abusive co-worker, for example, picture your workplace as though you were seeing it on a movie screen. Feel the texture of the chair you're sitting in; smell the odors of leather and coffee. See your antagonist's face; bring to memory an outfit he or she often wears. Hear the sound of his or her voice. The closer to actual experience your imagination can bring you, the more effectively your subconscious mind will perceive the images you create.

5. *Imagine yourself being successful.* It doesn't matter how you've handled situations in the past. In the theater of your imagination, you're going to see yourself acting and responding the way you always "thought you should"; the way you always "wished you had"—the way you pictured it when you told yourself "Next time I'll..." It doesn't matter whether you believe you're going to act and respond that way the next time the situation comes up. Just see yourself *being* that way *now.* Picture yourself moving through your environment "as if" you had already achieved your ideal self-image—confident, poised, happy, your spine erect and your head held high.

6. *Make your right brain work for you.* Your left brain is going to intrude from time to time with typical left brain thoughts: Did I turn off the oven? Did I remember to feed the dog? Is the copier going to be fixed in time for me to copy the sales reports? Your left brain is a lot like HAL, the computer in *2001: A Space Odyssey.* It believes that everything will fall apart if it can't maintain control. Just tell your left brain to shut up; you'll deal with its problems later. Then make a conscious choice to return to the theater of your imagination.

You have the power to use your creative imagination to find your own best self. It's simply a matter of replacing the old, negative pictures you carry in your subconscious mind with new, positive pictures. Your present self-image is based not on "reality" but on what you imagine to be reality. Just remember that it's based entirely on images you've allowed your automatic mechanism to zero in on, and that those images can just as easily be creative as destructive. Through reflective relearning, your ideal self-image will become reality in good time.

Targeting on Ideas

- Your attitudes, feelings and behavior change in the direction of what you *believe* to be true.
- Through your imagination you can create positive images of yourself that with time and repeated practice will become your actual self-image.
- "Fake it till you make it"—act as if you have already achieved success and your feelings, attitudes and behavior will become consistent with actual success.

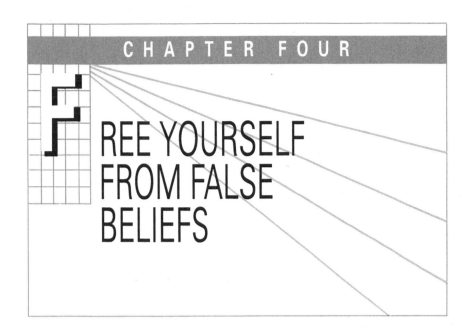

CHAPTER FOUR

FREE YOURSELF FROM FALSE BELIEFS

[I]f you have accepted an idea—from yourself, your teachers, your parents, friends, advertisements—or from any other source, and further, if you are firmly convinced that idea is true, it has the same power over you as [a] hypnotist's words have over the hypnotist's subject.

—*Maxwell Maltz, Psycho-Cybernetics (1960)*

Be careful what you say to your children. They may agree with you. Before calling a child "stupid" or "clumsy" or "bad" or "a disappointment," it is important for a parent to consider the question, "Is this how I wish my child to experience him- or herself?"

—*Nathaniel Branden, Honoring The Self (1983)*

If you believe you're limited to a particular way of living, then you are. Just ask any elephant trainer.

If the circus doesn't happen to be in town this week and you're not planning a trip to India, imagine this scene: you've got a full-grown elephant with a two-inch band of steel around her hind leg, attached to a chain perhaps six feet long. The chain in turn is fastened to a stake that's been driven into the ground. Now, it's obvious that the elephant could pull up the stake any time she wished. But she doesn't. That elephant was first chained to the stake when she was a baby and wasn't strong enough to move it. She soon learned the futility of trying to yank the stake free and began to accept it as a condition of her life. By the time she was strong enough to free herself, she had stopped trying. As long as she got her hay, water and an occasional peanut she was content to live out her life within a six-foot radius. Elephants have been known to die in fires while chained to stakes they could easily move.

Many of us human beings are constrained by beliefs as false as that poor elephant's. We allow our abilities to be defined by chains we could snap and stakes we could pull out of the ground. Our automatic mechanism needs a goal to strive for. If false beliefs keep us from setting goals, it becomes impossible for us to reach any. We tell ourselves, "I'm not smart enough for a high-paying job"; "I don't deserve to have someone love me"; "Change is too scary." Yet often the only thing that keeps us from breaking out of our confining life patterns is a *belief* that a chain is holding us back. It doesn't matter where the belief comes from. Once it's planted in our subconscious mind we *accept* it as true and behave in a manner consistent with it.

"An elephant never forgets." We, however, have a couple of tools an elephant is lacking—a rational mind and a creative imagination. Our subconscious mind never forgets, either—unless we consciously choose to *make* it forget.

This chapter is about your belief system: how it was formed, how it keeps you confined, and how you can change it in ways that will empower you to break your chains. You'll learn:

- how to use rational thinking to *challenge* the false beliefs that prevent you from achieving happiness and success.

- how to use reflective relearning to *replace* those self-limiting ideas with "new memories" that are realistic and positive.

- how to use your automatic mechanism to *take control* of your new memories and incorporate them into your basic concept of yourself.

What You Believe Conditions What You Can Do

Every one of us has certain ideas about ourselves and our environment that we "know" are true, even when they're not. These beliefs have been a part of us for so long that we may not even be aware of them, but our subconscious mind keeps on saying "yes" to them just the same. Most of the time they remain hidden to our conscious mind, and all we're aware of is their negative results.

A five-year-old girl sits at a table drawing a picture. Her grandmother comments, "You certainly don't have your mother's eye for color and balance." When she is grown, friends wonder why her home and personal style are so conspicuously drab despite her lively personality.

A boy is called "selfish" any time he asks for something for himself. "Who do you think you are—the Prince of Wales?" his mother says. "Be grateful for what you have." As an adult he's learned to settle for a marginal, minimal life, subconsciously believing that he doesn't deserve money, respect, or love.

A boy grows up in a household with a violent father. By the time he's a teenager, he's subconsciously adopted as a fundamental tenet of his belief system, "The way to deal with frustration is to hit someone weaker than you."

A Native American girl from New Mexico moves to Ohio to live with her half-sister after the death of her parents. Though she was a straight-A student on the reservation, her grades plummet during her first semester at her new school. A shy and hesitant thirteen-year-old, she is taken under the wing of a school counselor who discovers that her encounters with racism have left her with the belief that she is "less capable" than her new classmates.

In the last chapter we looked at the power of beliefs to condition our attitudes and behavior. When beliefs become part of the fundamental way we regard ourselves and the world around us, they become very powerful indeed. Our belief systems begin in early childhood with "reflections" we receive from our parents. These reflections serve as our first indicators of our personal worth. As we grow and develop, other mirrors are held up to us by family members, peers and teachers. These reflections form the basis of our self-image as we grow to maturity. Yet if we bring these beliefs to consciousness and look at them critically, they rarely hold up under scrutiny. By challenging our false beliefs and using our imagination to create new ones—new *memories,* in effect—we can change our attitudes and behavior and discover new abilities within ourselves.

How False Beliefs Keep You Hypnotized

Maxwell Maltz regarded belief systems as a form of self-hypnosis. "It is no exaggeration," he wrote, "that every human being is hypnotized to some extent, either by ideas he has uncritically accepted from others, or ideas he has repeated to himself or convinced himself are true. These negative ideas have exactly the same effect on our behavior as the negative ideas implanted into the mind of a hypnotized subject."

Hypnosis is a heightened state of awareness in a narrow focus of attention. It engages the right brain's ability to vividly realize images and tune out left-brain distractions. As you know, people who appear to display unusual abilities under hypnosis have actually possessed those abilities all along. They were previously unable to use their power, as Maltz put it, "because they themselves did not know it was there. They had bottled it up and choked it off, *because of their own negative beliefs....* [I]t would be truer to say that the hypnotist had 'dehypnotized' them rather than to say he had hypnotized them." People operating under a self-limiting belief system, *"without realizing it consciously...are working against themselves... [T]hey cannot express, or bring into play their actual available strength."*

Even our physical health can be affected by such self-hypnosis. In their book *Getting Well Again*, Dr. O. Carl Simonton and Stephanie Matthews-Simonton described the connection between a patient's beliefs about his or her illness and the subsequent progression of the disease. In *Love, Medicine And Miracles*, Dr. Bernie Siegel demonstrated a link between the attitude of cancer patients toward health and their prognosis for recovery. If subconscious, even cellular processes can be positively affected by changing beliefs, why not your ability to achieve success?

How to Identify Your False Beliefs

To get an idea of what your false beliefs might be, get a pencil and paper. Read the following questions and jot down your answers.

1. Do you become anxious or fearful in situations that pose no actual threat? What are the situations? Calling strangers on the phone? Confronting a mechanic who overcharged you for fixing your car? *Why* do you feel that such situations are likely to cause you physical or emotional harm?

2. Do you feel that "things just happen" that prevent you from achieving success? What were you striving for? What were the specific circumstances that thwarted you? Express your answers this way: "I would have _____ if _____ hadn't prevented me."

3. In pursuing goals, do you ever find yourself blocked by such thoughts as "I can't," "I'm no good," or "I don't deserve to..."? In what circumstances has this happened? What were your goals? What, specifically, did you tell yourself? Express your answers this way: "I felt that I couldn't _____ because _____."

71

4. Do you sometimes feel that you're moving toward some desired outcome only to find yourself stymied by procrastination, leading to blame-casting and a sense of hopelessness? What desired outcome—a career move, a relationship, a personal project? What, exactly, were your feelings that led you to give it up? What were the circumstances? Be specific.

Finished? Take a look at the reasons you gave for your non-success. The fears, doubts and self-punishment you expressed are the results of self-hypnotism. They are like old tapes that were recorded long ago and are replayed over and over in your subconscious mind. They are clues to your false beliefs—the dead-end paths your horse has been conditioned to follow.

Not convinced? Perhaps you're telling yourself, "But they're *not* false. Confronting Ernie *is* scary—I'll be humiliated"; "I'm *not* organized enough to get that office manager's job"; "I *am* too dull to attract an interesting mate."

Well, don't put away your pencil just yet. You're about to find out how to *recognize* the falseness of your beliefs so that your rider can blaze a new path. The following questionnaire will help you identify and understand the source of your belief system. Think hard and answer as honestly as you can.

Exploring Where Your Beliefs Come From: A Questionnaire

1. What is your first memory of being alive?
   - What was the event?

   _____

   _____

   - How old were you? _____
   - Who was with you? _____
   - What emotions do you remember feeling? _____

   _____

2. What were you like as a small child?
   - What family stories were told about you?

_____

- Did you feel that you were a "wanted" child? ❑ yes ❑ no
  What memories support this feeling?

_____

_____

- What nicknames did your family give you?

_____

- Did you "fit" in your family? (Some examples of "nonfits": the only girl in a family of five boys; the "dreamer" in a household of "practical" people) ❑ yes ❑ no
  If "no," what memories support this feeling?

_____

_____

- How would you evaluate your overall "success" in the years before you started school? _____

3. What were your elementary-school years like?
   - What memories do you have of kindergarten?

_____

_____

- What do you remember your teachers saying about you?

_____

_____

- What was the general "message" of your grade-school report cards?

_____

_____

_____

- How easily did you form friendships?
  ❏ very easily   ❏ had a few close friends   ❏ did not have many friends
  Explain:

  _____

  _____

  _____

- How well do you feel you "measured up" to your peers?
  ❏ very well   ❏ moderately well   ❏ poorly
  Explain:

  _____

  _____

  _____

Now compare these answers with the ones you wrote to the four questions on pages 71-72. Do you see any correlations? Did your answers trigger memories of other experiences that connect with your beliefs about yourself?

"Mirror, Mirror on the Wall": Understanding How Your Beliefs Were Formed

"For the first five or six years", wrote family therapist Virginia Satir in *Peoplemaking*, "the child's [self-esteem] is formed by the family almost exclusively. After he starts to school, other influences come into play, but...[o]utside forces tend to reinforce the feelings of worth or worthlessness that he has learned at home."

Your early-childhood memories are often clues to your belief system. Your earliest memory of life is often indicative of the way you see yourself. A child whose earliest memory is one of security and joy will tend to have a more positive self-image than one who remembers uncertainty and fear.

A friend of mine remembers a story retold to the point of embarrassment by her family. At the age of two she climbed out of her playpen one day, opened the front door and wandered off intrepidly down the street. Her frantic parents found her safe and sound six blocks from home. Now she travels world-wide for an oil company and mentions this incident jokingly as a way of explaining "why I have jet fuel in my veins." Whether she recognizes it or not, the frequent repetition of this story probably had a great deal to do with her choice of careers. Another person remembers being told repeatedly by his well-meaning adoptive parents how lucky he was to have been chosen by them. "If we hadn't picked you out," they said, trying to reassure him of their love, "you would have been doomed to a life of poverty and misery." As an adult this man never seemed to be able to save money. He made choices about his life that consistently led him to see himself as "miserable."

Childhood nicknames can often be clues to adult self-perception. When a client told me she felt awkward and self-conscious about her body, I wasn't surprised to learn that when she was a child her older brothers had called her "Bigfoot." A man who was self-conscious about being "too short" turned out to have been called "Munchkin" as a child. And do you remember the woman we met in chapter 1 who'd been called "Laura Dammit" as a toddler?

How did you "fit" in your family? Joel, a successful architect, was a "workaholic." He saw himself as someone who had to work long hours to accomplish even the simplest task, to the point where it was negatively impacting his health and his marriage. It turned out that when he was a small child his mother had married for the second time. She and his adoptive father had three children together, all of whom were labeled "natural learners." Joel, while a good student, was spoken of as one who had to "work for his grades." At 42 he still saw himself as plodding away, needing to put in extra time if he was going to keep up.

Your memories of school may also tell you a great deal about how your belief system was formed. A man whose fear of failure and expectation of disapproval has him living a marginal life recalls a (singularly incompetent) kindergarten teacher's critique of a fingerpainting he made as a Mother's Day gift: "Oh, your mommy isn't going to like that at *all!*" A woman whose self-image tells her that she just isn't *entitled* to success remembers teachers throughout her school years expressing their disappointment when comparing her with her two older sisters. A woman who thinks of herself as a "bore" and a "compulsive talker" remembers that every teacher from first grade through sixth wrote on her report card, "Janice is a good student, but she bothers those around her with her incessant talking." And do you remember the alcoholic loner we met earlier who repeatedly heard "Shut up, Greg" from his schoolmates?

Whether your memories of childhood consciously correlate with your own belief system is of little importance. The thing to be aware of is that your self-hypnosis was accomplished at an early age. What your parents, teachers, peers, and early experiences "taught" you about yourself became the curbs for your automatic mechanism. They became programmed in your subconscious mind as defining limits. "Our errors, mistakes, failures, and sometimes even our humiliations, were necessary steps in the learning process," Maltz wrote. "However, they were meant to be means to an end—and not an end in themselves. When they have served their purpose, *they should be forgotten*." How much more true is this when the "errors, mistakes, failures, and humiliations" are no more real than the elephant's belief that she can't free herself from the stake?

It's time to start learning to forget.

⊞ How You Can Free Yourself from False Beliefs

The first step toward challenging your false and limiting belief systems is to understand that you are a human being who deserves better than to be constrained by unreasonable fears, expectations of failure, and feelings of unworthiness.

The second step is to remember that false beliefs are nothing more than habits that you have learned. Like any habit, a false belief can be changed by using your rider to create new memories for your horse. Remember, the subconscious mind can't evaluate the information. It merely agrees and complies with what the conscious mind tells it. By playing back images of inadequacy and failure, you program yourself to fail. By consciously challenging such images and replacing them with pictures of competence and success, you can cancel your negative beliefs and replace them with positive ones. These new memories then define the scope of the targets your internal guidance system may aim for.

A story told by a woman at one of my seminars illustrates perfectly how we can dehypnotize ourselves from false, restricting beliefs. While on her honeymoon in Yosemite National Park, Andrea and her new husband found themselves hiking on a steep and dangerous trail with a sheer dropoff to the valley below. Not anticipating such a rigorous climb, she had left her hiking boots in camp and worn only tennis shoes. Now her ankles were feeling rubbery and her feet were slipping on the rocky trail. As she climbed Andrea began to verbalize her fears to her husband: "I should have worn my boots. I can feel my ankles getting weaker. These shoes don't have enough traction.... *I'm going to fall!*"

At this point her husband stopped and faced her. He put his hands on her shoulders and said, "Look directly at my eyes and say, 'I am sure-footed and nimble...I am surefooted and nimble.'" He had her repeat this statement for several minutes. Then he said, "Let's go, my sure-footed, nimble new wife."

Erasing those old tapes that belie your own strengths and abilities is often just a matter of recording a new tape—of convincing your horse that it's surefooted and nimble. Let's take a look at different ways in which false beliefs can hypnotize you and at the skills you can use to dehypnotize yourself.

Irrational Fears May Spring from False Beliefs

Sid was an intelligent, capable businessman in his late thirties who had become involved in a small-claims lawsuit. He owned a health-food store that shared a parking lot with a pizzeria. The pizzeria's owner had brought action against him, claiming that Sid's customers "hogged the parking lot" and drove off his own customers by making remarks about the low nutritional value of pizza. In California small-claims actions no attorneys are permitted in court; each party must plead his or her own case. Sid prepared himself well; he entered the courtroom feeling relaxed and confident. This attitude changed the moment the judge appeared. Suddenly Sid became very uncomfortable. His palms were moist and his breathing labored and rapid. He became increasingly anxious and confused. When it came time for him to state his case, he babbled incoherently, unable to connect one thought with another. The judge's attempts to reassure him only increased his discomfort. Finally she granted Sid a postponement to allow him another opportunity.

The event left Sid with his confidence shattered. He had no previous history of anxiety or panic attacks and no clue as to why this one had happened. As he remembered the scene of the judge on her bench, he became agitated, and his panic began to return. To reduce his anxiety he put himself through a twenty-minute relaxation procedure and began to ask himself what had frightened him about the judge. A middle-aged woman in a black robe sitting behind a bench on a riser before him—what did that image mean to him? He said aloud "Black robe reminds me of..." and completed the sentence: "Nothing." He tried again: "Black robe reminds me of...well, yeah—judge." He kept repeating the phrase, each time allowing himself to *see* the image he was describing. "Black robe reminds me of..." emperor, ruler, justice, court...teacher.

Suddenly Sid's mind became flooded with memories. "My word, that's it!" he exclaimed. "I haven't thought about Sister Margaret in years!"

Sid had grown up a Catholic and had gone to parochial schools. His teachers belonged to a religious order that required them to dress in black. Now Sid vividly recalled an incident that had happened when he was in the third grade. He had been called to the chalkboard to work on a math problem. He became embarrassed and could not think clearly. The teacher reacted impatiently and ridiculed him before the class. He returned to his seat red-faced and mortified. Even as he remembered the incident, he became anxious once again.

How to Tune Out Negative Beliefs
with Rational Thinking

Look again at the answer you wrote for question 1 on page 71. Does Sid's experience shed any light on the situations that make you irrationally anxious or fearful? Perhaps you fear pursuing your dreams because of a childhood incident when you were ridiculed by a parent or other role model. Perhaps you become anxious in the presence of authority figures because of a long-forgotten incident of abuse. You don't need to identify the source of your false beliefs in order to challenge them. But as in Sid's case, it can be useful in showing you just how false they are. Sid had been unable to figure out logically what had happened in the courtroom. Yet as he relaxed and felt reassured, he could recall an "old tape" that stood in the way of an adult goal. In his subconscious mind Sid believed that the judge was going to ridicule and embarrass him, and he reacted to that belief as if he were a third-grade child.

Maltz advised us to challenge such beliefs with rational thinking. "To root out the belief which is responsible for your feeling and behavior," he wrote, "ask yourself, 'why?' Is there some task which you would like to do, some channel in which you would like to express yourself, but you hang back feeling that 'I can't?' Ask yourself...'Why do I believe that I can't?'... Is this belief based on an actual fact...or a false conclusion?'"

Maltz saw rational thinking as the "control knob" by which you can "tune out" negative and inappropriate beliefs. He suggested that you ask yourself the following questions each time you catch yourself saying "I can't," "I'm not worthy," or "I'm afraid":

1. Is there any rational reason for such a belief?
2. Could I be mistaken in this belief?
3. Would I come to the same conclusion about some other person in a similar situation?
4. Why should I continue to act and feel as if this were true if there is no good reason to believe it?

Ask yourself each of these questions *out loud* and *answer* it out loud *every time* you catch yourself indulging in a negative belief about yourself. As your conscious mind actively implements your answers, your subconscious mind will come to agree with them. By using rational thinking to challenge your false beliefs, you pull your automatic mechanism back on course.

Consciously recalling the incident he had suppressed helped Sid to rationally challenge the belief that a woman in a black robe was a cause for anxiety and panic. Was there any rational reason for his fear? No. Could he be mistaken in believing that a black-robed woman in a role of authority was going to humiliate him? Of course. If it were Joe Blow up there before the judge, would Sid expect *him* to feel humiliated? No way. Was there any reason he should continue to act as though the woman posed a threat? No reason in the world. Dehypnotized from his false belief, Sid went back to court and successfully defended his case.

Consider the irrational fears you identified in your answer to question 1 on page 71. Apply the four questions on page 79 to these fears *right now*.

They don't seem quite so fearful, do they?

Feeling That "Things Are Beyond Your Control" Can Spring from False Beliefs

Carol was terribly discouraged over what she perceived as a weight problem. She was 21 and had been on roller coaster of binging and dieting for six years. As a high-school sophomore she had weighed 120 pounds. By her junior year her weight was up to 165. By her seventeenth birthday she was back down to 120. At her graduation she had ballooned back up to 165. And so on and so forth, up and down.

I asked Carol to describe how she felt when she was at the "120-pound" phase of her cycle. "Emotionally high," she responded. "Terrifically excited about life. And *hungry*—enormously hungry all the time. It's like my *body* is urging me to get back up to 165 pounds." Carol described a pattern that is quite common among intensive dieters. When she was determined to lose weight, she displayed an iron will about what she put into her mouth. But once down to her desired level, she seemed driven to eat anything that would fill her up—leftover pizza, soggy French fries, stale donuts. Every day she would will herself to stop, but her indiscriminate binging was "something that just seemed to happen in spite of myself." When she began to approach the upper end of the scale (no pun intended), her craving leveled off. She would still compulsively eat selected foods, but she no longer devoured everything in sight. Finally she would hit 165, go on a diet, and begin the cycle again.

As with many "overweight" people, Carol's problem was partly social and physiological. Because of the prevalent cultural attitude that "thin is beautiful," she felt compelled to maintain a weight below what was normal for her body. When she dieted, her body compensated by decreasing her metabolic rate so that fewer calories were used. At the same time, her body increased her appetite to ensure an adequate caloric intake.

But when Carol began to replay some of her old childhood tapes, another reason for her eating pattern became apparent. Carol came from a family in rural Arkansas for whom life was almost literally "feast or famine." When the crops came in, they ate well. But there were times when all they had were canned or dried foods, and they had to make them last. Carol remembered dreading the winter and its promise of only one meal a day. To a great extent her "weight problem" was a result of her early conditioning. Her old tapes told her, "Eat it while you have it. Live for today, for tomorrow may never come."

Two conflicting subconscious beliefs had led Carol to the false conclusion that her weight was something over which she had no control:

- "I need to weigh 125 pounds because 'thin is beautiful.'"
- "I need to eat as much as I can today because I may go hungry tomorrow."

As a result of the first belief, Carol dieted to the point where her body craved calories. As a result of the second, she binged to the point of unhealthiness. Carol discovered her false beliefs in the context of psychotherapy, but you need no such assistance to recognize and challenge your own. Take a look at your answer to question 2 on page 71—the things that "just happen" to prevent you from achieving success. Use your responses on the questionnaire to try to identify the old tapes that may be making you feel that "things are beyond your control." Does something "always seem to come up" when you have an important job interview scheduled? Very likely your horse is hearing an old tape that says, "You're not going to get the job (or don't deserve to get it, or will have to assume unwanted responsibility if you get it), so don't embarrass yourself by trying." Do you seem to have "more than your share of bad luck"? It could be that you're making your own "luck" by subconsciously complying with an old childhood tape—something like "You buttered your bread, now *eat* it!"

When Carol applied rational thinking to her false beliefs, she came to these conclusions:

- "There is no reason I 'should' weigh 125 pounds."
- "There is no reason to believe that famine is just around the corner."
- "I was mistaken in my belief that my weight fluctuation was something over which I have no control. When I look at the problem rationally, I can see that I was subconsciously in control all the time. Now I can approach the problem consciously too."

Carol set 140 pounds as a new, more realistic weight goal for herself. By applying rational thinking every time she caught herself anxiously dieting or compulsively eating, she consciously challenged her false beliefs.

What do you believe "just happens" to keep you from attaining your goals? Use rational thinking to challenge this belief *now*. Every time you find yourself thinking, "I could (lose weight, get a promotion, take that accounting class, meet Mr. Right) if it weren't for (friends imposing on my time, my mother, church work, my allergies, bad luck, circumstances beyond my control)," ask yourself the four questions on page 79. Make it a habit to challenge your false belief whenever you find yourself aware of it.

Feelings of Inadequacy, Unworthiness or Guilt May Spring from False Beliefs

It's happened again, Georgia thought miserably. Every guy I get involved with turns out to be a creep. If they don't play around or put me down, they disappear when I need them the most. My sister is dying of cancer, and where is Rick? This is the week he picks to go off camping with his buddies. I've always been around when *he* needed *me*. I thought Rick was different. I don't know what I'm going to do. I'm 38; I want commitment, and a baby...but I guess I just don't deserve to...

Georgia shook herself. Wait a minute, she thought. Why is this *my* fault? What do I mean, I don't *deserve* to? Where did I get such an idea?

Georgia grew up in a small Pennsylvania town. She was by several years the youngest of her parents' five children. Though she regarded them as a close, loving family, Georgia now found herself remembering contrary messages. She remembered her mother's tension and flare-ups of anger when her brothers and sisters were off at school. She remembered her father referring to her jokingly as "an accident" and her mother saying with a sigh to a friend, "I'd always wanted to go back to school and finish my B.A., but after Georgia came along it just wasn't realistic." At 15 Georgia became pregnant and chose to give the baby up for adoption. Though her family had been supportive, Georgia now remembered the disapproval of her community, how hurt she'd been at being kicked out of her church choir and barred from participation in the school play.

"Is *this* why I feel I 'don't deserve' a man who'll love me, and a baby?" Georgia asked herself. "Because I was an 'accident'? Because I was an 'unwed mother'? Would I feel that about someone else? Then why am I punishing myself? Whose voice do I hear when I tell myself, 'You don't deserve to be happy'? My mother's? Pastor Hildesheimer's? And why do I have to agree with them?"

Why, indeed? Whose voices do you hear on your old tapes? The messages may be something like these: "He's not his older brother; Lord knows we shouldn't expect too much of him."

"Here's Daddy's little tax deduction!" "You idiot! This is all your fault!" "You sure didn't get that from *my* side of the family!" "What a (wimp, lazy slob, selfish pig, useless piece of nothing)!"

Take a look at your answer to question 3 on page 71. Can you identify the old tapes that keep you falsely believing "I can't," "I'm no good," or "I don't deserve to..."?

How to Use Reflective Relearning to Create New Memories

Once you've used your left brain to challenge your false beliefs, bring your right brain into play to create new ones. Don't forget that the subconscious mind needs vividly realized images to agree and comply with—"new memories," as Maltz called them. You will be successful in training your horse away from an old dead-end path only if you have a new, positive path for it to follow. When false beliefs have led to deep-seated feelings of unworthiness, your left brain may resist the notion that you could ever feel differently about yourself. But if you are willing to spend six weeks of daily practice selecting new beliefs and eliminating the old, and if during those six weeks you "act as if" your new beliefs were already in place, *you will succeed.*

During those six weeks, apply the CRAFT process every day:

1. **Cancel** memories of your old, negative beliefs
2. **Replace** them with new, positive beliefs
3. **Affirm** your new concept of yourself
4. **Focus** on specific images of success
5. **Train** yourself to accept your new beliefs

Georgia found it easy to challenge consciously the notion that she didn't deserve a loving family life. Dehypnotizing herself from her subconscious images of unworthiness was more difficult. "I find myself attracted to men who will reinforce these feelings," she recognized. "I need to cast off this image of myself as an unwanted child if I'm going to make adult choices." Every time she found herself ruminating over negative thoughts about her place in her family or her teenage pregnancy, any time she found herself thinking I don't deserve to be happy," she said "Cancel!" She replaced the thoughts at once with the statement, "I'm a worthy person. It wasn't my fault my parents didn't want a fifth child. I'm not a bad person for giving my baby up for adoption. I was 15. I made the *right* choice. I'm deserving of a loving, fulfilling relationship." She placed her affirmations in private places where she could gently remind herself several times each day that she was in the process of change. She spent 15 minutes every evening in the theater of her imagination, visualizing images of a relationship based on mutual caring and respect—showing her horse that *this* was the path it was to follow. She had never been shy about meeting potential mates; her horse had just kept leading her to the wrong ones. Now, as she learned to accept her new attitude about herself, Georgia "acted as if" she had already freed herself from feelings of unworthiness. She spent a great deal of her working day in her car making sales calls, and she adopted the technique of reaffirming her new image to herself every time she turned the key in the ignition. She told herself, "I am an adult, and I'm not bound by negative messages I received as a child and as a teenager. I am free to make adult choices based on what I want and *deserve*."

Losing Your False Beliefs: A Worksheet

Consider the false beliefs that have impacted your self-image and how you could use reflective relearning to replace them with new, positive memories. Plan your own program by filling in the questionnaire below.

A false belief I'd like to dehypnotize myself from is:

_____

_____

A positive memory I'd like to replace it with is:

_____

_____

What negative self-thoughts will I CANCEL?

_____

_____

What positive statements will I REPLACE them with?

_____

_____

What will my AFFIRMATIONS be?

_____

_____

What images will I FOCUS on to create my new memory?

_____

_____

What attitudes and actions will I assume in TRAINING myself?

_____

_____

False Beliefs Can Build Invisible Walls

Wade felt older than his thirty-four years. He went about hunched over and eyes downcast. He couldn't seem to hold a job. Every venture seemed to defeat him before he got started. "What's the point?" he said bitterly. "Once you get ahead, someone will tear you down every time."

Wade had grown up in a small town in upstate New York. He had married his college sweetheart and gone to work in the family electrical supply business. His father, uncle and grandfather would talk ceaselessly about the business with particular emphasis on "the good old days." These conversations were a sore spot with Wade. Any time he suggested bringing any innovations into the business—computerized accounting or a FAX machine, for example—they would ridicule and scoff at him.

They were even more of a sore spot with Wade's wife Kathy. She had always been embarrassed by the way his family regarded him and outraged at the dismissive way they treated *her.* It was at her insistence that Wade left this negative situation. He acknowledged that he was unhappy. Despite the enormous "guilt trip" placed on him by his family, he and Kathy packed up and moved to southern California. He landed a job as a manufacturer's representative, and at first he did well. But around the time their first child was born, Wade began to have troubles with his boss, who, as he described it, "never took me seriously." By the time his second child came along two years later, Wade had been fired from no fewer than six jobs. At each one his problems would center around his inability to get along with his boss. "They're always stepping on me just as I start to make progress," he told himself.

Four years after leaving his home town, Wade returned on the occasion of his parents' 40th wedding anniversary. The experience left him depressed and almost suicidal. The rooms seemed cramped, almost suffocating. Specific and unspecific memories of fear, anxiety and rage emerged in his consciousness. He remembered how distant and rigid his parents had been. He remembered that his father's ridicule of him as "unrealistic" and "a dreamer" had begun years before he entered the business. He remembered his mother bragging to everyone (even into his adulthood) that he'd been "completely potty trained before he was a year old." He remembered how she'd had their family doctor remove his healthy appendix and tonsils before she and his father had taken a trip to Europe, just in case he might get sick and they'd have to interrupt their trip. And he remembered an incident that had happened when he was six years old.

He'd been playing on the linoleum floor of the kitchen, making zooming noises with a toy car. His mother was standing over an ironing board, telling him crossly to keep quiet. He could see the white shirt she was ironing, the rising steam. As many children do when they are embarrassed or unsure, he responded to her rebuke with a smile. She lifted the iron, thrust it toward him and screamed, "Do you want me to iron that smirk off your face?" Wade ran down to the basement and hid behind some canned foods. He remained there for what seemed like hours before his father found him sobbing and carried him up to bed.

Wade had repressed this memory for years, but the horror of it had remained in his subconscious mind. Now he remembered other instances when his mother had threatened him and his father had rescued him. Eventually Wade came to recognize the connection between these childhood experiences—his father's ridicule and his mother's need to control and terrorize him—and his inability to keep a job. His subconscious mind kept playing the same two tapes over and over again. One said to him, "Who cares about your ideas? They're not worth anything and they'll only set up conflict." The other told him, "If you assert yourself, you're going to be slapped down."

Like Wade, we may find ourselves running into the same invisible wall again and again—conflict at work, money slipping through our fingers, projects that we never complete, those villains who won't let us get ahead. We may blame the boss, our parents, our spouses, the church we grew up in, "the system" or ourselves, but we keep running up against the same obstacle. After a while procrastination and hopelessness set in. Yet all that may be necessary for getting past the wall is to open a *door* by casting aside our false beliefs.

Take a look at your answer to question 4 on page 72. That's your horse talking. Apply the four questions on page 79. Does your rationalization make sense to your rider? Or do you hear any old tapes playing?

Turn New Memories into Positive Behavior

Just as Georgia was able to free herself from false beliefs through reflective relearning, so Wade created new memories for himself:

- He CANCELED old beliefs whenever he found himself ruminating over thoughts that he was "nothing but trouble," "unrealistic," "unworthy of success," or "bound to be slapped down."
- He REPLACED these old beliefs with positive, constructive self-thoughts: "I am a worthy, pragmatic, competent person. I work well with people in authority and I deserve success and happiness."
- He AFFIRMED his new convictions by writing messages to himself and placing them where he would read them several times each day.

- He FOCUSED on interactions with the bosses who had fired him, visualizing their working together cooperatively. In the theater of his imagination, he created new memories in which he did not react antagonistically to his bosses and they did not "slap him down."
- After several weeks he began to TRAIN himself. He began a new job aware that he was not going to succeed by creating conflict. His rider taught his horse a new path by consciously acting as if his new memories were true and by repeatedly affirming them on a daily basis.

Wade converted his new attitude into action by setting a specific goal: to hold his new job for one year without creating conflict with his boss. Such a goal was beyond the limits imposed by his false beliefs, but his new memories established a new program that made it possible for him to move beyond those limits. Each small success in the direction of his goal (*e.g.*, accepting the boss's orders without a sarcastic rejoinder) was further proof that his new memories represented a true assessment of himself. By thus selecting the new program, his rider eliminated the old program. As success built on success, his horse came to agree with the new program as the only one to follow.

By freeing yourself from false beliefs, you expand the range of potential targets for your automatic mechanism. It's then up to you to turn your new positive self-concept into success on your own terms. In later chapters we'll be taking a look at how to translate expanded awareness of your abilities into the attainment of specific goals. But once you've broken the chain you thought was holding you back, chances are you'll spontaneously discover an abundance of new directions for personal movement and growth.

One individual who tapped this potential in herself and in others was Mary Kay Ash, founder of Mary Kay Cosmetics. She observed that there were many women who had developed a realization of their potential but who had not yet moved from personal empowerment to "getting out there and doing it." These were bright, productive women who had the energy and intelligence to be their own boss but hadn't had much exposure to independence. By offering experience in various aspects of running a business and by providing goal incentives (the legendary pink Cadillacs), Mary Kay built a successful business for herself and launched many other women on their own course to success.

⊞ How Your Positive Beliefs Can Further Your Children's Self-Esteem

The California task force on self-esteem listed as the first of its key recommendations that the state develop a media campaign to "educate all Californians regarding the primary role of parents in the development of healthy self-esteem...and provide appropri-ate...training in loving and effective ways to raise children." Cre-ating positive beliefs can lead to healthy parenting. If you're aware of your own negative beliefs and how they were formed, you're far less likely to make the same mistakes your parents did in raising you. Be sensitive about the things you say to, about, and around your children. "You made a mistake" is a corrective state-ment that can help your child stay on course. "You *are* a mistake" is an injurious message that too many people send their children, deliberately or not. Such a message can be conveyed by physical or psychological abuse (as with Wade), but it may also be trans-mitted through seemingly innocuous statements (as with Geor-gia). What message does a parent deliver with such statements as "Now look what you made me do," or "We shouldn't expect too much of him; he's the spitting image of his Uncle Roy," or, "Why can't you be more like your sister"?

If you're a parent with a negative self-concept, it's only a matter of time before your children start parenting *you*. Parents unwittingly lean on children for support because of their own needs. They do it by requiring their children to make adult deci-sions when they distrust their own ability to do it themselves: "What do you think we should have for dinner tonight?" They do it by soliciting the child's support in marital conflicts: "This is all Daddy's fault!" They do it by emotionally manipulating their children: "I do everything for this family, and *nobody cares!*" These are heavy burdens to lay on any child. Keep in mind that as you dehypnotize yourself from false beliefs, you may be contributing to your children's success as well as your own.

How to Overcome Your Built-In Resistance to Change

The greatest obstacle you will face in the process of creating new memories for yourself is your own self-doubt. Remember that it isn't *easy* to break old habits and replace them with new ones...but it is *simple*. When you find your left brain nagging you with such thoughts as "This is never going to work," visualize the horse-and-rider analogy. Every time you feel yourself resisting change in your beliefs or behavior, give a hard tug on the reins. It's not what you know about your resistance that's going to make a difference, it's what you do with what you know. If you persistently challenge your false beliefs with rational thinking, if you practice reflective relearning daily, and if you have a positive and realistic goal that's consistent with your new memories, you will experience your new beliefs redefining your attitudes, actions, and capabilities.

Once again, don't get discouraged if you fail to see immediate results. Allow yourself six weeks of daily practice to let your new beliefs take root. Meanwhile, here are a few techniques to help you plot a successful course:

Four Steps to Creating New Memories

1. View your old beliefs and negative memories as if they belong to another time and place—another life. Elicit help from your right brain to visualize the old memory as though it were at the end of a long tunnel and gradually fading away into darkness. See it actually diminishing in size.

2. During the 15 minutes you set aside each day for visualization, imagine how you would alter the old memory. Create a videotape of

your new memory in your mind. See yourself successfully completing a task; see someone compliment you on your achievement; see yourself accepting their praise with grace, sincerity and pride.

3. Consciously accept this new memory as the true one. Affirm repeatedly that you accept this "future memory" as a fact. Remember, your subconscious mind will eventually come to view it as if it actually happened.

4. Make affirmation cards stating your new memories as goals: "I am a worthy human being with (something special) to offer (a man, a woman, an employer, the world)." "I successfully complete (whatever task I undertake)." Consider them as written proof of your ability to view past memories differently. Put your affirmation cards in plain view so that they will constantly be reinforced in your subconscious mind.

Three Ways to Make Your New Memories Last

As you feel your new beliefs taking hold, there may be a tendency to slack off a little on diligence. Don't make that mistake! Don't give your horse a choice of paths to follow, or chances are it will go back to the old one. Encourage it to stay on the new path with these "carrots":

1. Program your dreams by focusing on your new beliefs as you go to sleep. You know the old saying, "Take a problem to bed and sleep on it"? This "dreaming by design" directly addresses your subconscious mind and helps install the new images in your right brain.

2. Program your daydreams every time you catch yourself dwelling on a negative memory or past mistake. Say "Cancel!" and redirect your daydreaming toward positive images that support your new beliefs.

3. Go about your daily life with an "I'll see it when I believe it" attitude regarding your new belief system. Remember, to your subconscious mind "believing is seeing." Your attitude toward success will strongly affect the progress of your servomechanism toward your goal.

Inevitably there will be setbacks. Don't forget that a servomechanism works by making mistakes, responding to negative feedback, and correcting its course. There will be times you find yourself making mistakes and responding to them with your old programming. The important thing is to remember not to *dwell* on the mistakes. Don't let them divert you from your goal. Use your conscious mind as a control knob to remind yourself that you're not defined by your mistakes, past or present, or by beliefs that come from old childhood tapes. Those beliefs are the stake and the chain that constrain your life. Isn't it time you yanked yourself free?

Targeting on Ideas

- Your self-image may be conditioned and your capabilities constrained by false and negative beliefs about yourself based on subconscious memories of early-childhood experiences.
- Use rational thinking to challenge your false beliefs. Use your imagination to create new memories that will lead to positive beliefs. Make these new memories permanent by taking positive action that is consistent with your new programming.

S ET
YOUR OWN
TARGETS

GIVE YOUR SUCCESS MECHANISM SOME SLACK: LEARN TO RELAX

[C]reative ideas are not consciously thought out...but come out automatically, spontaneously, and somewhat like a bolt from the blue, when the conscious mind has let go of the problem.... After [a person] has defined the problem, sees in his imagination the desired end result, secured all the information and facts that he can, then additional struggling, fretting, and worrying over it does not help, but seems to hinder the solution.

—Maxwell Maltz, Psycho-Cybernetics *(1960)*

Dr. [Georgi] Lozanov discovered something...in his years of studying people of supernormal abilities.... [A]t the moment these people performed astonishing mental feats, their bodies were in a state of rest.... They did not strain, will, or coerce the mind to function. It happened effortlessly. It actually seemed to happen *because* physical and mental effort weren't involved.

—Sheila Ostrander, Lynn Schroeder and Nancy Ostrander, Superlearning *(1979)*

As a 14-year-old student in Switzerland, Albert Einstein rode a street railway to school every day. He noticed how the speed of the moving car altered his perception of buildings along the route so that they seemed to be compressed. No doubt millions of others have observed this phenomenon, but this was Einstein. One afternoon while watching the scenery go by, he had an idea. "The question came to me in a state of quiet reverie," he later recalled. "'What would the world look like if I rode on a beam of light?'" It was this question that eventually led him to formulate the theory of relativity.

Several years ago I was working with a seven-year-old hemophiliac patient I'll call Timmy, whose parents had brought him to me for hypnotherapy at the suggestion of his hematolgist. After we had had several sessions together, Timmy's doctors observed that Timmy had developed a remarkable ability to control his bleeding. When asked how he did it, Timmy replied, "Oh, it's easy. I just close my eyes and get *mushy* all over my body. Then I see the little holes where the blood comes out, and I plug them up with Silly Putty, and it stops."

Einstein and little Timmy had this much in common: they both knew how to relax. Most people think of *relaxation* in much the same way Mark Twain defined *play:* it "consists of whatever a body is not obliged to do." You may feel "relaxed" when you're puttering around in the garden, reading the latest Stephen King thriller, chatting with friends, making love or watching TV. But the sort of relaxation Einstein and Timmy used is of a different order. It's the state in which your left brain decelerates and your right brain is allowed to roam free. It's the only condition in which you can access your creative imagination and do the work of reprogramming your automatic mechanism.

"Creative imagination," you'll recall, is a quality everyone possesses, not just artists, entrepreneurs, and (budding) rocket scientists. But it's important to understand that you can engage your creative imagination *only* when you're relaxed. In Einstein's case, his ability to enter "a state of quiet reverie" led to one of the most important scientific discoveries in history. In Timmy's, "getting mushy all over" may have saved his life. In yours, learning to relax is a key step in becoming the person you want to be.

"Physical relaxation," Maltz wrote, "plays a key role in the dehypnotization process. Our currently held beliefs...were formed *without effort*, with no sense of strain.... Our habits, whether good or bad, were formed in the same way. It follows that we must employ the same process in forming new beliefs, or new habits, that is, in a relaxed condition."

This chapter is about relaxation and its benefits. You'll learn:

- why the inability to relax might be the only thing standing between you and your desired success.
- how relaxation influences health, learning ability, creativity, performance and self-esteem.
- simple exercises and techniques for relaxing your body and mind.

Stress: Private Enemy Number One

"'Stress' has recently become a popular word in our language," Maltz wrote. "We speak of this as the age of stress. Worry, anxiety, insomnia, stomach ulcers have become accepted as a necessary part of the world in which we live."

If Maltz thought *he* was living in the age of stress, imagine what he'd think of our time. Between 1959 and 1988, according to Department of Labor statistics, the average American's working hours per week increased by nearly 20 percent. In 1960, Wall Street hotshots with six-figure incomes weren't starting fistfights on streetcorners over who got the next taxi. People weren't shooting each other on California freeways. Women weren't trying to cope with the system overload that can result from trying to climb the corporate ladder and raise a family at the same time. Office workers weren't trying to monitor computer, Audex, and FAX machines simultaneously. Corporate employees weren't lying awake nights worrying whether their job would vanish in the next restructuring. Managers and professional people weren't biting their nails over whether a procedural oversight or offhand remark might result in a lawsuit.

Our ancient "fight or flight" response, genetically and culturally programmed into us for survival, has become our Achilles' heel. Many of us today live in a chronic state of fight-or-flight anxiety. Hormones such as adrenaline and cortisol, "designed" by nature to be released from our glands as needed to serve these survival-related functions, now slosh through our systems on a constant basis. These "stress-related" hormones are potent inhibitors of the immune system, making us easy marks for viral and bacterial diseases.

Stress may also inhibit the remission of cancer and accelerate the development of AIDS.

Stress is recognized as a key contributing factor in heart disease.

Stress has been shown to lead to the impairment of learning and memory by accelerating the aging of brain cells.

And stress, as Maltz pointed out, can "jam" your automatic mechanism and prevent it from working as a success mechanism.

How Stress Jams Your Creative Mechanism

When you're tense, anxious, or in any of the other states we describe as "stressed out," you approach problem-solving with your left brain. Correction: you try to *force* problem-solving with your left brain. The left brain does a fine job of analyzing problems. It's not much good at *solving* problems, except those of the conscious, procedural, or verbal variety. It can't create, intuit or invent. That's the right brain's job. When you take a left-brain approach to problem-solving, the resulting frustration only increases your stress.

There's a story about baseball great Yogi Berra trying to teach a rookie his batting techniques. "It's very simple," Yogi explained. "You want to be sure you got your feet..." Berra paused, confused. Just how did he place his feet in the batter's box? "Well anyway, when you swing you want to break your wrists just like..." Yogi stopped and scratched his head, unable to find the words to describe the natural, physical process. "Well of course, you want to step into the pitch like..." It was useless. The more he thought about the minutiae of his swing, the more confused he became. "Ah, hell," he finally told the puzzled rookie. "Just watch me and do everything I do."

The story may be a sportswriter's fable, but as Ken Kesey once wrote, "It's the truth even if it didn't happen." Habits are merely the byproducts of subconscious thinking and repetitious behavior. You don't break a habit and form a new one through "iron-jawed willpower"; you do it by creating clear mental images of a desired result and by acting as if it has already been achieved. This is the case whether the habit is a hitch in your batting stroke or a negative way of perceiving yourself. Yes, it takes conscious, repeated practice to learn a new habit. But if you worry about every detail of thought and action, you're guaranteed to "strike out" at learning new habits or beliefs as surely as a ballplayer who goes up to the plate tense and worried about body mechanics. If your left brain is going a million miles an hour over a problem that requires a subconscious, right-brain solution, you're in trouble.

Everyone has heard of the dread condition known as (speak it softly) *writer's block*. This terrifying cycle of paralysis, frustration, and anxiety affects just about every writer at one time or another, from Nobel prize-winning authors to supermarket-tabloid stringers. "It gets to where I can't even find the courage to sit down at my desk," says one survivor. "I'm like the new kid in the neighborhood, afraid to go outside because the gang of bullies down at the playground will beat me up again." Another writer calls it "impoetence," likening the condition to sexual impotence. "In fact, I'd rather be impotent," he maintains, only half joking. "My wife understands that *that's* only a transient thing. Try telling that to an editor when you're under deadline."

In fact, writer's block (like many cases of sexual dysfunction) is nothing more than an inability to relax. The left brain refuses to let the right brain do its job. "I almost see [the two sides of my brain] as my little kids," says best-selling mystery writer Sue Grafton. "My left brain is my editing function.... It always thinks it knows how to write, so it is always saying, 'You can't do that, you don't know what you're doing. I'll take over.' Right brain is much more childlike. If you criticize right brain too much, it'll quit playing."

Use Relaxation to Oil Your Success Mechanism

As with athletes who "lose it" due to overconcern with body mechanics, as with writers who "lose it" because of excessive self-criticism, your only obstacle in getting your rider to retrain your horse may be an inability to relax. Only when you relax the forcing, demanding aspect of your thought can your insightful, intuitive self emerge. Only when your conscious mind frees itself from worrying, fretting, stewing and "awfulizing" situations is your subconscious mind susceptible to reprogramming. If you approach reflective relearning in a state of relaxation, your automatic mechanism will keep you on course to success—and you may be amazed at how little effort it takes. The following examples illustrate how the relaxed state can provide the key to unlocking your creative imagination, solving problems and achieving personal growth.

How Relaxation Sparks Creative Insight

An associate of mine recently told me about an entrepreneurial brainstorm that came to him when he was on vacation, relaxing beside a hotel swimming pool in Hawaii. Dion owned a chain of seven day-care centers. He had been trying to think of ways to expand the concept, to offer something more than just the usual babysitting for working parents. There was a business conference in progress at the hotel where he was staying, and Dion had heard a group of women executives discussing it over lunch. "I didn't really want to come to this conference," one of them said. "I have a small child at home, and I hated to leave him for a week, but what alternative did I have?" Now as Dion lay beside the pool, the lightbulb went on over his head. When he returned from his vacation, he launched his new business: selling day care to business-conference planners as a service to conventioneers with children.

Lest you think such insight is limited to executives with money to invest, consider Karen. She was a homemaker with four children under the age of six. Her husband worked as a long-haul truck driver, and she was often home alone with the kids for days at a time. This situation frequently left her feeling tense, irritable, and trapped. When a friend suggested, "You should get out more often," Karen snapped back, "And who's going to take care of my kids?"

One afternoon after putting her youngest daughter down for a nap, she found herself in a state of relaxation for the first time in weeks. She had just read the children a story from *Winnie-The-Pooh*. As she drifted off into a dream-like reverie, she seemed to hear the voice of Eeyore the donkey saying to her, "Karen, find a way to get out more. Start a co-op."

Karen sat up, her eyes open. Later that day she called two friends who also spent their weekdays alone with their children. "Let's start a babysitting co-op," she suggested. "You and me and Vivian. We'll swap kids three days a week. That way you can take that art class at the college, I can go ice skating and Viv can take those guitar lessons she's always talking about."

"That's a great idea!" her friend said. "Whoever made you think of it?"

"Eeyore the donkey!"

How Relaxation Helped Save a Friendship

Relaxation can often provide the solution to those "unsolvable" personal dilemmas. Lydia was being driven to distraction by her friend Jean, a lonely, unhappy woman who had "adopted" her. Lydia was a retail-store designer who worked out of an office in her home, and Jean would frequently call to invite herself over during the day. "What time would be most convenient?" Jean would ask. "Shall we have lunch, or shall we get together later for coffee?" *None of the above*, Lydia would think, but she didn't want to hurt her friend's feelings. Then, since Lydia's work schedule seemed so busy, Jean began finding excuses to drop by during the evening. To be sure, she always called first to "see if it's okay," but she did it so frequently that Lydia couldn't always find a gracious excuse. Any time she scheduled an activity with someone else she felt compelled to keep it a secret from Jean, who would resent not being included. Lydia truly liked Jean, but she was angry about having her privacy invaded so relentlessly. She tried to think of a way she could ask Jean to back off without damaging her self-esteem, but there was no way. She began to feel stressed whenever the phone rang, thinking, "Oh, God, how am I going to put her off this time? Why doesn't she just get a life?" She had "awfulized" the situation to the point that she felt she no longer had any control over it.

One afternoon Lydia was riding her bicycle in the park. She was aware that she had left her studio and turned off the answering machine because she didn't want to hear from Jean. She was angry at herself for letting her friend take control of her life. As she rode along, she found herself breathing deeply, looking at the patterns made by the shadows of trees on the pavement, not thinking about Jean, not thinking about much of anything. It was then that the solution came to her. "It was like I was seeing it on a television screen," she later marveled. "There Jean and I were sitting at my coffee table, and I was calmly and tactfully telling her what I needed to say. I could hear the script in my mind. When I actually did sit down for that talk with Jean, I went for another bike ride first just to duplicate the experience and rehearse my talk. Jean and I are still friends—in fact we're better friends than ever."

How Relaxation Can Keep You Healthy

Brett was a 52-year-old printer for a daily newspaper. It was his job to keep the machinery in operation, and any hour of the day or night he might be called in to repair a printing press. A routine physical examination indicated that he had an irregular heartbeat. When an electrocardiogram confirmed that he indeed had a heart problem, he had become so anxious that he hyperventilated and nearly passed out in the examining room. The physician urged him to consult a psychologist with the aim of reducing his stress. Although Brett had no history of heart problems, his father had died of a sudden heart attack at 55, and he knew his stressful job made him doubly a candidate for trouble. He had long dreamed of quitting his job and becoming a tree farmer. Nevertheless he decided he was "too busy to waste time talking to a shrink." With two kids in college, it was "foolish to give up a well-paying job to go chasing a dream."

Four mounths later Brett suffered a heart attack—fortunately not the Big One. As he lay in the hospital recovering, he admitted to himself that it would be wise to take his doctor's advice. For the next several months he met with a psychologist on a weekly basis. They focused on practical considerations of leaving his job for a less-stressful lifestyle, but they also spent time each week on progressive relaxation. This is a technique for relieving tension developed by a psychiatrist, Dr. Edmund Jacobson, and subsequently adapted by other practitioners as a treatment for a variety of psychological problems. A major advantage of relaxation is that people begin to see results almost immediately. Within weeks Brett was feeling noticeably better psychologically as well as physically. Within months his EKG was showing normal. Progressive relaxation was still part of his daily routine when he bought a partnership in a tree farm with the help of financial backers he met through his cardiologist.

⊞ Relaxation: A Key to Reflective Relearning

By now it should be obvious why little Timmy's bleeding became controllable when he got "mushy all over." Unencumbered by conscious interference, his automatic mechanism was directed toward taking control of the situation, not by force or will power but by yielding to his body's innate ability to heal itself. By finding your own most effective path to relaxation, you can consciously address the subconscious, right-brain processes that are the key to Psycho-Cybernetics.

"Progressive relaxation" such as Brett used is one of the simple techniques you'll find described later in this chapter. If you've tried starting your daily program of reflective relearning but have felt frustrated by your inability to become relaxed enough to focus, these techniques can provide the key. Reflective relearning, as you know, generally takes six weeks to take effect, but you should begin to feel the benefits of relaxation from day one.

When you were in school, chances are your teachers at various levels had you memorize and recite poetry. Remember how you sweated over memorizing those long passages from Longfellow, Frost and Shakespeare? Remember any of them today? Didn't think so. Now, depending on your age, see if you can remember the lines that follow any of *these* verses:

"Pepsi-Cola hits the spot..."

"Oh, I'd love to be an Oscar Mayer wiener..."

"Here comes the king; here comes the big Number One..."

"You deserve a break today..."

It may be as long since you've heard these commercials as it's been since you were called upon to recite "The Wreck of the *Hesperus*" for Mrs. McDougal, but chances are you remember every line of the jingles and none of the poetry. That's because you learned the poetry through force of will, while you learned the commercials through subconscious repetition. Amazing how much incidental learning occurs when you're not even paying attention, isn't it?

Relaxation: The Gateway to Learning

When you're relaxed, your mind is capabale of accelerated feats of learning and memory. This principle can be used for significant learning as well as advertising jingles. A Bulgarian psychiatrist, Dr. Georgi Lozanov, has developed a method of instruction that uses deep-relaxation and breathing exercises combined with music to induce a state of heightened concentration. Widely used in European schools, "Superlearning" expands learning and memory capacity by "keep[ing] the left brain, body, and right brain from working against each other and hamstringing your abilities." When people in such a state of relaxed concentration are "fed" information, they are able to absorb and retain it at an astonishingly accelerated rate.

Such techniques are particularly useful for learning the new habits necessary for changing your self-image. In fact, in developing the Superlearning method Lozanov acknowledged a debt to self-image psychology. In order to learn faster and release our inner potential, he maintained, we must first overcome limitations in our thinking. "We are conditioned to believe that we can only learn so much so fast,...that there are certain rigid limits to what we can do and achieve," he said. "We're all bombarded constantly, from the first day we're born, with limiting suggestions." Like Maltz, Lozanov drew analogies with cybernetics in showing how feedback affects results: "If the teacher felt depressed, or thought the students were stupid, or that the method wouldn't work, students might realize it, and this would affect performance."

In other words: relaxation is the key to freeing the mind for creative, holistic, right-brain problem-solving. If you're physically tense or mentally distracted, your automatic mechanism cannot function. *It can only operate effectively when you're in a relaxed state.*

How Relaxation Can Change the Way You Perceive Yourself

Thanarat was a promising young computer whiz who had come to the United States from Thailand at the age of 15. After his graduation from college he obtained a job with a Silicon Valley corporation and advanced rapidly up the high-tech ladder. Then at age 24 he was promoted to a managerial position. Disaster struck. Thanarat found that asking procedural questions of his superiors made him extremely uncomfortable, and having to discipline his subordinates, no matter how mildly, made him even more anxious.

Thanarat had been in the United States for nine years and had been educated in American schools, but he came from a close-knit extended family with roots in traditional Thai culture. One of the cardinal "social sins" of that culture is what an American might call "pushiness." As a result, one of the essential aspects of Thanarat's personality was low-key deference. He would never embarrass himself or his family by appearing pushy—which to him included such behavior as bothering authority figures with questions or ordering people around. He had always had anxiety about such behavior, preferring to learn by observing rather than by asking, but since his promotion the demands of his job were running directly counter to his feelings.

Thanarat, in short, had a self-image problem. Clearly his self-concept wasn't "negative," but it was inappropriate for a manager in a culture which assumes more forceful ways of demonstrating leadership. He used progressive relaxation combined with reflective relearning to develop a self-image that allowed him to be comfortable in two roles. When he was completely relaxed, he would first visualize himself in his traditional role as a passive recipient. Then, still deeply relaxed, he visualized a new version of himself emerging as from a shell. He saw himself in specific *work-related* situations asking questions assertively without aggressiveness and confronting subordinates firmly without hostility. He repeated this activity daily until he was able to be comfortable in a work role that was consistent with his responsibilities while still maintaining a role in his personal life that was compatible with traditional Thai culture. Relaxation allowed Thanarat's rider to retrain his horse to follow two paths.

⊞ How to Unjam Your Success Mechanism: A Few Relaxation Techniques

The paths to relaxation are numerous, and it may take you some time to find the one that best engages your creative imagination. Any form of mental concentration that effectively places you in a profound state of rest will do. Dr. Herbert Benson calls this the *relaxation response:* "When this response is called upon, heart rate and blood pressure drop. Breathing rate and oxygen consumption decline because of the profound decrease in the need for energy....

Blood flow to the muscles decreases, producing a feeling of warmth and rested mental alertness." When the relaxation response is engaged, the fight-or-flight reponse is shut off. To achieve it, try some of the following techniques:

Zen Breathing

"Zen Breathing" may sound like some esoteric practice that belongs in a Japanese monastery, but it isn't. It is based on meditation techniques long used in Asia, but it has nothing intrinsically to do with religion. "Slow, rhythmic breathing can turn an anxious mental state into one of relative tranquillity and release the body from many of the other adverse effects of anxiety," as Dr. Kenneth R. Pelletier has written. I introduce this technique first because it's perhaps the simplest relaxation method there is, as natural and as easy to learn as...well, as breathing. Just follow this procedure:

1. Find a quiet, comfortable place to sit.
2. Breathe *deeply, slowly* and *through your nose.*
3. With each breath you take, concentrate on the feelings, sensations and changes you experience through breathing. Listen to your breath. Hear the life-giving sounds of breathing in and breathing out. This process helps you to tune out other sounds and to forget distracting left-brain thoughts.
4. After about 15 minutes, take one last deep breath and end the session. You should feel completely relaxed and refreshed in body and mind.

An important thing to remember about this or any relaxation technique is that individual preference is an important part of the process. Experiment with variations in your breathing and find a method that is right for you. For example, you may find that instead of the sound of your breathing, you prefer to concentrate on an external sound with a regular rhythm, such as the chirping of crickets on a summer evening or the pulse of waves on a beach.

You may find that repeating a single sound as you exhale, such as the word "one," is an alternative to listening to your breathing.

You may find that covering one nostril while you inhale and then covering the other while you exhale heightens your concentration. If you decide to use this technique, switch off every few minutes. If you've been inhaling through your right nostril and exhaling through your left, try inhaling through your left and exhaling through your right. Some researchers suggest that breathing through the left nostril may activate the right side of the brain and vice-versa. To facilitate breathing through the left nostril, lie on your right side when you do your breathing exercises.

You may find that counting backward from twenty (one number with each breath) helps you relax. When you reach "one," cue in on a key word or words from your affirmations, such as "calm and confident." Repeat your key word or phrase several times with successive breaths. After a while your subconsious mind comes to associate the process with the key words ("calm and confident"), and you become receptive to these feelings whenever you repeat the procedure.

Focusing your vision on a mandala while you breathe can help you tune in your right-brain thoughts. A mandala, such as the one illustrated on page 109, is a symmetrical pattern that focuses on a central point. Mandalas occur in such natural forms as snowflakes, flowers, gemstones, and the human eye. They are common figures in art, architecture and religious symbolism. The stained-glass "rose windows" found in many churches are mandalas.

Focusing on a mandala helps you relax because your left brain can't comprehend its purely spatial, visual input. It's especially useful for quieting the verbal distractions—the "inner dialogue"—that interferes with relaxation. Remember, your left brain hates being left out. It wants to be in control all the time. You may find your left brain analyzing the pattern of the mandala by breaking it down into circles, lines and triangles. "You can keep this from happening," advises Marilee Zdenek in *The Right-Brain Experience*, "by concentrating on the center of the pattern and trying to see as much of the peripheral design as possible *without analyzing it*. Soon the left brain will acquiesce to the powers of the

right brain. In effect, the mandala is being used to outsmart the left hemisphere so that you can shift to the right-brain mode."

Progressive Relaxation

This method of relaxation involves the progressive disengagement of different parts of your body combined with some of the same techniques as in Zen breathing. Follow these simple steps:

1. Find a quiet, comfortable place to sit. Remove your shoes.
2. Sit comfortably with your feet on the floor and your hands in your lap. Do not allow your hands or feet to touch one another. Close your eyes.
3. Without speaking, successively tell each of the following parts of your body to relax. As you feel each part relax, go on to the next.

Toes of left foot	relax
Toes of right foot	relax
Left foot	relax
Right foot	relax
Left ankle	relax
Right ankle	relax
Lower left leg	relax
Lower right leg	relax
Left thigh	relax
Right thigh	relax
Groin area	relax
Buttocks	relax
Abdomen	relax
Chest	relax
Left shoulder	relax
Right shoulder	relax
Right arm	relax
Right hand	relax
Right fingers	relax

Left arm	relax
Left hand	relax
Left fingers	relax
Neck	relax
Face	relax

Now you are completely relaxed all over.

4. Listen to your breathing. Repeat the word or sound of your choice. Try not to let your mind wander from the chosen word.
5. After about 15 minutes, take a deep breath and slowly bring yourself out of relaxation. Stand up and stretch like a cat. You should feel totally renewed.

You may find you prefer doing progressive relaxation while lying on your back on a mat or firm pad—just don't fall asleep.

You may find that you relax more deeply if you deliberately make your body tense before you begin:

1. Lie on your back and raise your left leg a few inches off the floor. Tense the muscles. Flex your foot so that your toes are pointing at the ceiling. Hold this position for about 15 seconds, then relax.
2. Repeat the procedure with your right leg.
3. Raise your left arm an inch or two off the floor. Extend your arm and tense the muscles. Squeeze your hand into a tight fist. Hold this position for about 15 seconds, then relax.
4. Repeat the procedure with your right arm.
5. Open your mouth and eyes as wide as you can. Stick your tongue out. Hold this position for about 15 seconds, then relax.
6. Follow the procedures for progressive relaxation, as above.

The Radiant Light

This variation on progressive relaxation is often taught in childbirth classes as an aid to women in advanced pregnancy and labor, but it can be used by either sex at any time.

1. Sit or lie in a comfortable position with your shoes off. Close your eyes. Breathe slowly and deeply for a minute or two.

2. As you inhale, visualize your breath as a radiant light filling your body. As you exhale, feel your body relax. Continue for several breaths.

3. Now as you inhale, direct the radiant light to your left foot. As you exhale, imagine the light passing out of your body through the sole of your foot, bearing the tension away.

4. Repeat step 3 as many times as needed, directing the light in turn to each part of your body listed in the instructions for progressive relaxation.

5. Enjoy the feeling of complete relaxation for a few minutes.

6. Take one last deep breath, open your eyes and stretch.

Dr. Lozanov's Listening List

Music is a key aspect of the "Superlearning" relaxation procedures of Dr. Georgi Lozanov summarized earlier in this chapter. It's beyond the scope of this book to describe these procedures in detail, but you might want to try using music to accompany your own relaxation exercises.

This is not "background music." Lozanov observed that a specific kind of music with a specific kind of rhythm helps induce a state of relaxed concentration by synchronizing processes of the body with the music. He used classical music from the Baroque period (about 1610 to 1750)—specifically, the slow movements of concertos by such composers as Händel, Vivaldi, Telemann, Corelli and J. S. Bach. This music has a slow, stately rhythm of about sixty beats per minute. If you're familiar with this type of music, you can make a tape of about 20 minutes in length using appropriate selections of your choice. If you're a stranger to it, ask a friend to help you in your selection or consult the music librarian at your public library.

Maltz's "Five Rules for Freeing Your Creative Machinery"

Daily relaxation exercises help keep your automatic mechanism functioning smoothly. But what about those everyday situations on the job or in interpersonal relations that typically leave you tense and self-conscious? How can you free yourself from the constant worry and self-monitoring that seems to accompany such situations?

"Conscious effort inhibits and 'jams' the automatic creative mechanism," Maltz wrote. "[S]ome people...are painfully conscious of every move they make.... We speak of such persons as 'inhibited,' and rightly so. But it would be more true...to say that the 'person' is not inhibited; but that the person has 'inhibited' his own creative mechanism. If these people could 'let go,' stop trying, not care, and give no thought to the matter of their behavior, they could act creatively, spontaneously, and 'be themselves.'"

Maltz proposed these five rules for disinhibiting the creative mechanism:

1. "Do your worrying before you place your bet, not after the wheel starts turning." Maltz derived this image from the game of roulette, but it's a concept I can easily relate to. Years ago when my husband was climbing the corporate ladder, I was playing the role of supportive wife and attending a lot of company functions I would just as soon have skipped. During one tedious luncheon I was sitting there wishing the time would go by faster and thinking of all the things I'd rather be doing when a woman seated next to me put her hand over my watch and asked me what time it was. I felt invaded and embarrassed—my left brain was saying things like "Where does *she* get off?"—but I smiled and told her I would be very happy to tell her what time it was if she would take her hand away. "Bobbe," she said to me, "don't you know how many times you've looked at your watch in the past half hour?"

That woman was a great teacher. Among the lessons she taught was: "The time to worry about the decision is *before* you make it." By deciding to attend the function in support of my husband, I had already cast my lot. I was *there*—there was no sense in trying to change what was. It may be appropriate to fume and fret over the consequences of a course of action before deciding on it. But once the decision is made, go along for the ride and accept responsibility for the decision. All fretting can do is jam your creative mechanism.

2. Form the habit of consciously responding to the present moment. This is the principle behind Alcoholics Anonymous's famous watchword, "One day at a time." Your automatic mechanism can only respond in the present. You can't approach a situation that's happening *now* by worrying about how you'll feel tomorrow or how you may have mishandled a similar problem in the past. If you're a beginning skier and have selected to brave the intermediate slope for the first time, do you worry about the times you've fallen as you hurtle down the mountain? Do you worry about what's coming up three turns ahead? Of course not—if you do, you'll be digging yourself out of a snowbank. When you're worrying about past failures, you're focusing on—failure. You're watching the curb. When you're worried about something coming up down the hill, you're focusing on something over which you have no control—*yet*. Meanwhile, you may be missing something crucial in your present environment that you *can* control.

3. Try to do only one thing at a time. In our busy world there often seem to be a dozen or more projects demanding our attention at once. We let ourselves become so anxious over the overwhelming prospect of having or wanting to complete all of them that we end up not doing any of them. This is why people become so cynical about New Year's resolutions. We start the year determined that we're going to get those résumés out and look for that new fulfilling job, *and* take that art class, *and* bicycle off 15 pounds, *and* spend more quality time with the kids, *and* build those shelves for the spare bedroom. "I *have* the *time*," we tell ourselves; "all I have to do is get out of bed a little earlier and not watch so much TV." We try to concentrate on all the projects at once; we make a little progress toward one of them and feel anxious that we haven't done anything about the others. By January 15 panic has set in; by February 1, discouragement and self-punishment.

Your automatic mechanism can only handle one goal at a time. No matter how busy you are, time comes to you at a rate of only sixty minutes to the hour. Even a computer that can do millions of calculations every second cannot execute two programs simultaneously. Focus your awareness on one project at a time and don't worry about the ones you're not doing. Making progress on one project will raise your self-esteem far more effectively than worrying about six.

4. Sleep on it. Always remember that your right brain works best when there is minimal interference from your left. At no time is your left brain less engaged than when you're sleeping. This is why "sleeping on it" when there's a problem you're trying to solve is *not* an empty cliché.

Entertainer, writer and composer Steve Allen describes how his most famous song, "This Could Be the Start of Something Big," came to him in a dream: "I just reached over while I was still waking up and wrote down the few lines I had dreamed and the melody was basically all there."

Industrialist and engineer R. G. Le Tourneau had been trying for several months without success to solve a problem involved in the design of a new piece of earth-moving equipment. The answer came to him while taking a nap on an airplane. He woke up, jotted down his solution, and fell right back to sleep.

5. Relax while you work. "You can induce something of 'that relaxed feeling,' and the relaxed attitude," Maltz contended, "if you will form the habit of mentally *remembering* the nice relaxed feeling that you induced." When tension and anxiety are blocking the operation of your creative mechanism, stop what you're doing and focus on a memory of relaxation. Form a detailed mental picture of an occasion on which your body and mind were totally at peace.

When you're feeling anxious about a specific situation—pressures at work, an impending confrontation with your boss or your spouse, an important interview—recall a similar episode that ended successfully. Focus on the sense of relaxation and well-being that accompanied your success. Remembering a past episode of success and its accompanying sense of well-being reinforces your awareness that relaxation and success go hand in hand. Once you've made a habit of linking such memories, recalling the feeling of relaxation will also induce your subconscious mind to recall memories of success.

Observe Your Take-a-Break Signals

Dr. Ernest L. Rossi has made a detailed study of ultradian rhythms, the mind-and-body cycle of biochemical activity we experience several times throughout the day. In *The 20-Minute Break*, Rossi describes how most of us experience a basic rest-activity cycle of about 110-120 minutes, "a cycle of arousal, peak performance, stress, and rest in many of our key physical and psychological processes." It is when we try to maintain activity during the typically 20-minute "down time" of this cycle, the period during which "our conscious mind apparently needs to take a break from its outer labors so that the deeper parts of our mind can catch up and pull everything together," that stress, agitation and impaired performance occur. Rossi suggests that to the extent that it is realistically possible we try to synchronize our breaks, meditations and "inner rejuvenation" activities with these 20-minute lulls. He lists the following cues as signals that our mind and body need restoring:

- feeling a need to stretch, move about, or take a break
- yawning or sighing
- finding yourself hesitating and procrastinating, unable to continue working
- noticing your body getting tense, tight, and fatigued
- pangs of hunger
- awareness of a need to urinate
- feeling "spaced out"; your concentration is poor, your mind wanders
- feeling depressed or emotionally vulnerable
- being distracted by fantasies, perhaps sexual
- slight memory problems; forgetting words "on the tip of your tongue"
- making careless errors in spelling, typing, or counting
- sharp drop in performance and output

Six On-the-Job Stress Reducers

In *Whole-Brain Thinking,* Jacquelyn Wonder and Priscilla Donovan recommend these "quickie" relaxation exercises for the workplace:

1. *Time-out for eyes.* Turn your face to the wall or look out the window (whatever is less conspicuous). Close your eyes and roll your eyeballs upward. Take two deep breaths.

2. *Mini push-ups.* Put your arms at your side, hands pointed forward. Now bend your hands backward as far as possible and hold them rigid. Count to 20 (if you have time) and release. Put your hands in your lap for a few seconds and enjoy the feeling of release.

3. *Roll-arounds.* Roll your head in a circle several times and then reverse direction. Repeat for as long as you can comfortably, each time rolling more slowly and fully.

4. *Lean-tos.* Lean from side to side in your chair until your hands are touching the floor with each lean. If observed, you can always pretend you're picking something off the floor.

5. *A mini mind-vacation.* Close your eyes and visualize yourself in your favorite place—the mountains, bed, etc. Stay there until your body feels it's there too. If you have cold hands or feet, visualize yourself in a warm, friendly place and warm those extremities.

6. *Standing room only.* If you must stand for extended periods, shift from foot to foot, exaggerating the movements by bending your knees and ankles.

Seven Tips for Making Relaxation a Way of Life

The important thing to remember about any program of relaxation is that it is most effective when practiced on a regular daily basis. You'll find it much easier to slip into the relaxed state for visualization and reflective relearning once you've made relaxation a part of your routine. Here are a few guidelines that will help you do it:

1. When you awaken in the morning, be aware of your thought patterns. If you find yourself thinking in a negative mode ("Oh, God, it's Monday!" "I just don't want to face this day!" "Five seconds awake and I already *know* it's going to be a miserable day!"), say "CANCEL!" *Restate* and *Reframe:* consciously allow yourself to see a different mental picture. If it's pouring outside, see Gene Kelly singing and dancing in the rain. See flowers growing. If you find yourself dreading the consequences of a mistake you made yesterday, visualize another time when you were effective. If you find yourself playing the "If only I had..." game, reframe and focus on something positive that you *do* have.

2. Get some relaxation tapes to play when you're feeling anxious on awakening in the morning, while driving in your car or before going to bed at night. Such tapes may present a guided relaxation exercise accompanied by music or "natural" sounds such as waves breaking on a beach. You can find them in the health, psychology or self-improvement sections of bookstores, in the "new concepts" section of record stores, or through catalog sales. Evaluate a variety of tapes, if possible, to choose the ones that are right for you.

3. Take a class in hatha yoga from your local YMCA, recreation and parks department or community college. Hatha is a basic, "physical" form of yoga involving flexibility, breathing and relaxation exercises. It poses no conflict with any religious or spiritual beliefs you may hold.

4. Approach relaxation techniques not as something esoteric—such as something a turbaned mystic sitting on the pinnacle of a mountain would do—but as a natural part of your life and an aid to problem-solving.

5. Schedule an appointment time for practicing relaxation. Mark your calendar or Daytimer and honor the date the same as you would honor an appointment with a doctor, dentist or business client. Save your social and recreational commitments for another time.

6. If your work situation allows it, set aside ten to 15 minutes for relaxation instead of taking a coffee break. Tell the receptionist to screen your calls (if you're fortunate enough to have a receptionist); hang a DO NOT DISTURB sign on your door or cubicle—do whatever is necessary to assure that you won't be interrupted.

7. Arrange a tradeoff with a co-worker. Agree to handle his calls for a specified time period while you handle his for an equal time.

Once you initiate a program of relaxation as an aid to reflective relearning, you'll soon discover that it's made you better able to handle the stressful situations that pop up in your everyday life. You'll find yourself feeling less fatigued at the end of the day and less anxious about concerns at work and in your personal life. And you'll find that relaxation is yet another "fake it till you make it" condition. After a few weeks of consciously practicing relaxation techniques, you'll find that you've made relaxation a habit.

Targeting on Ideas

- Relaxation is an aid to health and problem solving as well as a necessary condition for the work of reprogramming your internal guidance system.
- There are numerous effective procedures for achieving relaxation. Find the one that's most effective for you.

SET
YOUR OWN
TARGETS

CHAPTER SIX

JUST SAY YES: DE-STRESS YOURSELF WITH DRUG-FREE TRANQUILIZERS

[O]ur disturbed feelings—our anger, hostility, fear, anxiety, insecurity, are caused by our own responses—not by externals.... Thus, relaxation is nature's own tranquilizer, which erects a psychic screen...between you and the disturbing stimulus.

—*Maxwell Maltz*, Psycho-Cybernetics *(1960)*

When fear...has become an overpowering force on patients, we take them through a generic fear neutralizing procedure...which entails helping the individual get into a relaxed state and then call upon their imagination to confront their fears.

—*Vida C. Baron, M.D.*, Metamedicine *(1990)*

What sets off your stress alarm? What circumstances tend to send you into an unreasonable state of anxiety, panic, rage, despair? Too many file folders in your "in" basket? Certain individuals who push your buttons? A police car in your rearview mirror? Screaming kids? Crowds? First dates? Job interviews?

Wrong. The correct answer is: none of the above. They're all events, situations. Your stress comes not from any event but from your response to it—and that response is nothing but a habit you can replace.

Notice the catch? In order to learn new habits, we need to visualize them clearly in our imagination. In order to engage our imagination, we need to relax. And if we're feeling "stressed out," by definition we aren't relaxed. Psychologists call this *reciprocal inhibition:* we can't be stressed and relaxed at the same time.

And so instead of eliminating stress, we cover it up. That's what tranquilizer drugs are for: covering up our stressful over-responses. "Tranquilizers do not change the environment. The disturbing stimuli are still there. We are still able to *recognize* them intellectually, but we do not *respond* to them emotionally."

Since Maxwell Maltz wrote these words, tranquilizers have become the single most-prescribed class of drugs. In 1981 Americans consumed more than one hundred *tons* of Valium alone. It's no wonder. When the effects of the drug subside, our anxieties are still there. And so we take another pill, and then another. Before long our nervous system is in a constant state of depression. If we go off medication, we find that the anxieties are still lurking around, causing excessive stress and preventing our automatic mechanism from functioning as a success mechanism.

An extreme case was a woman I'll call Diane, whom I treated years ago in a neuropsychiatric hospital. Her husband had brought her in because he felt he could no longer leave her unattended and feared for the safety of their two young daughters. Her speech had become rapid and unconnected, and she could not sit still for more than a few moments. She would wring her hands and swing her foot rapidly, pick at her nails and cry in sudden outbursts. There had been several attempts to integrate her into groups at the hospital, but without medication she became so agitated that she could not function.

And so she was kept on seven different drugs, including three so-called minor tranquilizers. When I first saw her she was lethargic and unresponsive, staring at her food and nodding her head from time to time. She would neither speak nor make eye contact. I asked that she be taken off the tranquilizers. It took us several sessions, but eventually we reached the point where she could control her agitation through progressive relaxation. Once she was able to maintain her emotional stability without constant medication, she could begin to work on changing the way she responded to her anxieties.

Your anxieties, whatever they may be, aren't nearly as debilitating as Diane's. But chances are you're trying to deal with them either by giving in to them, causing your internal guidance system to go haywire; or by covering them up with pills. There's a third way: to learn to respond to those stressful situations Psycho-Cybernetically, not by groping through the medicine cabinet but through natural self-conditioning techniques of the sort Maltz called "do-it-yourself tranquilizers."

This chapter is about those natural tranquilizers and how to use them. You'll learn:

- a five-step procedure for deconditioning yourself from stress.
- how to identify the true stress factors in your life, learn to ignore the false ones, and use visualization to reduce stress.
- an assortment of techniques and exercises that will aid you in preventing stress from building up in your life.

Stress: A Habit You Can Change

Maltz compared stress to the way we respond to a ringing telephone. "From habit and experience, this is a 'signal'...you have learned to obey," he wrote. "Without...making a conscious decision...you...jump up from your comfortable seat, and hurry to the telephone. The outside stimulus has...changed your mental state and your...self-determined course of action. You were all set to spend the hour [relaxing]. You were inwardly organized for this. Now, all this is suddenly changed by your response to the external stimulus...

"The point...is this. You do not *have* to answer the telephone. You do not have to obey. You can, *if you choose*...continue sitting quietly and relaxed...by *refusing to respond* to the signal."

It's easier for you to appreciate this analogy than it was for Maltz's readers, thanks to a device that hadn't been invented in 1960—the answering machine. If you don't care to be disturbed when the telephone rings, you can let it ring and play back your messages later—*once you've conditioned yourself to the presence of the machine*, that is. Chances are this isn't the way you responded when you first got an answering machine. If the phone rang, *you answered it*, even if the machine was turned on. Then probably there was a transitional period when you didn't necessarily answer at once but felt uncomfortable if you didn't play back the message right away. It took some time for you to decondition yourself from your habitual response to the phone.

So it is with the "stress alarm" that certain occurrences set off within you. Think of the expressions we use to describe our stressful responses: "I shouldn't have gotten so upset; Sarah just *rang my bell*." "When Clark does that, it really *pushes my buttons*." It's important to recognize that it's *your* bell and *your* buttons. The circumstances themselves have no more power than the ringing of the phone—unless you choose to *give* them power. Your responses to the bells and buttons in your life often make no sense when you are able to look at them critically. You overrespond because you've formed a habit of stressfully *reacting to* events instead of *acting on* them. It's your horse, not your rider, that's in charge.

"We can, if we wish, just as in the case of the telephone, learn to ignore the 'bell' and continue to sit quietly and 'let it ring,'" Maltz wrote. But as it is with learning any habit, your horse requires a firm and consistent tug at the reins whenever it's about to veer onto the old path.

And that's where do-it-yourself tranquilizers come in. As a commercial might say, they give you fast, temporary relief from the anxiety caused by emotional overresponse. When "taken frequently as directed," they can also decondition you permanently from your programmed, stressful response.

As you read the four examples below, ask yourself "What situations make *me* respond like this? What circumstances tend to send me into an unreasonable state of anxiety, panic, rage or despair?"

Sow SEEDS and Reap Success: Five Steps to Defusing Anxiety

At five o'clock on a Friday afternoon, Maria's boss called her into his office and told her that her services were no longer needed. He explained why she was being let go after six years with the firm, but she was in such a state of shock that she hardly heard him. Maria knew about the company's recent losses and had heard rumors of impending layoffs, but she hadn't considered that she, a CPA with a healthy salary, might be affected. She couldn't believe she had been so swiftly terminated. No one had ever suggested that her work was less than satisfactory. Her review three months earlier had assured her that she was a "team player" and right on target with corporate goals. How had she slipped up? "I can't imagine what I did wrong," she told herself as she drove home. "I didn't do anything wrong. This is so unfair." By the time she got home, she was crying. "How am I going to find another job? Who's going to take a chance on me now?" She flung herself down on the sofa, but she was too agitated to lie still. "What am I going to do?" she asked herself as she paced around her darkened living room. "What am I going to do?"

The key to avoiding stress when your bells get rung is to *reframe* the event that causes the overresponse. You can learn to avoid stress by developing the habit of consciously examining events from a different perspective. Let's take a look at the steps Maria followed to resolve her stress. It's easy to remember these five steps if you think of them as SEEDS that you sow in anticipation of reaping future success.

1. **S**-ituation
2. **E**-valuation
3. **E**-motions
4. **D**-o
5. **S**-elf-esteem

As you read about how Maria sowed her SEEDS, think about your own "push-button responses" and how her solution might apply to you.

1. See the *situation* as fundamentally neutral. After her first wave of despair had passed, Maria turned on the lights, drew a hot bath and called Lila, a friend who worked in the company's employee-relations department. "You too?" Lila said sympathetically. "Don't take it personally. It's panic time. There are cutbacks and layoffs across the board. I've been waiting for the axe myself all month."

Lila's reassurances helped Maria to depersonalize the situation. She was caught in a situationally specific event—company losses—and she had no reason to blame herself. "It's like being on a bridge when lightning strikes," she told herself. "That bridge was going to get struck whether I was on it or not." Yes, the situation was unpleasant—losing a job is a blow to one's self-esteem, not to mention one's bank balance—but it was fundamentally a *neutral* event that her own response had turned into an anxiety-producing event.

2. *Evaluate* the situation: who owns the problem? Maria's first reaction on being laid off was to blame her boss. Her next response was to blame herself. But once she saw the event as neutral, Maria was able to evaluate it realistically. She told herself, "I'm a good accountant, and I did a bang-up job for that company for six years. My performance reviews have always been outstanding, and my salary increases have been proof of it. It's not my fault, and it's not my boss's. He's a fair man with a business to run who was caught in an economic crunch."

Such an evaluation establishes what psychologists call *ownership of the problem*. As you examine your own stress-producing situations, ask yourself the question, "Who owns this problem?" Maria had no cause to feel at fault for what had happened—it was literally *not her problem*. If she'd been fired for dishonesty or incompetence, ownership of the problem would have rested with her, and she would have legitimate cause for concern about herself and her goals. If she'd been fired for unfair reasons, ownership of the problem would have rested with her boss: again she'd have no reason for blaming herself. As it happened, Maria's answer to the question "Who owns the problem?" was "Nobody." It was "just something that happened."

3. Shift your *emotions* to fit your evaluation. As she sat in the bathtub, Maria used the hot water and a few minutes of deep breathing to relax. She allowed herself to enter a quiet room in her mind—an "emotional decompression chamber," as Maltz put it. "It wasn't me, it was just an event, she affirmed to herself. "I'm an okay person in a not-so-okay situation." Gradually Maria felt her emotions shifting to fit her evaluation—from anger, fear and extreme hurt to disenchantment and disappointment. Of course it would have been unreasonable for her to feel *happy* about the situation—but it was equally unreasonable for her to feel anxious about it.

4. *Do* something about the situation. Instead of just *reacting* to an anxiety-producing situation, Maria *acted on it*. She called a friend for support and reassurance. As soon as she got out of her bath, she sat down at her kitchen table and wrote out a list of other things she could do:

- Talk to the boss and confirm that my layoff was just due to circumstance.
- Get a letter of recommendation.
- Call Fred and get the name of that headhunter who got him his job.
- Get a book from the library about updating your résumé.

By making such a list immediately and by following through subsequently, Maria put herself back in control of the event. It was no longer something that was happening to her—it was something she was consciously acting upon. Once her conscious mind made the choice to do something, her subconscious mind no longer responded as if the situation were out of her control.

5. *Self-esteem* **will follow.** When she went to bed that night, Maria still had a task ahead of her—finding a job. Yet by following the first four steps, Maria had relieved her anxiety over the situation and restored her self-esteem. It was no longer a stress-producing situation. Her self-concept regarding the situation had gone through the following stages:

1. "I'm unworthy—I got fired."
2. "I'm miserable—I've been rejected."
3. "I'm scared—I'll never get another job."
4. "I'm lonely—I'll call Lila."
5. "I'm frustrated—I got caught in a downsizing operation."
6. "I'm determined—I'll call Fred; he's always a good resource."
7. "I'm on the move—I'll start updating my résumé tomorrow."
8. "I'm worthy—I just happened to be on the bridge when lightning struck. *I'm still fine!*"

Whatever pushes your buttons—a personal conflict at work, meeting new people, being late for appointments, hassles with your spouse, traffic jams or bureaucratic foul-ups, you can use SEEDS to decondition yourself from anxious overresponse. Once you put the situation in perspective, you can tolerate disappointment without damaging your essential self-concept. It may take several hours to restore your self-esteem. It may take several days or even longer. But however long it takes you, you will have responded to a stressful situation by *acting*—not by anxiously *reacting* to the pushing of a button.

It is important to sow SEEDS *every time* you feel yourself reacting stressfully to an outside event. New habits are learned only through constant repetition. But once you get started, you will soon begin to experience inner peace and confidence in situations where you have habitually known anxiety and self-criticism. This is a path on which you will not be likely to turn back.

What's Stressing You Out? Guess Again!

Irene might have wished she had Maria's problems. She was a 39-year-old homemaker whose days were spent in constant worry, frustration, and anger about her children. Her nine-year-old twin boys were doing poorly in school; her daughter was a sullen 11-year-old whose room could have qualified for disaster relief. How would they turn out in life? What kind of jobs could they ever expect to find? She was too lenient, she thought; that's why they were so lazy and disrespectful. When they were home she screamed at them; when they were out she fretted about who their friends were and worried about gangs and kidnappers. Her mother-in-law was coming to visit next weekend, and Irene just *knew* she was going to criticize the new clothes she had bought them. If only she could share the problem with her husband! But not, him, not Burt, no, never. "It's his fault," she told herself angrily. "They're his kids too, but does he do anything to help discipline them? He sits there and listens to me scream and never says a thing. He's so closed off I can't even talk to him. I'm all alone with this. There's no time to take care of my own needs. I feel so frazzled, I think I'm going crazy. I'd love to take up aerobics, but who am I kidding? I don't even have time to take the kids to the dentist. And nobody cares."

One of the questions I am asked most often in my seminars on stress management is, "How can I identify where my stress is coming from? How can I tell what's causing my anxiety and what is just a symptom of it?" This is a question Irene might do well to ask herself. Is she really worried about her children's problems in school, how their difficulties might affect their future, getting her husband involved in disciplining them, or something wholly unrelated to her family?

How about you? What's "stressing you out" these days? What are the real causes of your anxieties? If you're interested in finding out, a good way to start is by taking the following STRESS-EVALUATION TEST:

1. Spend about 15 minutes doing one of the relaxation exercises outlined in chapter 5 or any other meditative technique you may choose.

2. Get a large piece of butcher paper (or any plain paper) and tape it across your desk or tabletop. This is to minimize left-brain distractions—a notepad would leave you too much room to look around. Start at the top and write:

   I'm worried about...

   I'm worried about...

   I'm worried about...

   Do this *without stopping* for at least five minutes. Let anything come: I'm worried about my kids, I'm worried about paying for the new Buick, I'm worried about whether this cold snap will kill the gladioli. Let your horse trot off unbridled.

3. After five minutes you should have quite a list. Now go over it with your rider in charge. Look at the list more critically. Which items are important and should be focused on and which ones are trivial distractions? Circle those which are genuine concerns.

4. Now copy the genuine concerns onto a new list. Divide it into two vertical columns. At the top of the list across both columns, write the problem you're most concerned with. Then head the two columns FUTURE FANTASIZING and IMMEDIATE ACTION.

Irene's list might look something like this:

I'M WORRIED ABOUT MY KIDS

Future Fantasizing	Immediate Action
1. How will they turn out in life?	1. Their current grades
2. They'll never find good jobs	2. Their manners
3. What if they join a gang?	3. Firm discipline now
4. Mother-in-law's disapproval	4. Set regular dental appointments
5. Am I too lenient? Too demanding?	5. Deal with them without screaming
6. What kind of parents will they turn out to be with the terrible example Burt is setting?	6. Involve Burt in daily disciplinary activities

There are three purposes to this exercise. The first is to create a checklist for determining which of your worries are true stress factors and which are mere "ego-investments." These are the buttons that get pushed when you let yourself be concerned about what your mother-in-law thinks—or your sister, or your uncle Ed, or the neighbors, or the Joneses. Irene might initially have circled "I'm worried about what my mother-in-law thinks" as a true stress factor. Seeing it written down among all those genuine concerns might lead her to realize that it's really a trivial concern about *herself*. Instead of recognizing that her mother-in-law owned the problem, Irene let it become "awfulized" to the point where it became a bigger-than-life cause of anxiety.

Once you recognize these ego-investments for what they are, how do you keep them from overburdening you? This is a "what-if" question: "What if Burt's mother gets on my case about the kids' clothes?" Turn the what-if into so-what-if: "So, what if she does? That's *her* problem. My self-concept as a parent doesn't depend on what she thinks of my taste."

In fact, you may find that some of your "true" stress factors are only different aspects of the same question: "How does this reflect on ME?" Did Irene's concern about her sons' grades really arise from worry about how they would turn out? Or had her I'M-A-BAD-PARENT button been pushed? Irene's job was to model good behavior for her children, not her mother-in-law. Generally whenever you let your ego become involved, you're taking a protective stance. When you become conscious of such a situation, ask yourself, "Who am I trying to impress? Whose evaluation am I protecting myself from?" Once you've uncovered your ego-investment, you can use so-what-if to turn your evaluation into something more positive. Irene, for example, might have made a list of "good stuff" about her children in an effort to discover what was important to *them*.

The second purpose of the exercise is to separate what seems like one BIG problem into smaller, more manageable component problems. Remember in chapter 5 where we talked about breaking down problems into solveable units? Big problems—"I don't know what to do about my kids!"—are vague, formless and unsolvable. Small problems—"My kids talk back to me!"—are specific and manageable. Remember: *you will reduce your anxiety far more effectively by addressing one problem than by worrying about six.*

The third purpose is to discover *which* problems you can address and which are out of your immediate control. That's the reason for the FUTURE FANTASIZING and IMMEDIATE ACTION categories. The IMMEDIATE ACTION listings are your true stress factors, the ones you can successfully address *right now*. The FUTURE FANTASIZING listings are those you can put off. There was nothing Irene could do about things that *might* happen. They were fictional worries that distracted her from confronting the problems she could solve by prompt and present action. Right now, she could call the school and make an appointment to talk to the boys' teacher. She could set aside 10 minutes each day to discuss specific aspects of behavior with her children. She could insist that her daughter clean up her room before going to the mall. She could call the dentist and make appointments for the children. She could sit down with her husband and tell him specifically what support she needed from him in disciplining the kids.

By determining which of your anxieties are true stress factors and which are distractions, ego-investments, awfulized trivialities, vague generalizations, or concerns beyond your immediate control, you can reduce or eliminate your overresponse to them. By addressing these stress factors as solvable problems, you can take a large step toward restoring your self-esteem.

How to Visualize Your Stress Away

Frank, an assistant manager of a supermarket, had come to dread going to work. The anxiety would begin to build up in his stomach even before he turned his car into the parking lot. Frank, 37, was married with two children—and a high-strung, detail-oriented boss who had the knack of pushing his buttons. Mr. Harris had a mania for paperwork and accounting, while Frank was a "people person" whose strengths were in customer service and employee relations. He admitted that he sometimes did a less-than-excellent job of recordkeeping, but that didn't make Mr. Harris's screaming, desk-pounding tantrums any easier to take. The boss would come charging into his office, red-faced and veins popping, and scream about how he was "wasting time pampering folks instead of tending to your knitting!" Frank knew that his skill at pleasing customers and keeping up the morale of the checkers and box people had a positive effect on the bottom line, but there was no way to convince Mr. Harris of that. He felt like a wimp for not standing up to his boss, and he could feel his self-image slipping away with each confrontation. His anxiety had become such that even thinking of Mr. Harris could make his heart pound and his palms sweat.

Often you can give yourself a nonstressful perspective on a button-pushing event through creative visualization. As you read Frank's solution, consider how you could apply it to the people who push *your* buttons.

Frank tried this internal tranquilizer: the second he saw Mr. Harris coming toward him, Frank visualized him as a squalling two-year-old throwing a tantrum. Before he started screaming and pounding on the desk, Frank pictured him in a bonnet and diaper, banging a rattle on the edge of his playpen. He told himself, "This is what my boss *does*—wind him up and he has a tantrum."

This exercise kept Frank's stress at a manageable level. He could evaluate these situations when they occurred by asking himself, "How bad is it that my boss is acting like a baby? Does he have the right to make a fool of himself?" The answer, of course, was "yes." The problem clearly belonged to Mr. Harris—not to Frank. This evaluation helped Frank move from an emotionally negative response to an emotionally neutral one.

When Frank had reached the point where the thought of his boss no longer sent him into a cold sweat, he began to DO something about the situation: he followed each negative encounter with a positive interaction. He waited for his boss to calm down, went to his office and said, "You know, Mr. Harris, I really like my job here, but I'm finding it increasingly difficult to do it when these situations occur. I'd like to find another way for us to work together." After this had happened a few times, Frank began to notice a change in his boss's behavior. Oh, he would still come into Frank's office red-faced and screaming and pounding on the desk, but after a while he'd say, "Okay, I know I'm losing it, but you really should have..." Under such circumstances, Frank was far more willing to admit he'd made an error.

Remember: *The only way people can push your buttons is if you let it happen.* By doing this mental exercise, Frank inhibited his over-response. He now had a degree of control over the situation. Because he could now interact with Mr. Harris without anxiety, Frank was able to rehabilitate his battered self-image. Instead of telling himself "I'm a wimp," he could truthfully say, "The son-of-a-gun knows how I feel about his tantrums. He's admitted he was out of line. Who knows, maybe I can even get him to listen to me."

How to Get Rid of Imaginary Dragons

For a week Ted had burned the midnight oil over the new ad campaign he and Vera were developing for the Better Mousetrap Cat Food people. Next Tuesday was the big meeting with the client, and Ted was finally going home after leaving mock-ups on Vera's desk. They had had their differences over layout and copy, but Vera had left it up to his discretion and Ted felt confident that she'd approve. She'd better, he told himself as he drove home. I've worked my butt off on this campaign. Jeez, that's one tough woman. What if she doesn't like it? I'm going to have to work all weekend to do it over again—*her* way. And I promised to take the kids to the zoo Sunday. They'll be disappointed, but they'll just have to understand. What does Vera know about cat food anyway? She doesn't even *like* cats. Chain-smoking pig. Maybe I ought to have used the calico in the close-up instead of the gray one. What if she wants all the photos reshot? I should have thought about that. I shouldn't have taken such long lunches this week; that was irresponsible. She'll hate it; I know she will. I'd like to see her do better. She'd use my ideas and claim them as her own. *Who does she think she is?* SHE CAN TAKE HER @#¡%&*! GRAPHICS AND—!!!!!

Are there any such imaginary problems that leave *you* feeling stressed? As if we didn't have enough stress over real events, sometimes we allow ourselves to become anxious about monsters

134

of our own devising. Ted's anxiety is a perfect illustration of how your subconscious mind can't tell the difference between a real experience and one that is vividly imagined. He allowed himself to form a mental image of Vera's *most negative response,* and his servomechanism zoomed in on it as if it had been her actual response. "The more I think about it, the madder I get." The more you fantasize about catastrophe (whatever it may be), the more precisely you home in on the feeling as though the catastrophe had actually occurred. You expend emotional energy battling nothing at all.

Fortunately these imaginary dragons are the easiest stress-inducers to deal with. You can choose not to do battle with them. They're like the monsters in video games, the ones firing the laser cannons and karate kicks at you. *They're not real.* It's your choice whether to drop your quarter. It's your choice whether to stay hunched over the machine pushing your own buttons or to walk away. As he drove home, Ted might have benefitted by saying "Cancel. I don't *know* how Vera will respond. I'll find out tomorrow. I'll deal with it when the time comes. There's no point in stewing about it now."

As Maltz put it, "'Doing nothing' is the proper response to an unreal problem." Aren't there enough stress factors in your life without creating anxieties about what *may* happen?

How to Keep Stress from Taking Over Your Life

In each of these situations, the individual responded initially not to an event but to the way he or she *felt* about the event—in Ted's case, to the way he felt in anticipation of a *possible* event. Maria had legitimate concerns over losing her job, but she reacted as though she was sure she would never find another one. Irene let a parent's normal worries grow into a multi-tentacled monster. Frank allowed what was essentially a difference in management style to cause him to "lose it" whenever his boss approached. Ted

135

had the "what if?" game down pat, linking his self-worth to Vera's approval and blowing his stack over mere suspicion of what she might think. At this point it's a good idea to sit back for a moment and review these four examples: the activating events, the stressful ways in which the individuals responded, and the Psycho-Cybernetic techniques they used to alleviate their stress.

ACTIVATING EVENT	STRESSFUL RESPONSE	PSYCHO-CYBERNETIC RESPONSE
You lose your job	Blame the boss, blame yourself, PANIC	Relax, re-evaluate the situation, write options
Kids aren't turning out the way you want	"Awfulize" possibilities, blame spouse, DESPAIR	Address immediate, real concerns you can control
You think about your boss	Anxiety, physical illness, LOSS OF SELF-ESTEEM	Recognize situation as someone else's problem
You complete a task	Self-doubt, awfulize another's response, RAGE	Walk away from your anxieties—you've done all you can for now

Again, those Psycho-Cybernetic responses are:

- Sow SEEDS:

  1. View the event as a fundamentally neutral **S**-ituation.
  2. **E**-valuate the problem.
  3. Change your **E**-motions to suit the situation.
  4. **D**-o what is necessary to confront the situation.
  5. Feel your **S**-elf-esteem increasing as a result of your action.

- Evaluate your stress factors.
- Allow yourself to view the situation in a non-threatening context.
- Do nothing—you're only pushing your own buttons.

By taking a drug-free tranquilizer every time a stressful situation prevents itself—by taking a *proactive* instead of a *reactive* stance to the event—you decondition yourself from the habit of overresponding any time your buttons get pushed. Add a few of your own "push-button" responses to stress-producing events. Write down how you usually respond and how you intend to respond in the future.

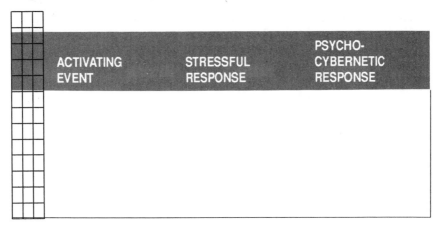

ACTIVATING EVENT	STRESSFUL RESPONSE	PSYCHO-CYBERNETIC RESPONSE

Four More Drug-Free Tranquilizers

In addition, you can go a long way to prevent stress from interfering with your life by practicing the following techniques:

1. Develop Immunity to Stress Through Exercise

A hundred years ago every American schoolchild learned the saying, "A healthy mind in a healthy body" right along with "My Country 'Tis of Thee." Our contemporary concern for health and fitness emphasizes the physical benefits of regular aerobic exercise—improved cardiovascular performance, weight loss, muscle tone—but we tend to underestimate the role of exercise as a stress reducer as well. When I was in clinical practice, I used to insist that my clients do some aerobic activity (of their own choice or their physician's) five days a week for a minimum of 20 minutes a day as an antidote to depression. Such activities—vigorous walking, running, swimming, bicycling or aerobic dancing—cause the body to release endorphins, the natural painkillers that relieve physical and emotional stress without the damaging side effects of drugs. Taking a long, brisk walk, weather permitting, is one of the best things you can do when stress threatens to short-circuit your internal guidance system. You can make it even more beneficial by repeating affirmations while walking. "I am calm, controlled, and relaxed" works very well.

2. Reduce Stress Through Altered States of Consciousness

"Don't medicate, *meditate!*" I tell people attending my seminars. Instead of taking a pill, decondition yourself from stress by taking advantage of altered states of consciousness. These are naturally occurring shifts in the patterns in which your mind functions, some of which you slip into every day of your life. Dr. Stanley Krippner, the leading authority on the subject, identified twenty different states of consciousness. Some of them are "hyperrelaxed" states that are particularly useful in dealing with stress.

Meditation.   This natural state of consciousness occurs on several levels. At one end of the scale is the "light" meditative state you're in when you miss your off-ramp because you're focused on another thought. At the other is a state of "pure consciousness" in which the mind is not aware of anything in particular. In between are states of relaxation that you can induce through the exercises you learned in chapter 5. Whenever your buttons get pushed, allow yourself some time to relax. When you're calm, quiet and breathing deeply and easily, begin to repeat to yourself with each breath, "This is only [an event, one person's opinion, my habitual response to Julie's criticism—whatever applies]. Next time I'll stay calm and confident." Repeat this affirmation six to 10 times and feel yourself getting more and more in control of your feelings. Remain in the meditative state for 15-20 minutes. Then end your meditation by repeating to yourself at least 10 times, "I can control my emotional responses at will." Don't be surprised as you come to discover that it's true.

Daydreaming. Daydreams are *not* an idle waste of time. They provide a window on your interests, an indication of what you would be doing "if only you could." The point is that in many cases, *you can*—if your self-image weren't holding you back. Daydreaming may be the "golden key" to eliminating stress from your life. It is similar to light meditation, except that we tend to remain in it longer and its patterns tend to repeat themselves. In chapter 7 you'll learn how to evaluate your daydreams and turn them into achievable goals. Meanwhile, pay attention to them—they're trying to tell you something.

Internal scanning. This state typically occurs in the "border area" between sleep and wakefulness. Unlike daydreaming, which tends to focus on one image, internal scanning is more like a collage of ideas, thoughts and desires. Ever notice the way your mind "freewheels" just before you fall asleep at night or just after you awaken in the morning? In this "twilight zone" of the mind, both sides of your brain are working together like meshed gears. Your left hemisphere is running through an "instant replay" of the events and impressions of the day while your right hemisphere is synthesizing them, letting them cook and simmer, fitting them together to form the day's "big picture." You have ready access to both of them at once.

You can use this rare state of harmony between the two often-condending sides of your brain as a sort of vaccine against stress. As you become aware of the collage of ideas and impressions forming and re-forming in your mind, affirm to yourself, "I can respond to the events of my life in any manner I choose." If your left brain is doubting the effectiveness of this technique, tell it to withhold judgment until you've tried it a few times. See how your stressful situations seem to evaporate when you've used the internal-scanning state to engage both sides of your brain that morning or the night before.

Dreaming. Dreams can provide a map to your internal guidance system. A thought implanted during internal scanning often becomes an element in a dream. Whatever is "on your mind" as you're falling asleep tends to appear in some form that night in your dreams. You can actually practice "programming your dreams" to find non-stressful responses to your anxieties. When your conscious mind is focusing on the stress-producing situation, your subconsious mind, that ever-agreeable horse, is whinnying and bucking and going nowhere. But in the dreaming state, your subconscious mind can be alerted to your stressors nonjudgmentally without magnifying and awfulizing them. It can find creative, intuitive solutions your conscious mind would never have thought of.

Use your internal-scanning state to program your dreams and pay close attention to them. Dreams of course are highly individualistic, and you may need to monitor yours over a period of time in order to understand the solutions they're offering you. Start a dream journal. Keep a notebook and pen by your bedside and write down your dreams on awakening. Almost everyone has dreams every night, typically five or six of them. It may be that you seldom remember your dreams, but there's a trick to that. Just affirm to yourself several times as you go to bed, "I shall recall at least one dream in living color tomorrow morning." Your subconscious mind will be only too glad to comply. Then first thing when you wake up, grab your notebook and pen and start writing.

3. The Power of Laughter

When was the last time you laughed so hard you were literally doubled over with tears streaming down your face? Remember how good it felt afterwards? Laughter induces the body to release endorphins and allows you to feel relaxed and at ease. Writer and editor Norman Cousins became an advocate of the theraputic and restorative effects of laughter during a painful and life-threatening illness. In *Anatomy Of An Illness* he described his "joyous discovery" (since substantiated by medical research) that "ten minutes of belly laughter" was effective in relieving pain. Cousins used "Candid Camera" reruns and old Marx Brothers movies to induce laughter. Something useful in containing your stress might be as near as your local video store.

4. Stress-Prevention Lists

A stress-prevention list is a checklist of those petty concerns you need to deal with before they turn into hulking anxiety-producing monsters. Getting the car tuned up, buying the anniversary card for the Gustavsons and installing pegboard in the family room are all trivial worries if you consider them one by one, but if you let them accumulate it becomes *when am I going to find the time to DO all these things?* You'll find the time and avoid stress if you make it a habit to DO something on this list every week—more than one thing if these minor, nagging items seem to be piling up faster than you can cross them off. You'll stay on top of the petty annoyances before they rotate to the top of the list and become stress-inducers.

Another way to use the stress-prevention list is to add one item daily that doesn't have to be done on that particular day. You arbitrarily make it a high-priority item as a precaution against accumulated stress. Ever notice how satisfying it is when you complete a task on Tuesday that didn't need to be done until Friday? Your subconscious mind feels that you're taking control of your environment before it can control you. If you make this practice a habit, I guarantee that your "stress index" will decrease.

⊞ Three On-the-Spot Stress-Reducers from the Doctor's First-Aid Kit

Maltz presented a number of "quickie" stress-reducing techniques he suggested we carry in our thoughts like a first-aid kit—a medicine chest of do-it-yourself tranquilizers. Some of his suggestions include these:

1. Delay the Response

While you're in the process of deconditioning yourself, you'll sometimes have your button pushed unexpectedly and be unable to avoid a stressful response. When this happens, try to *delay the response*. This is the theory behind "counting to ten" when you get angry. "Delaying the response," Maltz wrote, "breaks up, and interferes with the automatic workings of conditioning." Breaking up your response patterns makes it easier for you to decondition yourself from stressful responses on a long-term basis.

I had the occasion to use this skill on the morning of my youngest son's wedding. My only responsibility was to get myself and my mother-in-law to the church by 10:30. I had plenty of time (or so I thought), so I allowed myself to do my jogging, get the car washed and run a few errands before going home to shower and dress. It turned into one of those nightmarish mornings when everything seemed to take twice as long as I'd anticipated. Arriving home in my sweatsuit, I found the best man sitting forlornly on the curb in his tuxedo. Everyone else had left for a photo session at the church, and somehow in all the excitement he'd been left behind. I had to run him over the church and drive home, which left me only 10 minutes to make myself presentable and get back in time—a difficult task, considering that the church was 30 minutes away.

As I stepped into the shower, every nerve in my body screaming with stress—*I'M HOLDING UP MY OWN SON'S WEDDING!!!!*—I took a deep breath and told myself, "I'll delay this frustration until later. I'm not going to arrive at his wedding all stressed out and frazzled." I dressed in a hurry and didn't bother about my hair. Everyone would be looking at the bride anyway.

The conscious decision to delay my stress delayed it right out of my day. As we pulled into the church parking lot, my mother-in-law marveled at my composure. "I teach this stuff," I remarked. "I guess it really works!"

2. Build a Psychic Umbrella Through Relaxation

Practice the relaxation techniques introduced in chapter 5 until you're able to slip into a relaxed state almost at will. *It is impossible to feel anxious or "stressed out" when you are relaxed.* This may sound simplistic, like "It's impossible to get fat if you stay skinny," or, "I'd be more confident if I weren't so shy," but it's actually a fact about the way your body and mind work. It's more like saying, "It's impossible to get fat if you don't eat too much," or, "I'll be more confident once I've enhanced my self-image." Remember that anxiety, anger, fear and other feelings associated with stress are not caused by external factors but by your own responses. Avoid these responses by becoming adept at slipping into your "decompression chamber," that quiet place in your mind where stress and anxiety can't penetrate.

Maltz suggested that you think of this place as an actual room, fully realized in your imagination. "Furnish this room with whatever is most restful and refreshing to you," he wrote. "...[T]here are no distracting elements. It is very neat and everything is in order. Simplicity, quietness, beauty, are the keynotes.... From one small window you can look out and see a beautiful beach [or forest or riverbank, whatever natural scene is particularly restful to you].... Take as much care in building this room in your imagination as you would in building an actual room. Be thoroughly familiar with every detail."

A friend of mine, the CEO of a large corporation, builds his psychic umbrella by playing "mental golf." Just before he makes a major decision or goes into an important meeting, he closes his office door, turns his chair away from his desk, closes his eyes and plays one great hole on his favorite course. He sees it in minute detail—the lie of the fairway, the bordering trees, the hazards, the green, his perfect shots. It lasts only 10 minutes, but I have seen his face before and after he plays his imaginary hole, and I would swear it transforms him into a "new man."

3. Take a Little Vacation Every Day

Even when you're sailing through the day feeling no more than the usual "background-level" stress, it's not a bad idea to take a few minutes to retreat into your quiet room. "[In your] imagination," Maltz recommended, "see yourself climbing the stairs to your room. Say to yourself, 'Now I am climbing the stairs—now

I am opening the door—now I am inside.' In imagination notice all the quiet, restful details. See yourself sitting down in your favorite chair, utterly relaxed and at peace."

Such "on-the-spot escapism" has a positive effect on your physical well-being. Your blood pressure drops, your heart rate decreases, blood flows to the head resulting in clearer thinking. Where's it flowing when you're under stress? To your viscera; to your legs. That's the fight-or-flight response again: your body is preparing for an attack by a saber-toothed cat. It can't tell the difference between a life-or-death situation and a project that's overdue. When you consciously take time out for a mini-vacation, your body has no choice but to respond. The level of stress-related hormones in your bloodstream can't help but subside.

Use Drug-Free Tranquilizers to Cushion Emotional Blows

Josh was a 39-year-old firefighter who was suffering from a devastating loss and overwhelming stress. His wife had entered the hospital for minor surgery, developed peritonitis and died unexpectedly. In the depth of his grief, Josh wondered how he was ever going to give his children the emotional support they would need. He had two daughters ages seven and five and a three-year-old son, and however he might eventually learn to cope without Gloria, how could he be both mom and dad to them? After the initial shock wore off and his supporting friends returned to their normal routine, Josh's panic turned to despair. Gloria had been a full-time mom, and he felt that he wasn't even succeeding as a part-time dad.

Psychotherapy was not an option. Josh's medical insurance covered only a portion of what it would cost. As with most people suffering severe emotional blows, he knew would have to "go it alone." I met Josh at a stress seminar I gave in his home town in North Carolina three months after his wife's death. He was particularly inspired by the SEEDS model and saw its applicability to his situation. He asked if we could correspond, and I told him I'd be pleased to hear from him. Over the next few months he wrote me several lively letters chronicling his progress. Josh sowed his SEEDS whenever he found that the pressures of being a single parent were causing him to "awfulize" the situation.

S-ituation: "My wife died, and I took all the responsibility for what happened on myself," he told himself. "Now I can see it as a situation that happened. I was just the one on the bridge when lightning struck."

E-valuation: "Every time I sensed that any of the children were needy or deprived, I saw it as my fault," Josh noted. "I felt I wasn't doing enough for them. But with Gloria gone, they're needy all the time. I'm doing everything I reasonably can for them."

E-motions: By evaluating the situation, Josh was able to shift his emotions from negative reaction—"I can't give my children what they need"—to positive self-evaluation—"It's a tough job being both full-time provider and full-time nurturer, but I'm DOING something on both fronts."

D-o: Josh found help for taking care of the children while he was at work and quality time to spend with them on his days off. As he worked a schedule of 24 hours on, 48 hours off, this was relatively easy to arrange once he decided to do it. He committed himself to spending two hours each week alone with each child to do his or her favorite thing—rollerblading with Jeanie, painting and drawing with Sarah and unstructured play with Josh Junior.

S-elf-esteem: As he worked his way into this routine, Josh found his self-image as an effective and loving father restored.

Josh also made a checklist of practical things that needed to be done for the children and for himself. He felt stressed at first because he didn't know where to start, but by having a running to-do list and crossing out items as they were accomplished, he was able to avoid responding stressfully to the tasks that *didn't* get done. Here is his initial list:

1. Show the girls how to help Josh Jr. get dressed. Make it fun—not a chore.

2. Put a chart in girls' room—award points for beds made, lunches packed, etc. On Friday let them trade in points for small rewards such as a sleepover at a friend's house.

3. Interview babysitters. Hire someone to come in on my days at the firehouse.

4. Fix back-door screen.

5. Get new clothes for kids.

6. Mow lawn or hire Cody [a teenage neighbor] to do it.

7. Make dates for private time with each child this week and mark them in the calendar.

8. Talk to Denise [his late wife's unmarried sister] about coming over for occasional visits—the children love her, and she'd be willing to help out.

9. Do the vacuuming.

10. Set aside an hour each day I'm home for private time to myself.

Like most people undergoing emotional healing, Josh found that there were times he needed to be with people and times he needed to be alone. He joined a Bible-study group which he attended on his evenings off. During the typical 24-hour shift at the firehouse, there were "down times" when the crew had a chance to relax. Josh took some of these occasions to reinvolve himself in the hearts game that was constantly in progress. He frequently found himself laughing with his buddies almost like old times, and he discovered that laughter could indeed relieve his anxiety over how the children were faring in his absence. Previously he had felt guilty about having fun—Gloria was dead, and how could he sit around swapping jokes with the guys as if nothing had happened? It was his friend Ned who pointed out that Gloria would be the first one to "kick him in the pants" about getting on with his life. "Hey, why are you feeling guilty about being *alive?*" Ned asked him. Why indeed, Josh thought.

Josh also used those lulls at the firehouse to take mini-vacations. He would sit on his bunk upstairs, block out the banter of his buddies and the sound of the radio and withdraw into the theater of his imagination. He thought about his favorite fishing place in a nearby state park, a place he'd often gone with Gloria. He imagined it in great detail, from the shadows of pine branches over the river to the texture of the ground to the hum of dragon-flies. By accessing this tranquil place in his imagination, Josh lowered the level of stress hormones in his bloodstream and conditioned himself to achieving relaxation at the touch of a mental button.

Josh initially felt uneasy about the idea of altered states of consciousness. He associated meditation with "oriental religion," and wondered if it would conflict with the Christian principles that guided his spiritual life. A conversation with his minister and a thoughtful self-talk assured him that there was nothing in the practice of meditation that conflicted with *any* religious beliefs— as ways to spiritual health, they were no more in conflict than were nutrition and regular medical check-ups as ways to physical health.

Because his firefighter's schedule interrupted his body's nor-mal daily rhythms, Josh often had trouble falling asleep at night. When this happened, he tried to use his internal-scanning state to his advantage. Whenever feelings of despair or panic surfaced, he redirected them toward positive action. "Okay, what can I do about it?" he asked himself. "If I can do something, I will. If I can't do anything about it, it needs no further attention from me."

By synthesizing all these techniques, Josh was able to cushion the severe trauma caused by the death of his wife. Deconditioning himself from anxiety through the use of SEEDS, checklists, psychic umbrellas, altered states and so on wasn't *easy*—but once Josh set out to do it, he found that it was *simple*. It was merely a matter of changing the habitual way he responded to stress.

Turn Stress into Success

"Inner disturbance, or the opposite of tranquility," Maltz wrote, "is nearly always caused by over-response, a too sensitive 'alarm reaction.' You create a built-in tranquilizer, or psychic screen between yourself and the disturbing stimulus, when you practice 'not responding'—letting the telephone ring." Here are a few skills you can practice while waiting for that call:

1. Use reflective relearning to practice nonstressful responses. Make a list of events that you wished you could have handled more calmly. Decide which of the techniques presented in this chapter is most applicable to each of those situations. Then go into the theater of your imagination. Visualize a situation as it occurred, only this time see yourself responding to it Psycho-Cybernetically. Any time you find yourself thinking regretfully about letting a situation push your buttons, CANCEL and tell yourself exactly how you'll respond next time.

2. Build yourself a decompression chamber, Maltz's "quiet room in your mind." Fill it with as much detail as possible.

3. Review the five steps of SEEDS regularly to maximize your chances of an immediate, positive response to a stressful event:

    ■ View the event as a fundamentally neutral **S**-ituation.

    ■ **E**-valuate the problem.

    ■ Change your **E**-motions to suit the situation.

    ■ **D**-o what is necessary to confront the situation.

    ■ Feel your **S**-elf-esteem increasing as a result of your action.

By *practicing* these responses under non-stressful conditions, you increase the likelyhood that you *will* respond unstressfully the next time your buttons get pushed.

Six Habitual Thoughts That Signal Stress

Be on the lookout for recurring thought patterns that may be indications of stress in your life. If you find yourself indulging in any three or more of them on a daily basis, take a do-it-yourself tranquilizer.

1. Overcriticizing yourself and/or others

2. Needing to control others

3. Expressing inner fears: playing the "what-if?" game
4. Obsessing on past mistakes: playing the "if-only-I-had" or "if-only-I-hadn't" game
5. Playing Chicken Little: going around telling yourself, "The sky is falling, the sky is falling!"
6. "Awfulizing and catastrophizing": making mountains out of molehills

Stress can sometimes be hard to recognize—especially when you've become habituated to its presence in your life. Look out for these "warning signals" to keep your automatic mechanism in good repair.

Five "Red-Flag" Signals of Overstress

Prevent "burnout" by being aware of these five warning signals:

1. *Changes in sleeping patterns:* You have trouble falling asleep at your usual time or awaken atypically during the night.
2. *Changes in eating patterns:* You can't seem to get enough to eat or can't seem to eat much at all.
3. *Frequent ailments:* Your back goes out, then your stomach acts up, then you develop a cold, etc., etc.
4. *Addictive cravings:* You want more coffee, cigarettes, alcohol, chocolate (whatever your poison happens to be) and it doesn't alleviate your anxiety the way it usually does.
5. *Increased feelings of futility and exhaustion:* You never seem refreshed, no matter how much rest you get, and you find yourself wanting to "give up."

If you identify three or more of these red flags during the course of a week, take positive action:

1. *Take better care of yourself emotionally.* Be aware of your negative feelings. Practice saying CANCEL a lot.
2. *Take better care of yourself physically.* This is a time when your body needs more positive attention than usual. Add some easy exercises to your daily routine. Force yourself to eat a small amount of some-

thing healthful. Take extra time to relax. Reset your priorities and rotate YOURSELF to the top of your to-do list.

3. *Don't whip yourself for giving in to your vices.* Recognize that you're in a temporary crisis and therefore allowed to slip a bit.

Remember that Psycho-Cybernetics is a goal-striving process. On your path to your chosen goal, there will be times and places where your reactions to external events threaten to send you veering off course. "Do-it-yourself tranquilizers" are your internal controls that allow you to stay on course even though the events may be beyond your power to change. You don't need drugs to stay on course. You only need to avoid pushing your own buttons.

Targeting on Ideas

- Stress results from the way you respond to outside events, not from the events themselves.
- There are many techniques you can use to learn how to avoid stressful overresponses in the same way you learn any new habit.

ET
YOUR OWN
TARGETS

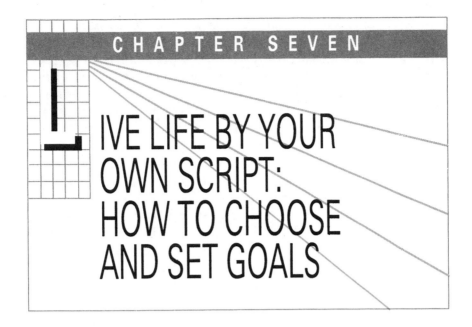

CHAPTER SEVEN

LIVE LIFE BY YOUR OWN SCRIPT: HOW TO CHOOSE AND SET GOALS

We are engineered as goal-seeking mechanisms. We are built that way. When we have no personal goal which we are interested in and which "means something" to us, we are apt to "go around in circles," feel "lost" and find life itself "aimless."…. People who say that life is not worthwhile are really saying that they themselves have no personal goals which are worthwhile.

—*Maxwell Maltz*, Psycho-Cybernetics *(1960)*

A man or a woman without a goal is like a ship without a rudder. Each will drift and not drive. Each will end up on the beaches of despair, defeat, and despondency.

—*Zig Ziglar*, See You At The Top *(1974)*

151

Most of us plan our vacations with more precision than we plan our lives. Take Jerry, a stereo-equipment salesperson from Kansas City who quit his job and moved to Los Angeles with the idea of writing for the movies. Now, you have to understand about the screenwriting thing in L.A. It's an old joke that if you randomly stop a hundred strangers on the street, police officers and accountants and secretaries and mechanics, and ask them, "How's your screenplay coming," eighty-five of them will say something like "My agent says Twentieth [sic] is about to take it under option," or at least, "I had to put it aside to concentrate on my day job, but I'll be getting back to it soon." Jerry was innocent of this. He rented an apartment in Santa Monica and signed up for a screen-writing course at UCLA. He bought a copy of Egri's *The Art of Dramatic Writing*, subscribed to the *Hollywood Reporter* and got a list of agents from the Writers' Guild in Beverly Hills. "I've got a thousand ideas," he told himself. "I only have to decide which of them has the most potential."

Eight months later, Jerry got a call from a friend in Kansas City. "How's your screenplay coming?" she asked him.

"Oh," Jerry replied, thinking of the half-dozen three-page "starts" in his filing cabinet, "I had to put it aside to concentrate on my day job, but I'll be getting back to it soon."

Then there was Lauren, a divorced mother of two living in Atlanta. Her job as a bank clerk enabled her to make ends meet, but there was little left over for luxury or savings. "I hate this rut I'm in," Lauren told her friend Dee one morning over coffee. "I feel like life's passing me by."

"You could always get another job," Dee said. "Send out some résumés."

"Yeah, but I'm not qualified for anything."

"You could take some classes. There's all kinds of evening courses at the local college—data processing, paralegal—"

"Yeah, but I couldn't learn any of those things. They're too hard."

"Sure you could. I've worked with you for three years. You're brighter than most of the managers at this bank."

"Yeah, but what about my kids? What am I supposed to do, neglect them while I do homework? They've already got one absent parent. The jerk."

"Well, anyway, you could always look for a better job?"

"Yeah, but who has time? How am I supposed to go on interviews when I'm here all day?"

"Well then, what do you want to do?"

"To get out of this rut I'm in!"

There's a special joy when you find yourself overcoming old mental programming and breaking out of "ruts." It is one of life's most exciting experiences to find yourself achieving things you may only have dreamed about before. The problem, as both Jerry and Lauren eventually recognized, is that you can't grow, you can't dig yourself out of a rut and move forward, unless you have clear and specific goals. Otherwise it doesn't matter how hard you strive. If you don't know what you want, you're guaranteed not to get it. If you want to hit a target, you've got to have one. If you mistake wishes for goals, you end up with a file drawer full of three-page screenplays. If a negative self-image keeps you aiming for curbs instead of destinations, you end up complaining about the rut you can't get out of. Finding a better job, establishing a more fulfilling career, meeting the love of your life, spending more quality time with your children, running a marathon or quitting smoking—it doesn't matter *what* your goals are, it only matters that you *know* what they are.

"Remember," Maltz wrote, "the creative guidance system within you is a goal-striving mechanism, and the first requisite for using it is to have a clear-cut goal or target to shoot for.... Time and time again I have seen confused and unhappy people 'straighten themselves out,' when they were given a goal to shoot for and a straight course to follow."

This chapter is about setting goals; about how to determine the direction of your life and how to get moving in that direction. You'll learn:

- what habits may be holding you back from establishing attainable goals, and how you can break them.

- how to assess what goals are appropriate for you.
- a five-point plan for setting realistic and practical goals.
- a seven-point program for action that can get you from goal-setting to achievement.

⊞ Goals—Your Set Point for Success

In the question-and-answer periods during my seminars and speaking engagements, I am struck by one particular paradox that is repeated again and again. People are always asking me for a magic formula, a list of "how-tos" for reaching goals, yet they fail to define what those goals are. Although "how-to" is a legitimate concern, it is the cart before the horse—and by now you know all about that horse! There is a direct relationship between setting goals and achieving success, no matter what "success" might mean to you. The goals you establish determine your *set point* for success.

A set point is a central tendency, like the setting on a thermostat, a pre-established *status quo* you keep returning to. Think about your physical set points. If you've maintained a weight of 150 pounds for several years and then suddenly lose 20 pounds, your body will strive to return to 150 pounds, its set point. When strenuous exercise causes your body to overheat, its cooling system will work overtime to maintain its set-point temperature of 98.6 degrees.

So it is with your mind. There is a direct relationship between what you strive for and what you actually achieve. If you consciously establish a set point, your automatic mechanism has a tendency to adjust toward that set point. If you have no clear and specific goal—a definition of success on your own terms—printed on your subconscious mind, your set point is essentially zero.

How *do* you define success? Do you feel that you truly deserve success? Do you dare to dream of success? How willing are you to take risks? The answers to these questions help determine your set point.

154

How to Avoid the Dead-End Trap of Magical Thinking

As you've learned, a poor self-image can trap you in limited thinking. For the person with low self-esteem, goal setting is throttled by such notions as "I can't." "I'd like to, but..." "If only I had..." "If only I hadn't..." And perhaps the most common of all, "Yeah, but..." Do you know what a yabbit is? It's someone like Lauren, who wanted to get out of her rut but kept making excuses not to: "Yeah, but I don't have the skills." "Yeah, but I don't have the time." "Yeah, but I'm too short." "Yeah, but..." "Yabbit..." Instead of setting goals, a yabbit sits around wondering when life is going to get better.

When *is* life going to get better? Think about the way it was when you were a child, looking forward to life's milestones. "Life is going to be really good when I'm 16; then I can get a driver's license." That's what you thought, wasn't it? Then you got your license and you found yourself looking up the road at another milestone. "Life is going to be good when I have the money for gas and insurance, money to *go* places and *do* things." And so you took a part-time job, flipping hamburgers or babysitting or pumping gas. You got a little money together, and that felt good. "Now life is really going to get better. All I have to do is find someone to *love*, gotta fall in *love*, man..."

See what a dead-end trap this is? It's not goal-setting, it's wishful thinking—"magical thinking," as Freud called it. "Step on a crack, you break your mother's back," so if you can avoid stepping on cracks you can rest secure that Mommy will be fine. Life will get better once you pass that next milestone: get married, have kids, get them grown up and gone, retire and get the motor home...die and go to heaven. "When I'm dead, that's when life is *really* going to get better"? This isn't goal setting, it's stagnation.

Yet you have set and achieved goals. They just may not have been particularly positive and fulfilling. *Everything you have done so far in your life has been the realization of goals,* whether or not you've recognized them as such. Think for a moment how effective you could be if you turned goal achievement into a conscious, purposeful act.

When is life going to get better? *Now,* this moment. *Now* is all you have. There's no such thing as life-will-get-better-at-the-next-milestone. Milestones are millstones. Life gets better when we know we've *made* it better.

Now read on and find out how to do it.

Getting Started: How to Avoid Living Someone Else's Script

I want to share a personal story about goal setting. Years ago I attended a lecture-discussion that was part of a seminar called Life Planning—a course to help grown-ups decide what they wanted to be when they grew up. I was sitting there with five hundred other people listening to the speaker ask us, "What do you want out of life? What do you really want out of your life?"—when all of a sudden the question stopped being hypothetical for me. Of all the faces in the auditorium, the speaker chose mine to point at. "Yes, you," he said. "What do *you* want from life. What do you really want to do with your life?"

"I, uh..." I stammered. "Well, I—I want lots of things!"

"That's not an answer," he said. "What do you *really* want?"

I was embarrassed. "I really want you to leave me alone," I said.

"I won't do that because it would be a disservice to you," the white-haired gentleman shot back. "*What do you want?*"

I finally managed to blurt out, "I want to be a public speaker."

"Great," he said. "You know what you want; you will be a public speaker. I affirm that for you."

The man, as you may have guessed, was Maxwell Maltz. That was the lecture that transformed my life.

On the way home I had the strangest feeling inside me, a mixture of confusion, fear, and excitement. "What did I say; what have I committed myself to?" I asked myself. "It just came bursting out of me." Then the old tapes started replaying themselves in my head. "Who do you think you are? Public speaker!?

Why don't you go for showbiz next; why don't you direct a movie?"

I come from southern Missouri, a town not far from the Ozarks. Neither of my parents had more than a high-school education, and it was their dream that I should go to college and on to medical school. They had written this script for me before I was out of my playpen. I ended up at the University of Colorado, where I was enrolled in pre-med. As I drove home from Dr. Maltz's lecture listening to all those old negative tapes, I found myself thinking about the day I had realized I wasn't going to become a medical doctor after all.

It was a beautiful Saturday morning in spring. I was looking across the campus from the chemistry lab where I was doing a makeup class. I never seemed to be able to keep up with my lab work. I was standing there in my apron and goggles, watching the centrifuge going around and around and saying to myself, "I don't get it? Why am I here?" Out the window students were walking in the sunshine, laughing, and enjoying themselves...and all at once I started to cry.

The lab assistant came hurrying over, full of concern. "What's the matter with you?" he asked.

"I don't know," I said, weeping. "All I know is, my life's not working."

The lab assistant urged me to go to the student health center where, as luck would have it, there was a psychologist on duty. I repeated the what's-the-matter-my-life's-not working conversation with him, and he told me to come back Monday for some testing. I was run through the usual battery of tests, and after they'd been evaluated the psychologist sat me down for a talk.

"There's certainly nothing wrong with you," he said. "You'll have no trouble making it through medical school with your ability. But your tests all indicate one thing very strongly: you have no interest in being a physician."

I said, "Huh?"

"Don't you see, all your scores are high in social science," he said, pushing a page full of bar graphs at me. "You're more people-oriented. You belong in another field, like sociology or psychology. You wouldn't be nearly as happy as a medical doctor as you would being a sociologist or psychologist."

It was as if someone had slapped my face. It took me a while to get it. I remember saying to him, "I didn't know I was supposed to *like* it." I had been entirely conditioned to the life and career that had been planned for me. It had never even occurred to me that it was a matter for like or dislike.

I'll spare you the scene with my parents when I told them I was switching from medicine to psychology. What made me think of it on my way home from Dr. Maltz's lecture was the notion that I was *still* letting someone else script my life. "What do you want out of life?" the doctor had asked me. "What do you really want?" I was getting my Ph.D. in psychology; I didn't know where that public-speaker thing had come from. All I knew was that when Dr. Maltz asked me his intimidating question, I had blurted out something completely off-the-wall.

Or was it? Whose goals was I striving for anyway? And whose was that voice inside me telling me what a self-deluding fool I was for thinking I could be a public speaker?

Why What You Believe Conditions Your Goals

Enough about my goals for now; let's have a look at yours. We all have that voice inside us, playing and replaying the old tapes, telling us "I CAN'T." That's your belief system talking, that set of chains and stakes forged by your self-image. Every time you consciously replay those old tapes—"I could never be a public speaker; it's too hard"—*that's a goal*, as far as your automatic mechanism is concerned. It's a negative goal, and it's not even your own. *It's someone else's*—your parents' most likely. Yet your subconscious mind, that faithful old horse, is heading right for it, straight down the I CAN'T path.

Try something right now. Get a pen and paper and see if you can get an idea of what your life's script is like. Write down some of the things your parents or other early role models told you about life. What was it supposed to be like? What was your role in life supposed to be?

Having trouble coming up with anything? See if any of these set that old tape recorder whirring:

"Life is tough."

"Life's not fair."

"What will the neighbors think?"

"You'll never amount to anything if you don't..."

"Be satisfied with what you've got. When *I* was your age..."

"Better to be safe than sorry."

"You can't have your cake and eat it too."

"A bird in the hand is worth two in the bush."

"Be careful what you wish for—you might get it!"

"You've buttered your bread, now *eat* it!"

"You've made your bed, now *lie* in it!"

"You can't teach an old dog new tricks!"

And one of my all-time personal favorites:

"I hope when you have kids they'll be rotten just like you!"

I wonder how many of us ended up fulfilling *that* particular prophecy? I certainly did. I had a rotten kid...just like me.

The point is that a lot of us didn't have very good role-modeling when it came to setting goals. Your early-childhood scripting may have programmed in a lot of negative feelings and assumptions, and your subconscious mind has been agreeing and complying with them ever since. When you replay the tape that goes "Who ever told you life would be easy," you're subconsciously complying with the notion that life is...*difficult*. If you're constantly replaying the tape that goes "What will the neighbors think," then every time you get it into your head to do something risky and out-of-the-ordinary, you start worrying that someone is peeking over your back fence and judging you.

By now you should be an expert on what to do when those old negative tapes start playing: *restate and reframe.* Exercise your CRAFT:

- Say "Cancel!"
- Replace the old tape with positive data.
- Affirm your ability to attain your goal.
- Focus on attainment of the goal in your imagination.
- Train yourself in a new role: act as if the goal has already been achieved.

And most important, have a clear, positive goal to strive for.

How Your Self-Image Conditions Your Goals

One of the things I learned about human behavior during my years as a psychotherapist is that there aren't too many victims in life. There are a lot of volunteers.

Consider how you may have volunteered to hold yourself back. Do any of these rationalizations sound familiar?

"It's _____ fault that I can't get ahead in life."

"I can't; _____ doesn't want me to succeed."

"I can't; I don't have the (time, money, education, intelligence)."

"I can't; I'm the wrong (sex, color, size, age)."

"If I do that, I'll lose _____."

"I could, if only I had _____."

"I could, if only I hadn't _____."

"I know my limitations."

It goes on and on, the intrapsychic dialog that keeps us immobile. If you know your limitations, sure enough, you're chained to them. You can build a great case for failure. You tell yourself that so-and-so "really makes me angry"; that someone or other "upset me so much I just lost it." Or another of my all-time favorites: "Now look what you made me do."

The reality is that no one "makes you" unless you let them. The only person who really stops you—the only person who ever truly "makes you" do anything is—you already knew what I was going to say, didn't you?—yourself.

Now your left brain, that infuriatingly logical little pest, is probably already arguing with me: "Where does she get off saying it's my fault? How am I supposed to set positive and realistic goals with (my eighth-grade education, my four kids, my abusive father, my demanding mother, my husband who wants to keep me dependent, my wife who's terrified of losing me to a younger woman, The Real World Being As It Is)?" In a few minutes, when you sit down to write out your goals, old Jiminy Cricket's really going to be sounding off: "What's she *talking* about, all this intuition and dare-to-dream stuff? This is dumb. This is bullpuckey. Who's minding the store?"

All this may be true, as far as your left brain is concerned. Assure your left brain that it's going to get its at-bats, but for now we're going to approach goal setting as a right-brain job.

⊞ Plan Your Work Before You Work Your Plan

It's important to write down your goals. It's been my experience that those who don't write down their goals don't achieve them. If you can't commit to writing them down, you won't commit to following through. If you won't connect to paper, you won't connect to reality. The act of writing down your goals is a signal to your conscious mind, like a TelePrompter. It forces your conscious mind to look at and consider your goals. It translates daydreaming and wishes into actual goal setting—and eventually, into a plan of action.

So get a pencil and pad right now. Read the rest of this chapter in a place where you'll be able to write comfortably. First you're going to give yourself an idea of what goals would be appropriate for you—by desire and (possibly hidden) talent. *Then* we'll get to the action plan.

Determine What Your Goals Need to Be

There's no single best way to decide what your goals ought to be. Don't, don't, *don't* allow the following exercises lead you to feel that you're restricted to a particular strategy of goal setting. *Do* let them guide you in suggesting what *may* be the best approach to goal setting for you. *Do* let them provide some insight into why you may have been thwarted in the past because your approach to goal setting happened to be in conflict with someone else's. There are many different paths to the same end, and you needn't feel intimidated or discouraged if your way happens to be different from your spouse's, your boss's or your Uncle George's.

Too many people try to set goals backwards. Jerry, the would-be screenwriter, is a perfect example. His approach to goal setting was, "To be a screenwriter, what do I need? Well, let's see, I need to live in L.A., I need to take a class, I need a list of agents, I need the right software, I need to know what producers are buying these days. If I have all these things, I can do what a screenwriter does, which is to visualize camera shots and write dialog and sell my scripts for a lot of money and do lunch with producers at Spago and cruise the Pacific Coast Highway in my Alfa-Romeo—"

—And *hogwash*. This is backward thinking. *Be* first, *then* do, *then* have. What Jerry needed first of all was to be a screenwriter inside.

What does this mean? You have to have a burning passion, a conviction that a screenwriter is *what you are*. You need to say, "I have something I need to say, and I have to express it through images on film." Then you can do what screenwriters do and have what screenwriters have.

Which is what? Pride, satisfaction, fulfillment.

It's time for you to determine what you want to *be*. Take a pencil and complete the sentence below. Write down the goal you'd most like to achieve, even if it seems no more than a dream. What is your burning passion, the goal that would be so fulfilling you'd *pay* someone for the privilege of doing it?

The thing I most want to do with my life is

Now, *don't* write, "I want to be happy." That's not a goal any more than "I want to get out of this rut" is. Be specific about what's going to *make* you happy. Do you want to find the person of your dreams and get married? Write it down. Do you want to leave a relationship that's gone stale? Write it down. Do you want to go back to school and get your degree? What school? In what field? Write it down. Do you want a new job? A different career? Write it down, but be sure you're specific about the job or career you want. Do you want to chuck the job thing altogether and go off and be a beachcomber in Tahiti? Write down what you want, whatever it may happen to be.

At a loss for words? I'm sympathetic. For me it took Maxwell Maltz pointing his finger in my face—but I'll get back to that story later. What do *you* want? Put your right brain in charge. Don't watch the curbs. Don't be thinking, "This is only a fantasy," or "I can't have my cake and eat it too." If your left brain *must* get its two cents in, let it consider that whatever it is you want, there's someone, somewhere in this world who's *doing* it and probably making a lot of money at it. Why shouldn't that be you? Let your right brain determine what that all-consuming passion of yours is and write it down. We'll be coming back to it from time to time throughout this chapter.

Dare to Dream: Draw a Map of Your Subconscious Interests

Dreams and daydreams get a bad rap when it comes to the practicalities of goal setting. How often have you expressed your deepest desires to a friend only to have him come back with a derisive "Dream on!" or "You must be daydreaming!"? In fact dreams of both the day and night varieties are useful in pointing you toward your goals. They are subconscious methods of goal setting that can convey messages about where you ought to be heading.

What do you find yourself daydreaming about? Let me tell you about Michaela, a woman in her late thirties who had a lucrative career as a speechwriter and consultant for public officials and business executives. Michaela had always had a passion for music. She'd played the flute in a city-wide youth orchestra, sung in choral groups, and worked her way through college playing in a rock-'n'-roll band, but the "impracticality" of a musical career prevented her from ever considering one. As she approached the Big Four-Oh, however, she found herself experiencing deep regrets about not having become a musician. "Of course it's too late now," her left brain told her. "How can I give up my career to go chasing after daydreams?" Still, in her quiet times she found herself thinking more and more about music. On a visit to her mother, she found her old flute in a box in the cellar and began to relearn it. She took a summer workshop at a college, where she met several professional musicians and dedicated amateurs. She still was not consciously thinking about changing careers, but she began to spend less time with the politics-and-management crowd and more with the musicians.

We'll be coming back to Michaela and her story shortly. Right now, I want you to think about your own daydreams. Pay attention to them. What specific steps would you have to take to translate them into attainable goals?

Think about your sleeping dreams too. Have you started keeping a dream journal as I suggested in the last chapter? Be aware of patterns in your dreams that may be suggesting certain goals.

Are you still having trouble remembering your dreams? Then make one up. No kidding! Make one up and write it down. Whatever you invent in your conscious fantasy is likely to yield something that's in your subconsious mind. It's a seed mechanism. Very soon you should be able to recall many dreams.

Learn to Trust Your Intuition

It's sometimes hard to accept that your right-brain thoughts are equally as valid as your left-brain thoughts. This is particularly true when it comes to setting goals. The left brain sees no point to visualizing goals; it thinks in words and procedures. It will try literally to talk you out of any intuitive feelings you may have about what your goals ought to be. Don't ever forget that your right brain has its own skills that are equally useful. It reads signals beautifully. It understands subtle nuances. It can interpret a sigh or a raised eyebrow that your left brain may not even have noticed.

Have you ever experienced *déja vu*—the feeling that something has happened before? Ever know what a person was going to say before he or she said it? Ever have what you thought was a clairvoyant experience? Scared the bejesus out of you, didn't it? Your left brain doesn't even want to think about these things. It tells you, "Uh-oh. This is paranormal. ESP. I don't believe in that stuff." The fact is there's nothing "extrasensory" about it at all. It's only your right brain receiving and processing signals that don't happen to be verbal signals. A recent study at UCLA determined that 93 percent of all communication is nonverbal. And a great deal of this non-verbal communication is subconciously sent and subconsciously received.

That's why it's important to trust your intuition when you're taking new steps toward personal growth. It may be trying to tell you something, no matter how strongly your left brain may be resisting the message. "That which we resist will persist," says an old Chinese proverb.

Here's a formula I follow. Pay attention to your intuition whenever:

- the intensity of the feeling is strong (your body is telling you, "Go for it!").
- the impression is persistent (occurs more than three times).
- you feel an intense intellectual urge to ignore it.

Taking Stock of Your Set Point: A Questionnaire

Thank you very much, right brain. Now, if you would please sit down, it's time to let the left brain have its turn. The next step is a series of questions that will help you get an idea of your current state of success. After you've answered the questions, evaluate your answers to help you determine what your set point ought to be.

1. How do you define success in each of these areas?
   a. personal

   _____

   _____

   b. financial

   _____

   _____

   c. career

   _____

   _____

   d. social

   _____

   _____

   e. physical

   _____

   _____

   f. spiritual

   _____

   _____

2. How would you rate your success in each of these areas?

	highest	5	4	3	2	1	lowest
a. personal		❑	❑	❑	❑	❑	
b. financial		❑	❑	❑	❑	❑	
c. career		❑	❑	❑	❑	❑	
d. social		❑	❑	❑	❑	❑	
e. physical		❑	❑	❑	❑	❑	
f. spiritual		❑	❑	❑	❑	❑	

3. Evaluate the quality of your present relationships with:

	highest	5	4	3	2	1	lowest
a. spouse		❏	❏	❏	❏	❏	
b. co-workers		❏	❏	❏	❏	❏	
c. friends		❏	❏	❏	❏	❏	
d. other _____		❏	❏	❏	❏	❏	
e. other _____		❏	❏	❏	❏	❏	

4. Your current values:

a. Name the five people you most admire today.

_____

_____

b. With whom would you most want to trade places?

_____

c. How do you spend your leisure time?

_____

_____

5. Rate your productivity:

a. Are you ❏ more or ❏ less productive than you were 10 years ago? (Check one.)

b. How do you produce in relation to your co-workers?

highest 5 ❏ 4 ❏ 3 ❏ 2 ❏ 1 ❏ lowest

c. How do you produce in realtion to what consider your potential?

highest 5 ❏ 4 ❏ 3 ❏ 2 ❏ 1 ❏ lowest

6. Which of these approaches best describes the way you handle change? (Check one.)

❏ the *fearful stance* (Chicken Little): "The sky is falling; the sky is falling!"

❏ the *courageous stance* (The little engine that could): "I think I can, I think I can!"

❏ the *waiting stance* (Snow White): "Someday my prince/ss will come."

❏ the *prepared stance* (the third little pig): "I've built my house with bricks. Huff and puff all you want."

7. How do you confront your obstacles?

   a. Do you justify to yourself why you should settle for less than your ideal?

   _____

   b. What is your greatest fear about making changes and taking risks?

   _____

   c. In what circumstances do you allow your "shoulds" to take precedence over your "wants"?

   _____

   d. In what areas do you avoid taking risks because you've "always done it this way"?

   _____

8. Which of the following best describes the feedback you get from others with regard to how successful you are? (Check one.)
   - ❑ clarifies your values
   - ❑ allows you to be objective
   - ❑ permits a shift of focus
   - ❑ facilitates change

Take an Inventory of Your Skills

Now it's time for the two sides of your brain to work together. Go back and take a look at your answer to the question on page 163, your statement about the one thing you most want to do with your life. The question to think about now is: what skills do you *already possess* that would be useful to you in achieving that goal? What skills may be hidden from your conscious view—qualities to which the excuses "I can't" or "I haven't the time to learn them" don't apply because *you already have them?*

Consider your responses on the questionnaire as you think about this question. What skills does the questionnaire reveal to you that you might not have been consciously aware of? How closely do they parallel your dreams? Consider too the old childhood tapes that may have seemed like obstacles until you learned to look at them as stakes you could easily pull out of the ground—habitual beliefs you could change through reflective relearning. How far away are you really from realizing this deepest desire? It doesn't look like *quite* such a fantasy any more, does it?

Let's take an inventory of your existing skills. Take a sheet of paper and divide it into two columns. Head the left-hand column MY EXISTING SKILLS. Head the right-hand column TRANS-FERS.

In the SKILLS column, make a list of the skills you possess right now that would be of use to you, no matter how small, in achieving that "impossible" goal. In the TRANSFERS column, jot down how each of your skills could be transferred over and applied to your goal.

In appraising your skills, remember times you've been successful in the past. Think back—what about the time you found your way home when you were six? Didn't you feel like a success? What problem-solving skills did you have to use on that occasion? How are such skills applicable to your present goal? What about the time you got Karen Sue Crowley to go to the prom with you? You never believed she'd say yes, did you? Doesn't that indicate "people skills" that would be applicable to present goals? What about the time you patched up the feud between Aunt Ruth and Aunt Elizabeth? The play you wrote for the office party all those Christmases ago? You might want to make another list on a separate sheet of paper. Head it MY SUCCESSES. Evaluate how your past successes point out your present skills.

What are the three most important identifiable skills you possess? Don't be modest. If you've got a high level of creativity, write it down. If you're better at procedural detail, write that down. Some goals take a lot more perspiration than inspiration. What can you do *today* that would draw you closer to that all-consuming passion of yours—even just an inch and a half closer? What new skills could you learn in the near or immediate future that would draw you closer still—perhaps even put the goal within reach?

⊞ How to Set Goals the SMART Way: Your Practical Guide to Goal Setting

By now your left and right brain should be fully engaged in thinking about goals. You have a clear picture of what a goal is and isn't and why goals are essential to success. You're aware of the obstacles your self-image may have thrown in your way and what steps you can take to overcome them. You've done a self-exploration to evaluate your dreams and desires and how they might be translated into attainable goals. Now it's time to get down to practical considerations. How do you go about establishing the goals that are right for you, and how do you maximize your chances of achieving them?

It's important to think of any goal as a process, not a place to be. Think of it as the path your automatic mechanism is taking toward a particular end, not the end in itself. If you're going to reach your destination, you need to view the process as complete, fluid and dynamic. Otherwise you'll tend to view every little setback, slowdown or meander as a sign of failure. Remember that a servomechanism works through a series of course corrections. This is why it's a good idea to state your goal as an ongoing process—not "I will be a professional flute player," but "I am in the process of becoming a professional flute player," or, "I am currently...," or "I am allowing myself to..." When you make affirmations to yourself about your goals, this is the form to use.

When you sit down to determine your goals, start by considering all the areas of your life in which you want to make changes—job, career, romantic satisfaction, health, family life, education, creative endeavors, community work, spiritual development—whatever is important to you. *Don't* neglect your life's wish, the goal you wrote down as the one you'd most like to achieve. By combining practical considerations with your dreams and desires, you can get an idea of what's most important to you. If you wrote down, "The thing I most want to do with my life is end world hunger," consider that you could start on a smaller scale by working for a relief agency. If you wrote "The thing I most want to do with my life is to be pope," don't dismiss this as a complete fantasy—even if you're not Catholic. It may show a desire to achieve leadership while following a path to spirituality.

Once you've identified your areas for goal setting, write down a long-term, five-year goal in each category. Then break it down into shorter-term, one-year goals. As you write them, test each one against five criteria. Setting goals that are fulfilling and achievable requires a SMART approach—SMART in this case being an acronym:

S-pecific
M-easurable
A-ction-oriented
R-ealistic
T-ime-conscious

Make Your Goals *Specific*

Make each goal specific—none of this "I want to get out of my rut" stuff. When Michaela made the decision to pursue her musical aspirations, she didn't write "I'm going to be a musician." Instead she said, "I'm becoming capable of playing the flute at a performance-quality level." Specificity gives your automatic mechanism something to aim for. "I want to end world hunger" is not a specific goal. "I see myself working for an international relief agency" is. "I want to go back to college" is not specific. "I am taking classes at East Fishgill State to complete my degree in psychology" is.

It's important to state your goal in the present tense. This suggests that your goals are imminent. The here-and-now approach gives your automatic mechanism a time-specific target on which it may begin work *today*. *I will* rather than *I am* suggests sometime in the future. It gives your servomechanism no time dimension in its programming. Stating "I am in the process of gaining control over my weight" presents a clearer target than "I will lose weight."

Set **Measurable** Goals

Take the goal, "I want to be a better salesperson." What's wrong with this picture? Right: what do you mean by "better"? Let's rewrite this goal as: "I am becoming a salesperson who will meet and exceed my company's guideline of a 16 percent increase in sales volume during the coming year."

When your goals are measurable, you have a scale on which to gauge your set point. You can chart your progress in increments and approximate it on a day-to-day basis. If your goal is a 16 percent increase in sales, you know what your volume will have to average each month. If your goal is swimming a mile, you know how many laps you'll have to increase your workouts by each week.

What about those goals that don't readily lend themselves to numbers—for example, Michaela's goal of becoming a musician? She expressed her measurement as a hierarchy of musical skills. "I am mastering Bach's suite number three in b-minor" was a goal she selected, but the process involved learning a succession of ever more difficult pieces involving ever greater complexity of techniques.

And how do you measure a goal such as, "I am open to meeting a caring, honest and sexy woman by my next birthday"? One way would be to record the times you place yourself in situations in which you're likely to meet her. Goals that have no scale of measurement must be gauged by the continuity of the process. Are you doing something daily, weekly, monthly toward your goal?

Measuring your goals involves a paradox. You must learn to hang on tight with an open palm. You must to be tenacious enough to hold to your conviction about a 16 percent sales increase or mastering the breath control necessary to play a Bach suite. But you also must free yourself from the burdensome demand of doing things on a rigid schedule when hampered by external factors that will affect your course. January and February are notoriously slow months for sales. You need to take that into account and preplan more effectively for March and April. You have to balance tenacity with flexibility, or when your January sales figures fall short those old limitation tapes will start whirring around in your mind. There'll always be some unforseeable circumstance that can push your FAILURE button if you let it. Remember to think of your incremental measurements as signposts, not judgment calls. Measuring your goals does not mean personalizing the zigs and zags. Make your correction, get back as close to your heading as possible and get on with the business at hand.

Develop an **Action** Plan for Your Goals

The most important step in the goal-setting process is developing a plan of action. This will take time and thought, so it will please you to know you're already well on your way. Your action plan should begin with an identification and written statetment of your goals. You've already started that process or at least given it some serious consideration. An action plan includes an assessment of past experiences, skills and interests that can guide you toward your goals. You gave this assessment a trial run earlier in this chapter. Now you need to apply it to the specific goals you hope to attain.

There are any number of models for your action plan. When Michaela began working on her musical goals, she followed this seven-point plan:

1. Identify and write down your goals. Michaela started by writing down her five-year goal: "I am earning my living as a musician." She then considered the steps she'd have to take to complete this process and wrote each one as a short-term goal: "I am mastering Bach's suite number three in b-minor this year." "I will join a professional performance ensemble within two years." "I will perform a solo flute recital within three years," and so on. Next, she broke down her first year's goal into the steps she would need to achieve it; for example: "I am mastering the breath control and tongue placement necessary for flute technique." Writing down specific goals brings your conscious mind to full awareness of them, provides a reminder every time you look at them, and reinforces your commitment. If you don't take the trouble to write it down, how will you take the trouble to follow through?

2. Assign dates for achievement of your goals. Michaela took each of her goals and assigned a specific date to it: "I am mastering Bach's suite number three in b-minor by October 15, 1993." "I am earning at least $30,000 annually as a flute player and teacher by October 15, 1996." She then rewrote each of these goals on a Post-It and put it in the appropriate place on a large wall calendar. Displaying your goals conspicuously on a calendar or daily planner affirms to your subconscious mind that they're important.

Note that "autumn 1996" is not a specific date. "October 15, 1996" is a specific date. Specific dates provide specific targets for your internal guidance system. Remember, your subconscious mind will agree with a goal established by your conscious mind. If that goal doesn't include a time-specific dimension, your horse will find any number of excuses for continuing to graze in the pasture. After all, the rider didn't say *when*.

3. Identify possible obstacles. You can always find a dozen reasons not to go for it. Write down all the obstacles you can conceive of. Then separate the real obstacles from the fanciful ones. This procedure has much the same purpose as the stress-evaluation exercise you did in the last chapter. Facing your fears is the first step toward debogeying them. Whether they are real or imagined, when they are out in the open you're more likely to recognize them for what they are and be able to assign them to their rightful place among your concerns.

Michaela wrote down every obstacle she could think of that might stand in the way of achieving her goals. Her deepest fears were that she would fail utterly at her musical endeavor, her family and friends would abandon her and she would end up a homeless street person. This is a common nightmare fantasy—I experienced it when I first decided to give up the practice of psychotherapy to pursue the goal of becoming an international speaker. The reality was that I could always reestablish my practice, just as Michaela could always resume her speechwriting career. Did I want to? No. *Would* I, if I had to? You bet.

More real to Michaela (and to me!) was the prospect of living for several years on a sharply reduced income while she perfected her new skills. Real also was the likelihood that her family would exert enormous pressure on her to forget the idea. So was the possibility that she might devote five years to her goal only to discover that she didn't have the talent to be a professional flautist. But the point was this: if she went for the goal, about the worst thing that was likely to happen was finding herself back where she started.

4. Surround yourself with people who want you to succeed. First think of people to call, write or spend time with who can help you toward your goal—people in positions of influence, people who have achieved the goal you're striving for, people who know people. Michaela started with the musicians she'd met in the workshop. They led her to teachers, networks, a whole musical community she hadn't known existed. Interacting with these people gave Michaela a sense of direction and new ways of thinking about her goals.

Make a point of being with people who are supportive and avoiding people who will discourage you. If someone reacts negatively—"You've got to be kidding! You can't do that!"—the first time you share your goal with him, reaffirm your goal out loud: "I'm sorry you see it that way. I'm determined to make this thing work." Then avoid that person like the plague.

It may be that the people most hostile to your goal are your family or closest friends. Your goal may be in conflict with theirs. They may be jealous of your goals or fearful of changes in your relationship. It's not always possible to avoid negative people if they're family. It's important to take into account the lives of people around you and how they are affected by your goals. It's equally important not to allow guilt to throw roadblocks in your way. Whenever a loved one ridicules your goal, merely acknowledge his or her opinion. Then CANCEL it and repeat your affirmation: "I know my goal is attainable. Someone is going to achieve this goal—why not me?" Think of every negative comment as an opportunity for reaffirmation.

If your goal is a new career, avoid people who are unhappy in their own careers.

If your goal is improved relations with your spouse, don't turn to your ex-lovers for support.

If your goal is improved fitness, don't accept any invitations from that friend who's always pressing pastries on you.

If your goal is to give up marijuana, don't hang out with your old doper friends.

If your goal is to overcome shyness, don't try to accomplish it by sitting at home in front of the TV set.

If you're waiting for your ship to come in, why are you hanging out at the airport?

5. Focus on your skills. Continually update your inventory of skills. Assess and reassess your past experiences. Be aware of the skills you possess that are directly applicable or transferable to your current goal. Be aware of the skills you'll need to realize your goal and the steps you'll have to take to acquire them. A good resource for career-oriented goals is the *Dictionary Of Occupational Titles*, a U.S. government publication which is widely used in career counseling. It breaks skills down into categories and subcategories and enables you to recognize in detail the skills you possess and the skills you'll need. Similar resources may be available for whatever your goal might be. Ask the reference person at your local library for assistance. You may be amazed at the variety of available information pertinent to your goal.

6. Follow your plan of action. Once you've written down your goals, it's of paramount importance to have a plan and to follow through with it at once. I call it the "do-do principle": you *do* do it. In the next chapter, you'll be learning ways to ensure movement toward your goals. Make sure everything is in place and that you're ready to go forward. Nothing is going to happen through magical thinking.

Let me share with you some of the things I did when I finally decided to take that leap and become an international speaker. This was in 1979. I had a good income as a psychotherapist. I maintained two clinics and a private practice. There was no reason to change careers other than my desire to do so.

I wrote on a piece of paper, "I am becoming an international speaker by February 15, 1984" and taped it to my refrigerator. I did the right-brain task of "being" a speaker in my imagination. I followed the "fake-it-till-you-make-it" course. But to put my left brain at ease I also started doing things. I made phone calls. I joined a couple of speakers' organizations. I hung out with professional speakers. I went to conferences to learn what they did. I started looking for a mentor; I never found one, but I sure looked. I took assessment of my potential obstacles and separated my fanciful fear (ending up as a bag lady) from my genuine concerns (money, lack of guidance, the negative influence of well-meaning friends who told me I was crazy).

How did I overcome my obstacles? I started collecting ideas. I began telling certain people about my goals, people who said, "Of course you can, why not?" What about skills? I already had the skill of communicating verbally—that's a large part of what psychotherapy is, after all. I knew I had the ability to present my ideas. I had a deep desire to help people, and I felt I could do it more effectively by public speaking than by counseling individuals. The task at hand was how to transfer this skill to my own public-speaking business. I went to more people and asked more questions. "Where do I begin?" "What do you mean by a press kit?" "Where do you get one?" "How do you do this?" "Where did you learn that?" I bugged a lot of people. I also got a lot of help. *Networking:* it's a key to your action plan whether your goal is a new job, someone to love or a new hobby. A friend gave me the name of a new company that conducted seminars for business people. At once I started formulating my plan for approaching this company. I called them at once and followed their required procedures. I put together a brochure and made a demo videotape. Yes, this cost money. Sometimes you can't afford *not* to spend money in pursuit of your goals, whether it's for résumé printing, equipment, classes or new clothes. Think of it as an investment in yourself.

If I was going to have a new career, I had to release myself from the old one. This could not be a short-term goal. It is difficult for a therapist to walk away from the people she is counseling. I made the phaseout of my private practice a five-year goal. I told clients that if at the end of this time they felt that they still needed therapy, I would help them make the transition to another practitioner. I began to Let Go. I did it in stages. I found colleagues to come in and take over parts of my practice as I phased it out.

I started my first international speaking tour on February 15, 1984—the exact date I had written down as my goal five years earlier.

7. Ask yourself "What's in it for me?" Sell yourself a benefit statement: "Why should I want to carry this goal through? How will it help me? How would I feel if I were already there? How would I look and act? What personal satisfaction will it bring me?" You deserve to get what you're striving for. Someone will find a fulfilling career in music—why not you? Someone will break your company's sales records—why not you? Someone will find his ideal mate—why not you? Frequently reassure yourself that your particular pot of gold is attainable if you're willing to put in the effort.

Decide What Goals Are *Realistic* for You

So you've written your goals, set dates and developed a plan of action. The fourth element of the SMART plan is to consider how realistic your goal is. To be realistic a goal must be balanced between safety and risk. How far can you allow yourself to grow and stretch without snapping; how much emphasis can you place on security without falling back into procrastination and stagnation? This balance is a highly personal consideration, and you need to assess how it applies to each goal. Michaela didn't just write down her goals, network with musicians and set out to become Jean-Pierre Rampal. She assessed her skills and considered how quickly she could expect to become professionally competent. She phased in her musical career as she phased out her speech-consultant business. She knew she could expect no income from music the first year, but she also knew she was not going to realize even her short-term goals without giving up some work time for lessons and practice. She estimated how much money she needed to live and how much time she needed to achieve her goals, and she scaled back her work schedule accordingly.

Pay attention to your interests in assessing the realism of your goal. Even a fantasy goal may give you ideas about pursuing related goals. You might find it worthwhile to invest a little time and money in exploring how you might translate an impossible dream into an achivable goal. Go to the psychology department at a nearby college or (if you're willing to spend more money) a career placement service and take an interest-inventory test. It can provide insight into what you realistically can do.

The same principle applies to your personal goals. Don't expect your prince or princess to step off the movie screen and into your arms the way it happened to Mia Farrow in *The Purple Rose Of Cairo*. Know your absolutes—what qualities you require in a mate as compared with what you may desire. Consider where you'd be most likely to meet a partner with those qualities—a singles bar or a Sierra Club outing? There are no guarantees, but a realistic appraisal of your goals makes the prospect of achieving them that much more likely.

Set *Time-*Conscious Goals

Be sure the timing is right for your goals. If you plan to have three children, complete your degree in accounting and build your dream house all during the next four years, you'll have to give timing a closer look. You may have to set aside one or two of these goals or reassign them to the long-range category. Part of being an adult is the ability to go back, reconsider your goals and reclassify them to accommodate changes in your lifestyle. Keeping your goals time-conscious is a key to your success in attaining them. Be sure you allow yourself ample time to complete one goal before you move on to the next. If you don't, you're going to find yourself under intense pressure. Which course do you think is more amenable to your self-esteem—to have a few manageable goals or to be overwhelmed by too many?

⊞ Don't Lose Sight of Your Goals

By now you probably have done the exercises in the first part of this chapter and have started writing down your goals. Good. Don't stop. Goal setting is only a part of Psycho-Cybernetics. Your goals will be achieved in conjunction with relaxation, reflective relearning, responding to feedback, and building the self-image that will make achievement of your goals a reality. It will take you considerably longer to formulate your action plan than it will to finish reading this book. But it's never to early to start thinking about goals, establishing your set point and testing your goals against the SMART criteria.

Remember that no path is absolutely straight. Life doesn't work that way. The moment you start pursuing your course, you're likely to find yourself veering off target. Don't let it be an excuse for procrastination or self-punishment. Trust your automatic mechanism to make the necessary corrections. Keep vivid in your imagination the image of what you wish to make happen in your life while at the same time remaining open to the adjustments you may have to make along the way. If you set goals that are sincere and follow a specific action plan, you'll deserve the success and happiness you'll get. If you always do what you've always done, you'll always get what you've always got.

Targeting on Ideas

- Don't confuse wishful thinking with goals.
- Ignore old programming that prevents you from setting goals.
- Determine your own best approach to goal setting.
- Approach goals as a process, not as a place to be.

■ Make sure your goals pass the SMART test: specific, measurable, action-oriented, realistic, and timely.

CHAPTER EIGHT

MOVING AHEAD: FROM GOAL-SETTING TO GOAL-GETTING

Functionally, a man is somewhat like a bicycle.... A bicycle maintains its poise and equilibrium only so long as it is going forward towards something.

—Maxwell Maltz, Psycho-Cybernetics *(1960)*

Life is a moving vehicle with no brakes.... If you spend too much time looking in the rearview mirror, you'll hit a tree.... That is why your front window is bigger than your rearview mirror. If you set realistic goals...and balance self-support with appropriate self-criticism, you'll stay on the road.

—Terry L. Paulson, Ph.D., They Shoot Managers, Don't They?
(Lee Canter and Associates, 1988)

183

Al had always found it easy to quit smoking—he'd done it a dozen times. This time, however, he had a SMART plan to make it stick. Instead of going "cold turkey" he would cut down by increments. On November 1, 1992 he set as his goal, "I am a nonsmoker by March 1, 1993." Al's established level was two packs a day—40 cigarettes. If he cut down his intake each week by only three cigarettes per day, he would make it with room to spare. He told his wife, his friends and his colleagues at work about his goal. He kept track of his progress with a pocket calendar on which he marked off every cigarette he smoked.

By late January Al realized that his plan wasn't working. At a hockey game his friend Dave noticed that he was smoking cigarette after cigarette. "Hey, what happened?" Dave asked. "I thought you were quitting."

"I am," Al said, a bit defensively. "It's just, you know, sometimes circumstances make it hard to get started, you know what I mean?"

Dave, an ex-smoker himself, was dubious. "I certainly do," he said. "What, uh, circumstances are you talking about?"

Al told his story between puffs. First there had been the visit from his brother and his wife Thanksgiving weekend. They both smoked, and Al didn't want to make them feel uncomfortable. That was okay—he still had plenty of time to reach his goal. If he had to, he could adjust his action plan and cut down by four cigarettes a week. Then came the holiday rush at work. Al was in retail sales; he was working overtime five days a week, and there were times he needed to slip out to the parking lot for a smoke just to stay alert. At Christmas he'd paid a return visit to his brother's family. He'd been too tense trying to cut down with them lighting up every 15 minutes, and he couldn't very well ask them not to smoke in their own house, could he? Then there was his Wednesday bowling league. All the guys smoked, and he felt obligated to join them. "And what can I do with Jeannie?" Al said, lighting up another. "I get so grouchy around the house when I'm not smoking, it drives her crazy. Don't get me wrong, I want to quit. I've set up a plan to quit. It's my family, my job, my friends; they just won't let me quit. You see what I mean?"

"Al," Dave said, pointing down at the ice, "What I see is you're acting as your own goalie. Every time you shoot the puck, you dash to the end of the ice and block your own goal."

If you thought all you had to do to reach your goals was to let your automatic mechanism do the work, you were right—except it isn't quite as easy as that. As with most things in Psycho-Cybernetics, it is *simple*...but it isn't *easy*. You've written down your goals, evaluated them SMARTly and formulated your action plan, but achieving goals is seldom a straightforward process. You may find your horse meandering off the trail or stopping in the middle of it. Your conscious mind has established a set point, but your subconscious mind may have an agenda all its own. While it's the conscious mind that selects the target, it's the subconscious mind that must come up with the creative "how-to." If they're at cross purposes, the result can be procrastination, stagnation or self-sabotage. You become a Charlie Brown/Lucy team, with your conscious mind all revved up to kick the football and your subconscious mind forever snatching it away. You can end up punishing yourself for what you perceive as failure, with a diminished self-image that can inhibit you from setting any future goals.

The trick is to remember that goals are a process, not a place to be. You will encounter slowdowns, obstacles and diversions during the process, but there are steps you can take to anticipate, recognize and move past them.

This chapter is about those obstacles and about minimizing their negative effects. You'll learn:

- the two paradoxical reasons why people procrastinate, and what you can do to overcome them.
- six ways to keep your automatic mechanism from wandering off course.
- techniques for avoiding anxiety and discouragement as you pursue your goals by readjusting your set point.

▦ *Today* Is Another Day: How to Overcome Procrastination

"I won't think about it today," said fiction's most famous procrastinator. "I'll think about it tomorrow. Tomorrow is another day." Unlike Scarlett O'Hara, who certainly could not be accused of being afraid to go after what she wanted, most of us procrastinate because of a subconscious desire *not* to achieve a goal. We resist writing our goals down, we resist formulating an action plan, and we especially resist following through. Though consciously we may come up with any number of reasons why we procrastinate— "I don't have the time"; "I don't have the money; "_____ doesn't want me to succeed"; "I'm just not good enough"; etc.— the subconscious reason is invariably one of these two:

- fear of failure
- fear of success

Together these reasons seem paradoxical. Yet in a sense fear of failure and fear of success are the same thing. They're two sides of the same coin. Consider the single woman who believes consciously that she'd be more attractive to men if she lost 30 pounds but who puts off dieting because she fears subconsciously that no man would find her appealing even if she were thin. "If I stay fat," her horse believes, "at least I have an excuse for staying home Saturday nights." Does this woman fear failure, or does she fear success? Flip a coin.

Let's take a look at the dynamic of procrastination as it results from fear of failure. Toni was a college sophomore who had eight weeks to write a term paper. Yet she put it off and put it off until six days before the due date, and she got a predictable grade of D for her noneffforts. Toni was attending a top-rank academic institution. She had been a somewhat-above-average high school student who was accepted by the college as part of a nationwide "hidden talent search" program and found herself surrounded by former class valedictorians. She had never received much encouragement from her family regarding academics, and her self-image led her to perceive herself as a "ringer" in this high-achievement environment. Because in her subconscious mind she expected to fail, she used her time poorly so that later she could rationalize her failure. She could tell her peers and her parents, "Oh, well, I would have gotten a better grade if I had started early." If she'd worked hard for eight weeks and still come up with a D, her fear that she wasn't as smart as her fellow students would have been confirmed.

Okay, that one is easy to understand. We fear that our limitations will cause us to fail, and procrastination lets us avoid the humiliation of failure. The man who develops an action plan for writing the great American novel never gets started because he subconsciously believes no publisher will accept his efforts, and worse, his friends will see what a fool he's making of himself. The woman who wants to go for the managerial position is stymied before she begins by the fear that her skills just aren't up to the job.

Fear of failure. Most of us have experienced that at one time or another. But fear of success...it doesn't make sense, does it? Success is a *good* thing. Why would anyone fear success?

There are lots of reasons—as Al, the would-be ex-smoker could tell you. After his talk with his friend, he got to asking himself, "Why am I resisting going after my goal? I *want* to quit smoking. I don't want to be a coughing, wheezing invalid at 55. *What am I afraid will happen if I succeed?*"

As Al came to recognize, he was afraid of falling out with his social group. All his favorite relatives and friends were smokers, and he was subconsciously afraid of losing their companionship if he was the odd one out. "How will other people take it?"—this is a *big* reason we fear success. How will achieving our goals affect our relationships with spouse, colleagues, peers? Will my husband resent my making more money than he does? Will my wife feel uncomfortable about having to move to Albuquerque if I get this job? Will my co-workers stop being my friends if I'm promoted above them? Will my church group think I'm putting on airs if I go back to college? Will my bowling buddies think I'm rejecting them if I quit smoking? Will they reject *me?*

Another reason we fear success is that it can put us in the spotlight. When we're under scrutiny we tend to feel self-conscious. It can be safer to remain in the shadows, in the background. Take Christina, a twenty-nine-year-old artist who made ceramic jewelry that she gave away to friends. Christina worked as a checker in a large supermarket, but her friends were forever urging her to sell her jewelry at art shows as a step toward becoming a full-time artist. The idea seemed appealing to her. She got a schedule of art shows in her city and filled out applications for space. Yet every time a show came up, something happened to keep her from exhibiting. She had a cold. She had to work. She was up all night tending to her sick cat and was too tired to stand around smiling at customers. The real reason for her procrastination, as Christina came to learn, was fear of success. She was afraid that if she became successful with her jewelry, everyone would discover that she was a "fraud": not only did she lack formal training as an artist, she had never even graduated from high school. Somehow she connected success with "being found out."

Why else might we fear success? Early-childhood scripting can have something to do with it. Those same old tapes that block us from setting goals may also keep us from following through in pursuit of them. "Don't get too big for your britches." "What makes *you* think you deserve to...?" "Don't be so selfish; put other people first." "You can't have your cake," etc. Women especially, but also many men, are susceptible to fear of success because these old subconscious tapes keep telling them they're not entitled to success.

And then there's the what-will-I-do-for-an-encore syndrome. Suppose you *do* write the great American novel? There you are at the top of the bestseller list, signing autographs for the admiring public, discussing your book on TV with Oprah, raking in your royalty checks, signing a movie contract...feeling *pressured*. Ohmygod, what's next? What can you do now that you've achieved success? If you're at the top, there's nowhere to go but...*down!*

Are you beginning to see how fear of success and fear of failure are really two ways of not approaching the same problem?

How to Discover Why You Procrastinate: A Questionnaire

Here's a questionnaire I developed years ago when I was going for my Ph.D. and found myself playing the tomorrow-is-another-day game. Write your goal, then answer the questions as honestly as you can. Check all boxes that apply. Evaluate your answers to determine your own reasons for procrastination.

My Goal:

_____

_____

1. Why do I **really** want to achieve this goal?
   - ❏ prestige
   - ❏ more money
   - ❏ self-esteem; self-satisfaction
   - ❏ credibility
   - ❏ personal growth
   - ❏ future advantages
   - ❏ to prove to _____ that I can do it
     (fill in name)
   - ❏ other:_____

2. How might achieving this goal affect me adversely?
   - ❏ might go to my head
   - ❏ might threaten my spouse
   - ❏ might upset *status quo* of my family
   - ❏ might alienate my friends or co-workers
   - ❏ might compromise my privacy
   - ❏ might require a greater commitment of time and energy
   - ❏ _____
     (fill in your own reasons)

   _____

3. How might **not** achieving this goal affect me adversely?
   - ❏ might leave me without money or resources
   - ❏ might "set me back to square one"
   - ❏ might make _____ ridicule me
     (fill in name)

❏   might make me "feel like a failure"

❏   _____

(fill in your own reasons)

_____

4. What am I **unwilling** to do to achieve this goal or as a result of achieving it?

❏   unwilling to discipline myself to follow through

❏   unwilling to move to a new home

❏   unwilling to accept added responsibilities

❏   unwilling to change _____

(fill in specifics)

_____

5. How could I make myself more open to risk-taking in pursuit of this goal?

❏   openly discuss my fears of success/failure with family and friends

❏   consider my action plan as an investment of time, just as I might invest money in stocks or real estate

❏   consider how would I be spending my time if I were not pursuing this goal (how?) _____

❏   consider that change is inevitable over the next five years (how?) _____

❏   consider what is the **worst** possible result of my pursuing this goal (what?) _____

How to Put Your Success Mechanism to Work

Once you've recognized and evaluated your reasons for procrastination, you can put your automatic mechanism to work against it. In previous chapters you learned how to use CRAFT to change your beliefs about yourself and your environment by approaching them as habits that can be changed. If you approach procrastination as a habitual response to fear of failure or fear of success, you can use CRAFT to overcome it as well.

Cancel your rationalizations for procrastination.

Replace your rationalizations and excuses with positive, goal-oriented statements.

Affirm your self-image as a task-oriented person who moves forcefully toward your goal.

Focus on images of yourself in fulfillment of your goal.

Train yourself by taking positive action.

Christina used CRAFT to overcome her procrastination over becoming a professional jeweler. She said "Cancel!" every time she found herself ruminating ("What if they find out I've never been to art school?") or indulging in her usual excuses ("I've worked overtime this week; I'm too tired to get a show together"). Every time she CANCELed such thoughts, she replaced them with a positive statement such as, "I don't *need* formal education to be a jeweler," or, "I make wonderful jewelry, and I deserve to be out there making money with it." She wrote the statement, "I take action toward my goal" on three cards. She taped them to her refrigerator, the mirror over her dresser, and her cash register at work to remind her horse of her commitment. Every day she allowed herself 15 minutes to sit quietly, relax, and visualize herself at art shows. In her imagination she saw herself selling her jewelry, handing out her cards to interested customers, accepting awards from judges and experiencing the satisfaction of being financially rewarded for her talent. Most importantly, even before she felt comfortable about taking positive action toward her goal, she acted as if she did. She took repeated opportunities to remind herself that she was becoming a professional artist. As she crafted her jewelry, she reinforced her affirmations by telling herself, "Someone will pay thirty dollars for this pin, or "I'll put this in the center of the display next weekend."

By consciously choosing to be a task-oriented person, you eliminate the possibility of procrastination. Your subconscious mind comes to agree with this concept and to comply with the action plan your conscious mind has selected. You break the habit of procrastination and replace it with the habit of action.

Al was eventually able to use his creative talent to quit smoking. As he reflected on his friend's comment, he saw clearly how he blocked his own goal by making excuses. Al, however, faced a problem that was not a factor in Christina's situation, one that he had to overcome before he could use CRAFT to take control of his procrastination. He recognized that he was blocking his goal out of fear that his success would lead to loss of acceptance by the people who were close to him.

If you're holding back on pursuing your goal because you fear that success will negatively impact your personal relationships, you may have to lay some preliminary groundwork before you apply CRAFT. Often the only way to resolve such a fear is to meet it head on. Talk to the people you think may feel threatened by the change you desire for yourself. This can be a difficult step, but it may be a necessary one. You may find that your goal is not in conflict with your relationship after all. You may find that you have to balance one against the other and make a hard decision. But until you resolve the situation, you will probably continue to procrastinate—and to punish yourself for doing so.

Al talked to the people he felt might react negatively to his quitting smoking. "Look," he said to his brother. "I'll probably be acting a little weird for a while. I'm trying to quit smoking, and I'd really like your support in this."

"Sure, Al," his brother said uncertainly. "What, uh, do you want us to do? Are we not supposed to smoke around you, or what?"

"Nothing like that," Al said. "I don't want you and Charlotte to feel uncomfortable about smoking around me, and I'm sure not going to preach at you, but I'll be dying for a smoke whenever I'm with you, and whatever I say, *don't offer me one.* If I screw up, I want to do it on my own."

Al had a bit more trouble with his bowling buddies. "Sure, Al," they kidded. *"You're* going to quit smoking—Al, the human chimney?" One guy, who always had been a bit of a jerk, seemed to take great glee in offering him cigarettes and making such statements as, "What's the matter, Al, feeling a little nervous today?" But once he assured himself that losing his habit wasn't going to lose him his friends, Al was able to move ahead and apply CRAFT—to CANCEL negative thoughts about his goal, RE-PLACE them with positive thoughts, AFFIRM to himself that he was on his way to becoming a nonsmoker, FOCUS on an image of himself as nicotine-free and TRAIN himself to accept himself as a person who worked toward his goal instead of blocking it.

The Road to Success: Six Ways to Maximize Your Progress

Your internal guidance system *is* a goal-striving mechanism. If you have a clear and specific image of where you're going and follow your action plan for getting there, your rider will go where your horse wants it to go. There will be times, however, when progress won't be as rapid as you'd like. You may feel that you're drifting; you may find it difficult to recognize that you're moving ahead. To keep from getting discouraged, follow these six strategies to create a system of roadmaps, milestones, and direction markers.

1. Focus on Your Action Plan Daily

One of the surest ways to avoid anxiety and discouragement about goal attainment is to do a little something in furtherance of your action plan every day. At 42 Andy hadn't given up the hope of attracting his ideal mate. He was discouraged, however, by what he perceived as a lack of progress toward finding her. "I've given up trying," he said despondently the first time we met. On questioning him I found that Andy was actually doing many positive things in furtherance of his goal—he just wasn't keeping track of them. I suggested that he make appointments with himself and check his appointment calendar every day. On Monday at 10:15, for example, he would make an appointment to contact a nearby church to find out when their next "Musical Evening for Singles" was scheduled. On Tuesday he would mark off a half hour at lunch to go to the library and check out books on personal-image enhancement. Andy came to feel much less anxious and desperate when he was able to look back over his week and reassure himself that he was indeed doing something positive about his goal.

Observe these tips in focusing on your action plan:

- Reserve a few minutes each weekend to list the things you could do in furtherance of your goal during the coming week.

- Make appointments with yourself to spend at least ten or 15 minutes every day working on some aspect of your plan: making job contacts, practicing a new skill, researching and reading appropriate articles; whatever is appropriate to your goal. Mark your appointments in your calendar or daily planner and honor them as you would any commitment.

- Take note of your progress. Review your calendar weekly as evidence that you're actually doing something in pursuit of your goal.

2. Set Up a Self-Monitoring System

When Al decided to stop smoking, he established an incremental plan for quitting and kept track of his progress. At first Al hampered himself by procrastination, but he had the right idea. With a self-monitoring system to chart your progress—a calendar, graph, checklist or table—you can assure yourself that you're moving forward even if you experience a short-term setback. Such a system can also serve as a guidepost for readjusting your set point if you find long-range progress too slow or a short-range goal unrealistic.

The form of self-monitoring system you choose should depend on your personality and the specifics of your goal. Stu, an engineer who managed a department at a petroleum refinery, found himself working longer and longer hours to the detriment of his marriage and family life. He set as his goal to manage his work time more efficiently so that within six months he would be completing the same volume of work in 20 percent fewer hours. He made a chart dividing the work he did into task categories. He then made a bar graph for each category showing the amount of time he spent on each task every week. To be sure, the bars on every graph did not show steady progress downward. But by filling in his time increments daily and assessing the graphs at the end of each work week, Stu avoided focusing on his setbacks. By keeping continually aware of his progress, he steered clear of discouragement and self-punishment.

Larry and Marilyn had a built-in time constraint for their goal of buying their first house. They were apartment dwellers who had occasionally talked about buying but kept putting it off. They had any number of stated reasons to remain renters: they couldn't afford to buy; Larry might be transferred by his company; they would be responsible for all maintenance; they might get "stuck" in a neighborhood they couldn't escape from. All these reasons became inconsequential when Marilyn became pregnant. Suddenly their one-bedroom flat seemed VERY small. When they sat down to consider the reality of buying a house, they both recognized that all their objections really stemmed from one cause: it was a terrific hassle, one which neither of them had any desire to deal with. Now they established as their goal to be settled into their painted and furnished new house thirty days before Marilyn's due date. To monitor their progress they made a list of all the steps that would have to be taken: reading the real-estate ads, going to open houses, securing a loan and so on. Then they broke down each step into subtasks, set dates for the achievement of each of them and wrote them in on a four-foot long day-by-day calendar which they taped to their kitchen wall. Every Sunday evening they agreed on an action plan for the coming week and divided up the tasks. They readjusted as necessary depending on the previous week's progress and constraints on Marilyn's activity due to her pregnancy. Expecting a first child will put the fear of God into any couple, but Larry and Marilyn's self-monitoring system let them reach their goal without self-imposed obstacles, self-doubt or panic.

In devising and using a self-monitoring system, follow these guidelines:

■ Review your progress on a regular basis—daily, weekly, monthly; whatever is appropriate to you and your goal. If you're dieting, a daily assessment of caloric intake might be appropriate, balanced with a weekly reading of the scale. If you're looking for a new job, set a monthly quota of contacts to be made and résumés to be sent, then monitor your efforts on a weekly basis to make sure you're keeping up. If you've established an action plan for meeting Mr. or Ms. Right, make sure you schedule a specific number of social engagements within a given time period—and then check every month to make sure you're keeping them. If your horse is making excuses not to follow through, regular monitoring will keep your rider aware of it.

■ Set aside the same time each day, week or month to review your progress. Remember, habits are more easily established if practiced on a routine basis. Ask any dedicated jogger—if she misses her regular 6:30 a.m. workout, by eight o'clock she's probably "lost interest" or moved on to something else. If goal assessment is a normal part of your schedule, you incorporate it much more readily than if you have to "work it in."

■ Use your daily review as a one-minute routine checkup, not as a fault-finding maneuver. Reassure yourself if you've taken a small step toward your goal, but don't expect to find yourself making measurable progress seven days a week. Your weekly and monthly checkups may be more detailed and accountable.

■ Have some **objective** measure for assessing your progress: for example, "I smoked two fewer cigarettes today than yesterday."

■ At the same time give yourself a **subjective** assessment: "Am I pleased? Do I feel good about this?" The idea is to recognize that *any* progress is positive, even if it's not as great as you might have hoped. If your answer is "yes," well all right! You may even wish to stretch yourself a little further next week. If your answer is consistently "no," it may be a sign that you're procrastinating or need to readjust your set point. But keep in mind that even if you smoked two fewer cigarettes yesterday when you were shooting for three, you're still ahead of the game. Even if you're less than perfect, you're still making progress.

3. Make a Contract with Friends and Co-Workers

Another way to stay on course is to share your goal with a trusted friend or colleague. Any veteran of Alcoholics Anonymous knows the value of a "sponsor"—someone who will partner you, offer encouragement, and "throw you a rope" if you're in danger of drifting away. Choose someone discreet enough to keep your secrets, caring and secure enough to nudge you if he perceives you straying off your path, and nonjudgmental enough not to reject you if you don't succeed. Tell your friend about your action plan. Ask him if he'll sit down with you regularly for a heart-to-heart talk and progress report. Allow him permission to offer advice and criticism if he thinks you're stagnating or straying.

In choosing someone to share your goals with, it's important to exercise a little common sense. You can share your "give-up" goals with just about anyone. If you're trying to quit smoking or lose weight, tell everyone you know. They'll keep you honest, like Al's friend Dave at the hockey game. If they see you reach for that doughnut, they'll come down on you to remind you not to do it. Some people will come down *hard*—but that's what you want, isn't it?

Your "go-up" goals are a different matter. Suppose you're in sales, and your goal is to become a regional sales manager. That probably means you'll have to become the top salesperson in your office. So who are you going to share your goal with? Elaine may be your best friend, but you don't want to tell *her* because she's your colleague and *she* may be trying to become the top salesperson too! Share your "go-up" goals with someone who will champion your efforts and not be inclined to sabotage them. Tell people who believe in you, not those who tend to scoff at other people's desires or to be jealous of other people's accomplishments. Be selective.

You and a friend may agree on a contract to support each other's goals or a mutual goal. This is a common practice in workplace situations, but you can apply it in your personal life too. Groups of friends get together for mutual support in efforts ranging from giving up smoking to finding romance to coping with grief. In seeking out friends or colleagues to form such a group, follow these guidelines:

- Make sure you all want similar results.
- Share with each other your reasons for having this goal.
- Meet at the same time every week to discuss progress.
- Honor your commitments: if you have agreed to meet with your group at five o'clock Wednesday, keep the appointment just as you would an important business meeting.
- Make a pact: there shall be no blame or guilt directed at other members of the group, only positive support—even if they "fall off the wagon."

4. Use Progressive Self-Discipline to Stay on Target

As your assessments show you that you're making progress, you'll find your confidence growing. Now is the time to let success build on success: to commit yourself to greater self-discipline in pursuit of your goal. This process will vary greatly in time and procedure depending on your long-range goal. But whatever it might be, one way to upgrade your commitment is to begin pre-planning your incremental goals in more detail. Follow these guidelines:

- Outline your task. Break it down into component tasks. Give yourself a ballpark estimate of the resources—time, money, supplies—you'll need to complete each subtask.
- Set aside specific dates and times for working on each subtask. Enter them on a calendar or chart: *what* needs to be done *when?* What resources will I need to assemble in order to do it?
- Plan for miscalulations and mistakes. Allow for possible detours and setbacks by allocating extra time for each task.
- Minimize distractions. Plan ahead to make sure you won't have to interrupt your designated timeslots for food shopping, child care, chit-chat or driving your neighbor to the airport. Inform friends and loved ones of your nonavailablility at these times and request that you not be interrupted. Let your answering machine handle your phone calls, or just let the phone ring.

5. Design Your Own System of Motivational Rewards

Remember when you were in the first grade, struggling with the awesome task of learning your letters? Remember the scrawls you made and the satisfaction of passing each milestone—the alphabet, your name, the days of the week? Chances are your teacher praised and encouraged you by affixing a gold star or colorful sticker to the smudged piece of paper. It made you feel that you really accomplished something, didn't it? Now you're grown up, but a little reward now and then wouldn't hurt. That's why corporations hand out bonuses at the end of the year; that's why armies give medals to soldiers in combat. Your goal itself can be its own reward, but meanwhile why not motivate yourself with a series of little rewards along the way?

What might be an appropriate self-stroke—something you enjoy but normally don't indulge in because it's too frivolous? Dinner at a special restaurant, a new article of clothing, a bottle of single-malt Scotch, opera tickets, a weekend getaway, a new piece of furniture, a long-coveted "adult toy," throwing a catered party for a dozen friends? Such rewards may provide you with the motivation you need to turn your goal-striving into goal-arriving.

Here are some guidelines to follow in designing your system of rewards:

- Review your action plan for your long-range goal. Select three or four milestones that you consider to be the most significant intermediate goals.
- Decide what would be the best reward you could reasonably give yourself when you achieve your goal.
- Choose a series of rewards to give yourself at each milestone. If possible, have them relate to your final reward. If you've chosen to get a new dresser when you achieve your goal, you might pick out a tray that will eventually sit on top of it as one of your incremental rewards.
- Have discipline. Don't break down and give yourself the reward until you've reached the designated milestone.

199

6. Control Burnout by Setting Priorities and Narrowing Your Focus

Many people feel that their best chance of reaching their goal is to pursue every lead, try every angle, consider all actions, believing each has equal validity and potential. Susan, for example, was a sixth-grade teacher who was dissatisfied with the curriculum materials available in her district. She was sure she could create better workbooks, supplementary texts and learning aids and quite possibly make a little money at it. She prepared a set of samples in math, language arts, science, history and geography. She researched a couple of writers' market guides at the public library, compiled a list of all the publishers of educational materials in the United States and began sending her samples and her résumé to each of them, starting with the As.

Computer programmers call this the "brute force" method of problem-solving. They can instruct a computer to compare every piece of data with every other piece of data until it finds the best solution. They can, but they don't. With such an inefficient method, even a high-speed computer requires too much time and effort. When we slow-thinking human beings try to reach our goals by this method, we quickly burn out our chips. By the time Susan reached the Es, she was exhausted and frustrated. This publisher only dealt with grade three and below, this one specialized in mathematics materials, this one didn't use out-of-house writers; thank you for your interest and we'll contact you should anything come up.

Susan, however, had a couple of assets a computer is lacking: intuition and creative imagination. She refocused and prioritized her efforts. She reviewed her list and checked off the names of the twenty-five publishers that seemed most promising. She called the companies on her revised list and got copies of their catalogues to review the scope of their product lines. She browsed in a local teacher-supply store to get an idea of the various companies' approaches and editorial styles. She selected eight publishers whose lines seemed most in accordance with her experience and with the type of materials she wanted to develop. She made another round of phone calls and found out the names of appropriate editors at these companies. Then she redesigned her samples and sent them along witb personalized letters to the editors on her prioritized list. Within a year she had freelance contracts with three of the companies and was being offered more assignments than she could handle.

Whatever your goal may be, you can prevent burnout by abandoning the brute-force approach. Make your action plan more efficient by prioritizing and narrowing your focus:

- Make time to prepare and review your plan. Eliminate approaches that are least likely to be fruitful. Evaluate your tasks at hand to determine whether several of them may be combined into one.

- Evaluate feedback carefully. It will help you avoid making the same mistake twice. If an approach proves too time-consuming and unrewarding, try to determine whether your next attempt will be more efficient or whether the approach itself is unfruitful. Let each detour or setback provide clues for handling a similar task differently next time.

- Don't expect gratification at each step. If one path does not yield immediate rewards, you needn't necessarily go back to square one and try another path. You may only have to continue on the path a little further.

When It's Time to Reevaluate Your Goals: Some Practical Tips

Then there are those times when your rider is galloping along in pursuit of a goal, you look down...and your horse isn't there! It's wandered off to graze in a pasture. This image may sound like something from an old Bugs Bunny cartoon, but there's nothing funny about the hard landing you experience. Something's not working. You're networking and sending out résumés, but your interviews all terminate quickly and no one's called you back for a second visit. You're striving like the dickens to keep your "in" box empty, but the more effort you put in the less you seem to get done. You're attending all the right singles events; you're meeting lots of people but no one attractive or interesting enough to meet your standards. You're finally teaching yourself to use those woodworking tools you inherited from your uncle Henry, but giving a facelift to your kitchen cabinets as you've long anticipated doing is turning out to be...*boring!* Your conscious mind is following an action plan but your subconscious mind, for reasons of its own, is saying "Whoa!"

When this happens, there may be a tendency to give up your goal as a lost cause. Don't fall into that trap—the purpose here is to raise your self-esteem, not to diminish it by giving into failure. You may just need to work on coordinating the goal you've consciously selected with the disparate goal you're subconsciously aiming for.

How to Avoid the "Perfection Trap"

Milt was a high-school basketball coach in a small Wisconsin city who was aware that juvenile crime and gang activity had become a problem in his once-tranquil community. On his own initiative he set up a basketball program to keep troubled teenagers off the streets. He made the rounds of local churches and enlisted their support; he designed and paid for the flyers used to promote the program; he volunteered his time as coach and referee. The result was a successful program that provided recreation for the community's teens at the same time that it reduced crime.

Now, what do you suppose would have happened if Milt's goal had been to build a championship basketball team? Few of the kids in the program were particularly good at basketball. If Milt had striven for perfection, the outcome might have been measured not in wins and losses but in muggings and smashed windows.

While your conscious mind may recognize that "nobody's perfect," your subconscious mind may be trying to achieve a set point of one hundred percent. Of course realistically you can never expect to reach perfection. If you're putting off buying new clothes until you reach your "ideal weight," you'll never have anything that fits you. If you refuse to submit a project until it's perfect enough to pass inspection, you lose helpful input from others as well as a lot of sleep. If you put off planting shrubbery until you can afford to do the whole yard, you may be stuck indefinitely with an empty patch of ground. If you postpone your trip to Mexico until you can speak Spanish like a native, you'll never see the pyramids of Teotihuacán except in the *National Geographic*. The results of such futile striving can be discouragement, self-punishment and a loss of self-esteem where an adjustment of your set point from perfection to practicality might have resulted in success.

Learn to recognize and avoid the "perfection trap" by observing these procedures:

1. Erase any old "practice-makes-perfect" tape your subconscious mind may be playing. Replace it with a new tape: "practice makes *permanent*." Listen for critical self-talk. Say "Cancel!" whenever you catch yourself berating yourself for less-than-perfect results. Affirm to yourself, "I am making my goal of _____ a permanent part of my life. I do not expect perfection."

2. When you find yourself repeating a task out of dissatisfaction with earlier results, assess whether you're falling into the perfection trap. Step back and ask yourself "Is this trip really necessary?" If not, *don't take it!*

3. Wait a minute before giving in to the urge for perfection. Wait an hour. Wait a weekend. Force yourself to allow those water spots to remain on the window for a few days. Let the memo sit in your computer overnight before you retype it. You may find you're closer to your goal than you realized after you've allowed yourself time to reevaluate.

4. Continually remind your horse that you're climbing out of the perfection trap. Make a MODERATION & TOLERATION motto for your desk. Practice telling other people that you're a relaxed person who can let unnecessary things go.

5. Instead of setting your thermostat at a hundred percent, aim for making one percent progress in a hundred different ways.

How to Get More Done with Less Effort

Goals often seem elusive, particularly the long-range and time-consuming ones. The harder you strive, the further away they may seem to slip. When that happens, stress and discouragement may set in. Your left brain may prompt you to throw in the towel. "It wasn't so bad before," you tell yourself. "Why are you torturing yourself? Quit while you're ahead! Who needs this headache?"

It is important to remind yourself of the truth of the cliché, "A journey of a thousand miles begins with but a single step." Your initial steps may involve a certain amount of trial and error, delay and discouragement. This goes with the territory. Remind yourself that you're on for the long haul—the end result is worth a little frustration. Allow your right brain to visualize your future success in vivid detail. This will encourage your left brain to hang in there a little longer and take another shot at the planning and prioritizing tasks it does so well. Meanwhile, keep these thoughts in mind:

1. Being able to withstand disappointment and its concomitant stress will strengthen your self-image as you move toward your goals.
2. Delayed gratification is a hallmark of adulthood. The hours may be long, but the payoff is worth it.
3. Sharing your frustration with those who have struggled successfully with similar goals can help you stay focused.

How to Readjust Your Thermostat as Necessary

Any time you move out of your "comfort zone" into new areas of experience and growth, you should experience some tension. If you aren't feeling this essential tension, if you're finding progress toward your goal "too easy," it could be a sign that you're aiming too low. Remember the thermostat analogy: your set point is adjustable, and you can always turn up the heat.

A good rule of thumb for deciding when to adjust your set point upward is, "If it's not challenging enough to keep you thinking about it, it's not challenging enough." If this proves to be the case, go back and revise the "M" (Measurable) aspect of your SMART program. If you're cutting your smoking by one cigarette a day without much anxiety, try cutting it by two. If your boss is responding positively to your more assertive behavior, it may be a good time to negotiate for a higher salary.

What if you find you've set your point too high? It's one thing to deal with boredom; it's quite another to try to cope with frustration. Reconsider the "R" (Realistic) aspect of your SMART program. If you can't stand the heat, don't get out of the kitchen; just turn down the heat. If landing three new accounts per month is proving to be unrealistic, reset your point to two. If losing two pounds per week proves to be an unreasonable goal, it could be that monitoring your progress weekly is leading to frustration. Try resetting your point to eight pounds per month. If that works, readjust upward to ten pounds.

Don't be in such a hurry to lower your set point when setbacks or slow progress cause frustration and resentment. Before reconsidering your goals, take the following steps:

1. Sow SEEDS when you experience a setback.

   ■ View the **situation** simply as one event among many, not as an indication of failure. One loss won't drop you out of the league.

   ■ **Evaluate** the setback. Was it a result of unrealistic expectations or poor efforts? Or was it just a matter of circumstance?

   ■ Let your **emotions** about your progress change to become consistent with your evaluation.

   ■ **Do** something to set you back on course toward your goal.

   ■ Feel your **self-esteem** restored as a result of your action.

2. Can we stand one more old cliché? "Rome wasn't built in a day." Any goal represents the learning of a new habit, and habits are replaced, not broken. You spent years learning your old pattern. Don't be discouraged if it takes longer than you expected to learn a new one. There are no quick fixes.

3. Review your actual accomplishments on a regular basis. They serve as evidence to your subconscious mind that you *are* making progress.

4. Use your creative imagination to reinforce your goal. Use mental imaging to visualize yourself as having attained the goal. Be open to insights from your right brain that may point you toward new ways of approaching it.

5. Identify people with whom you might brainstorm new approaches to your goal.

The Secret Is to Keep Moving

Remember that your automatic mechanism moves you toward the things you think about. That's what a goal *is:* a target for your creative mechanism to act on. If you claim your goal in consciousness and have a workable action plan, you will move from thought to action to form. Don't forget to spend time every day in the theater of your imagination seeing yourself as having already achieved your goal. Put your affirmation cards where you can't help but see them several times each day. Even if you pay little conscious attention to these reminders, your subconscious mind will see them. Say "Cancel" every time you catch yourself indulging in negative self-talk and immediately reaffirm your goal. Remind yourself that someone is going to achieve this goal—why shouldn't it be you? If you follow these procedures, you'll find yourself making the necessary adjustments and course corrections without resistance. You'll find yourself moving toward your goal without any interference from the goalie within.

Targeting on Ideas

- Procrastination may result from fear of success or fear of failure.
- Use your internal guidance system to overcome procrastination.
- Tracking your progress on a daily basis will help you stay on course.
- Use slowdowns and setbacks as cues to reshape your action plan.
- Readjust your set point as necessary.

SET
YOUR OWN
TARGETS

YOUR SUCCESS MECHANISM REVISITED: DRAWING A BLUEPRINT FOR CHANGE

Our self-image and our habits tend to go together. Change one and you will automatically change the other.... When we consciously and deliberately develop new and better habits, our self-image tends to outgrow the new habits and grow into the new pattern.

—*Maxwell Maltz*, Psycho-Cybernetics *(1960)*

We do not consider self-esteem to be necessarily fixed at any point in the life span. We think it can be either static or dynamic, depending on the changing behavior dispositions of the individual across the life span.

—*R. L. Bednar, M. G. Wells and S. R. Peterson*, Self-Esteem *(1989)*

209

You now have all the tools you need to build a new self-image and an action plan for success. You may have begun to lay the foundation through relaxation, imagination and thinking about goals. You may even have begun the process of changing old habits through daily application of CRAFT. If so, good for you!

If you're like most of us, chances are you're feeling a bit overwhelmed. It's a little like trying to build a house without a blueprint. You've got the land cleared, you've got building materials arranged in neat stacks, you've got your bulldozer and your concrete mixer, your hammers and saws and trowels and wiring and copper pipes. But what you haven't got is a plan, and it's only by following a plan that you're going to turn your intentions into a house.

Of course the only person who can draw a blueprint for your self-image is you. Only you can design the plan; only you can decide how best to rebuild your personality to your specifications. The good news is that it doesn't matter what your design is as long as it's *your* design and you're diligent in following it. Your automatic creative mechanism is versatile enough to plot a course to any target you may set—provided you *make a habit* of applying the skills and techniques necessary to keep it running smoothly.

This chapter is about designing such a plan for yourself. To guide you in creating your blueprint, you'll find·

- answers to questions you may have about applying Psycho-Cybernetics in a systematic way.
- two model plans that show how others have integrated these skills into strategies for success and will aid you in designing your own.

⊞ Building a Sturdy Foundation: A Few Questions and Answers

During my speaking engagements this is the point at which I throw open the floor for questions. Since we can't quite do that, I'll review the most frequently asked questions and respond as if we were talking face-to-face. The answers to these questions will guide you in establishing a solid foundation that will serve for any plan you may devise.

This may be a silly question, but where do I start?

Not a silly question at all. If you're going to gain the full benefit of Psycho-Cybernetics, you need to start with *awareness.* You need to have the feeling that something in your life just isn't working. Chances are you've already made that start, or you wouldn't have picked up this book in the first place. Perhaps you've found yourself feeling depressed and dissatisfied. Perhaps you've told yourself, "There's got to be something better than this—if only I knew how to achieve it!" Perhaps there was some triggering event that made you realize your life just wasn't working. Perhaps you've picked up hints from friends, family or co-workers that "you just don't seem to be yourself these days." Such comments may be clues that there's someone else you'd like to be—a "better you." Recognition—becoming aware that change is desirable and attainable—is the first step toward getting your success mechanism functioning.

What exactly do you mean by "goals"? Do you mean the new image of myself that I visualize in my imagination, the achievement I'm working toward with my action plan, or both?

When I use the term *goals,* I'm talking about personal and career achievements. A new self-image isn't the goal in itself—it's just a necessary prerequisite if you're going to maximize your potential for setting and achieving goals. Unless your automatic mechanism has a target, a goal, it literally has nowhere to go. Your self-image comes into the picture because it sets limits on what you can attain. A poor self-image can keep you trapped in the belief that your goals are only fantasies, or it can discourage you from thinking about goals at all. Before you can realistically assess which goals are appropriate for you, you need to have a self-image that's positive enough to enable you to select a worthwhile and realistic target.

Then how do I integrate goal-setting with changing my self-image? Isn't it necessary to maximize my potential range of goals before I select one?

Yes, but that doesn't mean you can't start thinking about goals and developing an action plan while you're working on changing the habits that have limited you. You can start working on goals at any time and extend your reach as you feel your self-image being enhanced, your potential strengthened.

I've got so *many* tools in front of me—visualization, relaxation, stress management, SEEDS, CRAFT, SMART—I don't know which one to pick up first or how to use them in combination with one another. How do I choose?

It can be difficult to know which tool to use when—and a procedure that works for someone else might not be the best one for you. Generally, though, once you've become aware that change is both desirable and attainable, your next step is *assessment:* What are the beliefs that keep you habitually bound to limitations? What is the dead-end path your horse is following? Be aware of old tapes that keep sending you negative messages like "I'm a loser," "I'll never amount to anything," or "Nothing good ever comes my way." Where did such self-assessments come from? Whose voices are you hearing on those old tapes? How did you form the habit of believing them?

Once you've made such an assessment, you can begin to challenge and replace your negative beliefs through the CRAFT process. But in order for CRAFT to be effective, you first must learn to relax. The key to CRAFT is practicing new attitudes and behavior in your imagination, and for that you must be able to free yourself from tension and distraction. Begin your program of relaxation exercises at the same time as you initiate CRAFT—maybe even a little sooner.

It's never too early to start thinking about goals. Start writing them now, but understand that your perception of what's possible and how you might go about achieving it will be enhanced as your horse becomes habituated to new paths. Continue to reevaluate your goals according to the SMART test as your reflective relearning takes effect. Once you've been "acting as if" long enough to feel that you're actually "making it" instead of just "faking it," you'll be able to shape your plan into one that's even SMARTer.

I can see what my false beliefs are, but I'm having trouble identifying where the old tapes came from. Do I need to dig deeper?

No. Identifying the source of your old tapes can make change easier, but it isn't necessary. Your conscious mind will select new beliefs more readily if the rational side of your brain can realistically assess the old ones: "Okay, that's how my mom saw me *then*. This is *now*," or "Why should I care what *he* thought of me? I'm not a little kid in the playground any more!" But all you really need to go on to the next step is to reach the point of asking yourself "Hey wait a minute—where did I get *that* idea? Who *says* I'm no good?"

I can see how canceling old, negative self-statements and replacing them with positive ones can change my mind on a subconscious level. But those affirmations—writing them down and pasting them all over my house seems silly and embarrassing. Are they really necessary?

That's your left brain talking: "This is silly; why are you wasting your time?" If that's the message your conscious mind selects, then old Jiminy Cricket is right—it won't work. But if you eliminate such a message by consistently affirming your new self-image, then *that's* the message your subconscious mind will comply with. Write those affirmations and stick them everywhere. Let your rider register repeatedly that you are *entitled* to seek and find new ways of achieving happiness and success. It's the only way your horse will come to agree—and if you're diligent, it's inevitable that your horse will agree.

Just don't forget that affirmations alone won't do the job. Only by vividly imagining yourself in your new and positive role on a daily basis will you persuade your subconscious mind that the affirmations are really you.

I just can't find time each day to do my visualizations, let alone the same time every day. Why is this so important?

Because your horse loves routine. By practicing the "F" step of CRAFT every day at the same time, in the same place, you establish a familiar pattern, a focused direction that is much easier for old Dobbin to follow than a hit-or-miss approach. If your schedule makes such routine impossible, allow yourself to be flexible about time and place, but *don't* forego the daily practice. Routine is desirable, but daily focusing on your new self-image is essential.

I'm trying to "fake it till I make it," but I feel uncomfortable doing it. I *feel* like a fake, and I don't seem to be making it at all. Is there anything I can do?

"Patience is a virtue," but sometimes it's a tremendous challenge as well. You feel like a fake because your left brain doesn't see the point of what you're doing. It's not a fraudulent feeling; it's just not a useful one because reflective relearning is a right-brain process. That's why you repeat your affirmations every time you step on the gas pedal or brush your teeth: You're cueing your right brain that you're in an ongoing process, even though your left brain can't acknowledge it just yet. Remember, it took years of reinforcement to get you to believe your old tapes. Allow yourself the time it takes to learn the new ones. You'll find that your patience was well worth it.

You've said it takes six weeks to break an old habit and learn a new one. I have a lot of habits to break.... If I have to spend six weeks working on each of them, I'll be a senior citizen by the time I'm through. Isn't there a shortcut?

It depends on what you mean by shortcut. If you mean using CRAFT to change more than one habit at a time, the answer, unfortunately, is no. When you're trying to focus on too many things at once, you really aren't focusing on anything at all. If for example you try to challenge your procrastination before you're entirely comfortable about the new way you're learning to perceive yourself, you'll only end up confusing your horse. Let it learn one new path before you start teaching it another. It may take longer that way, but the result will be success and not frustration.

Now for the good news: Breaking a habit and replacing it with a new one are two simultaneous aspects of the same process. As you build a new self-image that makes room for new capabilities, you're also cancelling old habits that have kept you watching the curbs. Six weeks is a guideline; an average. Some habits may require only a few days to dislodge and replace; others may take months. You can "cut and paste" as needed. You are the sole judge of what's working and what isn't. I do recommend, however, that when you first get started you practice CRAFT religiously for at least a month and preferably a full six weeks. At the end of this time, contrast the old you with the new you. This assessment of your progress can serve as a baseline for determining how much time to allow for changing other habits.

You gave some suggestions for daily monitoring of my action plan. Is there a quick daily assessment I can use to monitor my reflective relearning too?

Not really. Again, you'd be asking your left brain to supervise a right-brain job. However, here's a checklist you can review daily or use as a starting point for devising your own list:

214

❑ When I woke up this morning, did I immediately focus on my affirmation? Did I tell myself, "I am a _____ person and am worthy to succeed in _____ or in anything else I may attempt"?

❑ Did I accompany all routine tasks—brushing my teeth, petting the dog, turning each page of the newspaper—with a reiteration of my affirmation?

❑ Did I spend a full 15 minutes relaxed and undisturbed in a quiet place, focusing on my new self?

❑ Did I practice my new behavior today as if I had already made it a part of me, even though it may still feel uncomfortable?

❑ Did I challenge every setback, every reminder of my old, negative self, by evaluating the situation from a nonjudgmental perspective?

Are the positive effects of CRAFT permanent? If not, how can I ensure *lasting* changes that will let me achieve my potential?

That's where SEEDS is useful. You can use this process as a booster shot, an ongoing testing ground for determining "how you're doing" with your new self-image. If you find yourself slipping back into old habits—"Lois dumped me; that means I'm ugly and a drag"; "Ms. Eng hated my report; I should have known I wasn't qualified for this job"; "I didn't follow throught on that interview; I'm still a spineless wimp"—use SEEDS to put the situation in perspective. If you find yourself slipping back *frequently* into old habits, it may be a sign that you need a refresher application of CRAFT. But in most cases a SEEDS evaluation will reaffirm your new self-concept.

Then SEEDS isn't just about dealing with stress?

Oh, no! I introduced it in connection with stress-producing situations, but it has much wider applications. SEEDS is an attitude adjustment tool, a reminder to your subconscious mind that you have a choice. You can apply it whenever you sense that your automatic mechanism is wandering off course; that you're reacting instead of acting. Any time an incident makes you wonder whether your old self-evaluation might not be true—an event that seems to reinforce old beliefs about yourself, an apparent lack of progress toward your goal—reevaluate it by sowing SEEDS. Remind yourself that the situation is just *that*—a fundamentally neutral event, not an indication of failure. Lightning strikes bridges. People get dumped. Bosses' opinions can be withering. It's no reason to revert to your old way of thinking.

Remember that your emotional reactions don't arise directly from an event but from the way you evaluate it. There's a lag there, though it may be difficult to perceive it. Often the evaluation seems so spontaneous that you're not consciously aware you made it. But the crucial step—subconsciously asking and answering the question WHAT DOES THIS MEAN TO ME?—has bent your feelings about the event. By evaluating it without judging yourself, you can gain great insight into your behavior. Pay attention to what you tell yourself when you evaluate the situation negatively. You'll hear those old tapes whirring around like helicopter blades. Who told you that you were "a drag"? That's not your evaluation—it's your brother's; he's the one who used to say you were about as interesting as a bologna sandwich. Why do you feel "ineffectual"? You don't have to choose that evaluation—it's your Uncle Fred's; he's the one who used to laugh at you whenever you tried anything new. You probably just caught yourself using his very words, didn't you?

Think of *emotion* as "*energy in motion.*" Because your behavior springs from the way you feel about an event, the appropriate response to your feelings is to take the bull by the horns and immediately DO something that reinforces your changing self-image. The event doesn't mean you're slipping back into old habits. You're doing just fine. You're no longer faking it; you've *made* it. Now go do something that *shows* you've made it, something consistent with the new concept of yourself you've so painstakingly built.

I'm trying, but my self-image is still the pits. I'm not ready to give up yet. Is there any way I can troubleshoot the process to see what I might be doing wrong?

Good for you! Being unwilling to give up and determined to find out what's wrong places you halfway on the road to success. A good way to do it is to apply the steps of SEEDS backwards. You might find that your trouble is a case of "as ye sow, so shall ye reap." By working backwards through SEEDS, you may find that you're *choosing* a negative outcome.

Let's take a hypothetical situation. Think of someone whose life appears not to be working at all—your aunt Delilah, perhaps. Lord knows *she's* lonely and miserable—just ask her. Her *self-esteem* is pretty poor. She's convinced she's no good to anyone. How did she get that way? What does she *do;* what has she done to become burdened with such a negative concept of herself? She blames others for her misery, she feels sorry for herself, she talks incessantly about her woes—choose any or all of the above; we could compile quite a list. Our formula tells us that what she has chosen to do in life is a reflection of her previous *emotional* states. It's a sure bet that her feelings must generally be negative to have resulted in her actions. Delilah does what she does because she's generally feeling angry, blue, resentful, victimized—again, the list of negative emotions could go on for pages. Remember your eighth-grade science, the first law of thermodynamics? Energy can neither be created nor destroyed, it can only be converted from one form to another or channelled into another system. The negative energy of Delilah's emotions is channelled into negative actions, and her negative actions in turn are transformed into negative self-esteem.

And what is the source of Aunt Delilah's emotions? The way she *evaluates* the events life deals her. She evaluates life as unjust, cruel, lopsided and generally out to get her. Now, whether or not these evaluations are correct is a moot question. The larger consideration is that she does not—cannot—see them as fundamentally neutral *situations.* Long ago she formed the habit of seeing them in this negative, self-impacting manner. Thus she can rationalize that men are no good, that people are essentially selfish and uncaring and that there's no use putting herself in situations where she's going to get hurt.

Fortunately, you haven't reached Delilah's state of misery—hers is a worst-case scenario. When your self-esteem is threatened, you can work SEEDS backwards to give your horse a hard tug at the reins.

1. At the end of the day, check the barometer of your *self-esteem.* How do you feel about yourself? Are you feeling drained, uneasy, maybe a little unhappy with yourself? Maybe a lot?

2. Next, explore why. Check out what you *did* today to induce such a feeling. You really lit into Debra for being late on her portion of the project—a step backwards from your goal of controlling your temper at work. Now, why did you do that? What were the feelings involved?

3. Your overriding *emotion* was anger. Well, then, in what way were you looking at the situation that caused you to blow your stack?

4. Here's how you *evaluated* Debra's action: "She does this to slow me down. She's lazy, and it makes me look bad in the boss's eyes..."

5. *Aha!* There's why you came home feeling bad! You evaluated the situation in a way that gave *you* ownership of the problem instead of assigning it to Debra. *Maybe* she's doing it to make you look bad. And if she is? Why, you

can approach the problem with your rider in charge. Next time it happens, your emotion will be concern rather than anger. You can *act* assertively instead of *reacting* aggressively. You can do something about the problem—approach your colleague as a responsible adult would do—and perhaps salvage her self-esteem as well as your own.

Use this technique to take your emotional pulse any time you feel you're not making progress, any time you find your horse wandering down old paths. You may be reacting negatively to one particular situation and discounting others you handled perfectly. Any day you find yourself feeling uneasy or depressed, give yourself the SEEDS-backwards test as a reality check.

Putting It All Together: Two Psycho-Cybernetics Success Stories

How you will integrate these skills and techniques depends entirely on you. The specifics will vary; the proof of your success will be success. You'll have to use your own intuition and rational evaluation to determine how much time to spend on each step. But since Psycho-Cybernetics is essentially about changing habits—habits of belief, habits of attitude and habits of action—the procedures any two individuals may follow will closely parallel one another. Only the habits are different. What works for someone else, with a few modifications, is likely to work for you.

In earlier chapters the illustrative examples have tended to focus on only one aspect of Psycho-Cybernetics—visualization, false beliefs, stress management, etc. Let's now take a look at the *whole program* as exemplified by two individuals. Though the self-image problems they had to deal with may be different in their particulars from yours, you'll see parallels with your own situation when you review the steps they followed. As you read their stories, think about how you might adapt the procedures for yourself.

Success #1: Retooling Your Self-Image for Career Advancement

Awareness. Doug, 36, was a bright, energetic engineer working for a fast-growing company that made computerized hospital equipment. He had lost enthusiasm for his work and come to doubt his capabilities. He was anxious and depressed and had difficulty sleeping more than two hours at a time.

Doug traced his negative feelings to an incident at work five weeks earlier. He had come up with a revolutionary software idea and was pitching it to the managerial staff when he was challenged by Peterson, one of the senior engineers. This man jumped all over his idea, calling it "not only untenable but downright stupid." He suggested that Doug was wasting the valuable time of the managers in attendance.

At first Doug was shocked, then angry. He endured the rest of the meeting in silence. As he drove home, however, his anger turned to depression and the humiliation of rejection. His wife asked him several times what was wrong, but he was too deeply wounded to answer. That night the insomnia began; the next day he found himself indifferent to his work. He could develop no enthusiasm for any of his projects. The senior staff member who had belittled his idea approached him with a slap on the back and a "Hey, I hope there's no hard feelings—business is business!" But this gesture did nothing to lift Doug's spirits. He had continued in a downward spiral until his supervisor took him to lunch and expressed concern about Doug's "apathy."

Identifying false beliefs. This talk led Doug to explore the feelings about himself that he associated with his apathy. He caught himself ruminating frequently, thinking such thoughts as "I'm never going to be successful, no matter what I do"; "I always screw up"; "I guess I'm just lacking in some essential qualities."

Doug probed further into these feelings by exploring his early childhood experiences. He had no trouble recognizing the source of his belief that he was "lacking in essential qualities." His father was an exacting taskmaster whom he could never seem to please. Whatever goal his father set for him, whether it was cleaning the garage, coming home with a perfect report card or having a cavity filled without fussing in the dentist's chair, Doug could never perform up to his expectations. His most persistent old tapes were of his father saying, "Doug, I'm disappointed in you," or "Doug, for the love of Pete!" or simply frowning and shaking his head. He remembered one particularly painful incident at age six or seven when his father, a skilled woodworker who had built much of the family's furniture, had asked Doug to help out in his garage workshop. Doug remembered how proud he had felt to be asked to help, and how he'd sought to please his father by doing his own creative woodwork with some pieces of scrap lumber and the toy tools he'd been given for Christmas. "To this day I don't know what I did wrong," Doug told his wife. "I just remember him shaking his head and sneering at me to stay out of his way and not to touch anything."

Doug could readily understand both where his negative tapes had come from and why the incident at work had started them replaying. It was painful to reconfront his father's unrealistic goals of perfection for him and the feelings brought about by his inability to attain them. Doug had long ago learned to dismiss the pain by thinking "Oh well, that was a long time ago—let's let bygones be bygones." Yet although the events were bygones, Doug's memories of them were not. While confronting his now-aged father might not have served any purpose, confronting his false beliefs was essential.

Rational thinking.   Doug challenged his beliefs by asking himself these questions whenever he found himself thinking he was "lacking in some essential qualities":

1. *Is there any rational reason for such a belief?*

No. The belief came solely from old tapes and from my habit of believing their message.

2. *Could I be mistaken in this belief?*

Of course. I've been successful at my job for ten years. There wasn't anything essential lacking in my proposal. Old Peterson just didn't like it.

3. ***Would I come to the same conclusion about some other person in a similar situation?***

Certainly not. I'd think "He just got slapped down by some jerk, and after all business *is* business."

4. ***Why should I continue to act and feel as if this were true if there is no good reason to believe it?***

No reason in the world.

Relaxation. Before he could begin learning a new habit to replace the old, destructive one, Doug had to be able to achieve the state of relaxation that makes right-brain learning possible. He read up on breathing exercises and progressive relaxation and experimented with a few relaxation tapes. With minimal practice he learned to enter a relaxed state at will. Part of his success was due to his choosing the same time every day for relaxation—in the evening, just before dinner. He made an agreement with his family that he would reserve this time slot for himself alone. From 6:15 to 6:45, he was not to be disturbed. He requested that the TV and radio be turned down; he went into his bedroom, positioned himself on a foam pad for comfort and let himself relax.

Reprogramming. Doug began to break his old habit of viewing himself as "lacking" and instilling a new habit of seeing himself as an effective person with valuable contributions to make. He spent six weeks reprogramming his automatic mechanism by means of the CRAFT system.

1. He said "Cancel!" every time he caught himself thinking of himself as inadequate.
2. He immediately replaced each negative thought with a positive statement: "I'm an effective engineer with excellent ideas to offer my company."

221

3. He wrote affirmations on cards and placed them on the sun visor of his car and on his bedroom mirror: "There is no essential skill or quality that I lack!" He copied his affirmation on a Post-It which he stuck in his desk calendar and moved from day to day.

4. Every evening during his reserved private time, Doug entered the theater of his imagination. He pictured himself in the conference room pitching his project ideas to the senior managers and winning their approval. He imagined the scene in detail: the faces and postures of the executives, the smells of coffee and furniture polish, his confidence in presenting his ideas and the enthusiastic approval of the staff—particularly Peterson.

5. For six weeks Doug trained himself for his new self-image, even though he did not yet feel comfortable in it. He prepared for staff meetings by evaluating the pros and cons of how others were likely to react to his ideas and anticipating how he might address the "cons." He approached his supervisor with a modification of his earlier proposal and received permission to reintroduce it at the next staff meeting. He practiced speaking assertively on behalf of his idea in his car on the way to work. He repeated his affirmations to himself every time he glanced in the rearview mirror of his car, looked in his bedroom mirror at home or consulted his desk calendar at work.

Goal setting. Doug needed a specific target, not just, "I want to feel that I'm not lacking in essential qualities." He knew his goal would have something to do with achievement at work. When he started his negative self-image wouldn't allow him to think of anything beyond "I want to gain some courage about presenting my ideas and not feel devastated if they're rejected." After several weeks of retraining, he sat down to choose a goal that was specific, measurable, action-oriented, realistic and timely. He wrote down: "I'm having one of my ideas selected for development by next October 1." He realized that by "acting as if" he had already achieved his new self-image, he had already gone a long way toward developing an action plan. He had set out systematically to win over the senior staff, identified possible obstacles and planned how to circumvent them. He had enlisted his supervisor's support. And he was aware of the positive effects achieving the goal would have on his career.

Stress management. The night before the next staff meeting, Doug experienced a panic attack. He began to anticipate Peterson's reaction, "awfulizing" it to the point where he expected the worst and was responding with anger and despair. When Doug became aware that his horse was bucking around the corral and snorting at nothing, he chose to walk away from the situation. He found a quiet place in his mind, a vividly realized image of a park where he used to enjoy walking during his college days. After 15 minutes in this tranquil place, Doug found it impossible to feel stressed about the impending meeting. Even so, as he drove to work the next day he found himself wondering uneasily, "What if Peterson ridicules my idea again?"

"So, what if he does?" Doug answered himself. "That's Peterson's problem. *I* know it's a good idea."

Progress check. The senior managers *did* respond negatively to his idea—but this time Doug did not allow himself to react as he had in his father's workshop. He had broken his old habit. "Look, I know this isn't the way things are traditionally done around here," he said to Peterson, "but I feel very positively that this idea has merit, and I strongly suggest that you hear me out. Anything you're feeling negative about I'd be glad to address, but please save your questions until after I've finished my presentation." When one of the managers interrupted him, he stood firm. "Please listen," he said. "I think that instead of considering my idea, you're just thinking about what you're going to say next. I know this is something new, but we can't really have a meaningful discussion until you've heard it fully."

Doug's idea was rejected—but not Doug. No more did he feel that he was "just lacking in some essential qualities." From that day on he asserted himself as a confident member of the engineering staff. On those occasions when some unexpected blow to his self-esteem sent his horse cantering down the old path, he was able to use SEEDS to confirm the reality of the situation:

1. This situation is fundamentally neutral—it doesn't impact me negatively.
2. When I evaluate the event from a neutral perspective, I can see that it isn't my problem at all.
3. There is therefore no reason for me to react with feelings of anger, despair or self-punishment.
4. I can take specific, positive action to put the situation behind me.
5. My self-esteem is restored.

During the next several months most of the senior managers came gradually to see the value of Doug's ideas. It was reasonable for him to anticipate that he would achieve the goal he had set. And if he didn't? Then his newly programmed self-image would empower him to shrug off the disappointment and either modify his goal or set another. He had made success a habit.

Success #2: Enhancing Your Self-Image for Personal Fulfillment

Awareness. For Peggy, 25, the road to success began the day she received a letter from her 18-year-old sister in Dayton, Ohio. "Great news!" Yvette had written. "I've been accepted at Goucher College in Baltimore. I'm going to have to work part time, but Mom and Dad have agreed to pay my tuition and half my room and board, so I'll have some free time, and I'm looking forward to spending a lot of it with you in D.C...."

At this point Peggy stopped reading. She began to cry uncontrollably. She worked as an airline flight attendant and was scheduled for a flight that evening. For the first time since she'd got the job, she phoned in sick.

That evening her neighbor, Jenny, dropped in to return a videotape she had borrowed and found Peggy weeping. "I don't know what's come over me," Peggy said. "Yvette's letter was so 'up'—and all it did was make me realize how miserable I feel most of the time."

"You?" Jenny said. "Come on. You're just having a bad day. You're the most upbeat, well-adjusted person I know."

"You don't understand," Peggy cried. "I'm just no good with people—no good at all. I let everybody down."

"What about these?" Jenny indicated the three framed certificates from the airline on Peggy's wall. "They don't give out citations for Exceptional Customer Service to flight attendants who are no good with people."

"Oh sure—that's the way they see me at work," Peggy said. "I get along just fine on the job, but I don't have any close friends. The crew goes out to dinner, and I eat alone in my room. And my love life—it's a joke. Any time a man lets me know he really needs me, I let him down!"

When Jenny checked back with Peggy several days later and found her still disconsolate, she suggested counseling. Peggy rejected the idea. She didn't feel comfortable about going to a therapist. "How about a pastor?" Jenny said. "The one at our church is an insightful, understanding guy." Peggy rejected this suggestion too. She didn't need counseling. She *knew* what her problem was—she let everybody down. "I just have to come to my senses and stop crying," she said. But as days went by and Peggy continued to feel miserable, she realized something was wrong. Why had Yvette's letter precipitated such negative feelings?

Accessing the right brain for creative insight. Peggy covered her kitchen table with white paper. She put on some relaxing music, sat comfortably at the table and spent ten minutes breathing deeply and slowly to calm herself and clear her conscious mind. Then she took a pen and began to write down all the random thoughts that came to her concerning her sister's letter. "Just let your consciousness flow," she told herself. She wrote:

> Yvette
>
> college
>
> favored one

...and that was as far as she got. Suddenly Peggy dissolved in tears as a flood of memories and emotions overcame her.

Identifying false beliefs.   Peggy was the oldest of four daughters. Her mother worked at home as a piano teacher, and from a very early age Peggy had been expected to assume a great deal of the responsibility of caring for her sisters. Yvette in particular had come to regard Peggy as her primary caregiver. By the time she was six she was depending on Peggy for everything. When 13-year-old Peggy protested that she didn't always want to walk Yvette to school, pack her lunches, and generally be responsible for "sister sitting," she was dismayed by her mother's response. "You're always letting me down," she yelled. She pointed out how Peggy had failed time after time to keep the girls quiet while she was giving lessons in the living room. Her father too chastised her for "upsetting your mother after all she's done for you."

During her adolescence more and more of the burden of caring for her sisters fell on Peggy's shoulders. She had little time for personal life. Yet she never seemed to be able to win her mother's approval. *You're always letting me down.* Every time she reflected on her situation, her resentment was quickly swallowed up in guilt. How can I be so selfish? *I'm letting my sisters down.*

By her 18th birthday Peggy couldn't wait to get away. Going away to college was out of the question. "There isn't enough money," her parents told her. "Why don't you go to the local community college? You'd still be able to live at home." Peggy was already packed and ready to go. She had found a job as a stable groom at a farm in Kentucky through an ad she'd answered in a magazine. Although she'd never had anything to do with horses, she was willing to do anything to get away from her family. "How can you do this to your sisters?" her mother cried as she left for the bus station. "Yvette will just die without you. *You're letting us down!*"

Peggy now understood where her negative self-evaluation had come from and why the letter from Yvette had precipitated her depression. Now she began to reflect on how this image of herself had affected her life. She'd always been a responsible worker; she'd had no trouble getting or keeping jobs. But she'd shied away from social involvements because of her subconscious belief that she was the sort of person who let her friends down.

Her disastrous love affairs, she realized, had been built on the same negative premise. She was always attracted to immature, emotionally needy men—alcoholics, "little boys"—men who could provide no nurturing but who required a great deal of it; men with whom she could fulfill her negative estimation of herself by letting them down. "*I* didn't let them down!" she told herself in a moment of insight. "They used me as an excuse for their own dependencies, their own weaknesses. And with that old tape playing in my head, I fell for it like a ton of bricks!"

Self-assessment. Over the next several days, Peggy used her relaxation procedure to access a quiet place in her mind where she could meditate and evaluate herself realistically. She confirmed to herself that there were many areas in her life where she *did* follow through. "In some areas I'm doing just fine," she told herself. "I've just got to learn to carry that over into my personal relationships. But first I've got to learn to *see myself* as a person who follows through in my relationships."

Goal setting. Peggy wasn't sure yet how she was going to change her self-perception, but she knew she didn't want to be made miserable by another man who couldn't take care of himself. She bought a notebook and wrote on the first page, "I see myself in a warm, balanced, mutually nuturing relationship with a man by New Year's Eve." Later, she evaluated her goal SMARTly:

1. I have a specific goal with a specific date for achievement.

2. I can measure my progress by the number of contacts I make and monitor myself by checking off appointments in this notebook.

3. I have an action plan for meeting this lucky guy. My job keeps me traveling a lot, but I won't let that be an excuse for not following through. I'll compile a list of places and organizations where I'm likely to meet the right kind of man, get calendars of their upcoming events, check them against my work schedule and jot down a few likely ones. I'll share my goal with Denise and Carol and see if I can get some good input from them.

4. Realistically, money's not an issue—I have a good job. I'm more concerned with finding someone with good spiritual values and whom I don't have to be rescuing from himself all the time. I want someone with whom there's a balanced emotional give and take.

5. I've set myself a time limit, so I'd better get started. These are the three things I'm going to do this month to initiate contacts:...

Reprogramming.   "Okay, this isn't just about meeting guys," Peggy told herself. "I have trouble establishing *any* close relationships because I've programmed myself to believe I'm going to let people down. If this is my image of myself, no wonder I've found it hard to make friends. I'm also likely to zero in on exactly the same kind of guy as always and realize my mistake too late. How do I change my programming?"

For the next six weeks Peggy practiced CRAFT:

1. She said "Cancel" every time she caught herself thinking "I let people down."

2. She replaced each such thought with, "I'm a worthy person whose main job is not to let *myself* down."

3. She wrote affirmations to remind herself she was in the process of change. Though it was difficult to place her affirmation cards where she could see them while in flight, she kept one in her notebook and one on her refrigerator door. She also kept one in her flight bag. Every time her schedule required her to spend a night in a hotel, the first thing she did on arrival was to tape this affirmation card to the mirror in her room.

4. Her schedule made it impossible to do her relaxed visualization at the same time every day, but Peggy made sure to reserve *some* time for it every day, no matter where she was. In her imagination she focused on herself in interpersonal situations as "a happy, open person who is willing and able to let others care for me as I care for them." Her favorite imagery was seeing herself and the (future) man in her life on a see-saw, balancing each other back and forth, lifting and being lifted, giving and taking.

5. For six weeks Peggy repeated her affirmations to herself every time she placed a food tray on a serving cart. On her time off, she sought

out social contacts with her crewmates to train herself to be a care receiver as well as a care giver.

Reality checking. From time to time Peggy found herself overcome by depression. It happened the first time Yvette arrived for a weekend from Baltimore. At first she felt resentment about having to "take care" of her sister again, then anxiety over not wanting to let Yvette down. (Yvette must have wondered why her big sister kept muttering "Cancel" to herself all evening!) That night as she prepared for bed, all the bitterness she felt toward her mother came welling up inside her. When she became aware of this feeling, Peggy sat on the edge of her bed and thought about SEEDS:

1. "I was put in a situation in which I was thrust prematurely into the role of taking care of my sisters," she said to herself. "Any child in such a situation would feel guilty and resentful. It just happened to be me."

2. "I used to evaluate the situation as though I owned the problem," Peggy realized. "But I don't, and neither does Yvette. It was Mother's problem, and it still is. She expected adult behavior from a child."

3. "Why should I feel guilty or depressed about letting my sister down?" Peggy asked herself. "I have the right to be *angry* about Yvette. She's getting the college education I never got. I can allow myself to feel anger."

4. The next morning, Peggy took action. Over breakfast, she told Yvette how she had felt when they were both living at home, and how she felt now. "I don't want *you* to feel guilty," Peggy said. "I don't want to drive you away. But I do want you to understand. I'd like to see you from time to time, but I'm very uncomfortable with the feeling that I *have* to take care of you—and I won't allow myself to feel that I'm letting you down. I've got to be taking care of *me* right now."

5. When Peggy discovered that she could have this interaction with her sister without experiencing guilt or depression, she realized the progress she had made in raising her self-esteem. "I'm a *grown-up!*" she told herself.

It wasn't always easy for Peggy...but it was *simple*. By reordering her internal guidance system, she erased the program that said "Letting people down is what I'm about" and replaced it with one that said "I can do what's best for me without feeling guilty about disappointing someone else." Within months she was dating a government economist whom she met in an art class at the National Gallery. She knew she'd found a winner the night she had to work a coast-to-coast flight that was delayed three hours by a medical emergency. He was waiting for her when she dragged herself home at two a.m. "Sweetheart, you look bushed," he said. "How about I go get a pizza and then give you a backrub?"

⊞ Your Psycho-Cybernetics Blueprint

"Plan your work before you work your plan." Use these two examples to guide you in formulating your own blueprint for change. Keep in mind that you don't need outside help to make you aware of your need for change, to guide you in identifying the beliefs that keep you following negative habits, to teach you how to relax, to set goals for you or to direct you through the procedures. All you need is the willingness to change and the patience to allow Psycho-Cybernetics to take effect.

You've got the "big picture" now. If you've been holding off on getting started, now is the time to do it. If you haven't answered the self-assessment questionnaires and filled in the worksheets, do so now. If you haven't started teaching yourself relaxation techniques, start today. If you're not exercising your imagination, this is the day to start. If you haven't started thinking about goals, what are you waiting for? If you feel blocked by excessive stress, why not start practicing some stress-management techniques right now?

Before you read the rest of this book, take an afternoon or evening to start developing your blueprint for change. Use the mini-index below as a guide to review highlights. Review the exercises at the end of each chapter. Then get a pen and some paper and start planning!

- Changing habits: worksheet, pages 85-86
- CRAFT, pages 25-27
- False beliefs: identifying, pages 71-74
- Goals: assessing your present set point, pages 165-168
- Goals: maximizing progress, pages 193-206
- Goals: overcoming procrastination, pages 189-193
- Goals: the SMART plan, pages 170-180
- Imagination, pages 46-49, 60-61
- Relaxation: exercises and techniques, pages 106-119
- SEEDS, pages 125-128
- Stress management, pages 123-137
- Stress prevention, pages 137-144

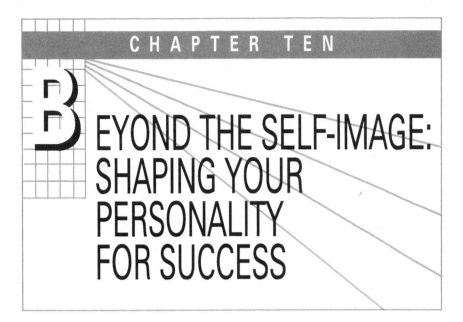

CHAPTER TEN

BEYOND THE SELF-IMAGE: SHAPING YOUR PERSONALITY FOR SUCCESS

I have found that one of the most effective means of helping people achieve [a] "successful" personality is to...give them a graphic picture of what the successful personality looks like.

—*Maxwell Maltz*, Psycho-Cybernetics *(1960)*

[W]e are not on earth to live up to someone else's expectations. To make our unique contributions to the world, we each need to prize our individual worth and pursue our dreams.

—*California Task Force to Promote Self-Esteem and Personal and Social Responsibility,*
Toward a State of Esteem *(1990)*

233

The word *success* comes from a Latin word meaning "to follow." It's a future-oriented concept. If you don't consider what's ahead when pursuing your goals, you may reach the place where you thought you would find success only to discover that it's not there. It's a little like a quarterback throwing a pass. He has to lead his receiver; to throw the ball not where the pass-catcher is now but where he expects him to be at some future moment. He must be able to improvise: if his primary receiver is taken out of the play he has to target on another before he's thrown for a loss. And he has to move the ball downfield: three completions don't mean a lot if they don't result in a first down.

You're engaged in a process of expanding your potential for achievement. But in a wider focus, you're also creating for yourself what Maltz called a "success-type personality"—one that will empower you to set and achieve goals throughout your life. "When we say that a person has a 'good personality,'" Maltz wrote, "what we really mean is that he has freed...the creative potential within him and is able to express his real self.... A good personality is one which enables you to deal effectively and appropriately with environment and reality, and to gain satisfaction from reaching goals...."

The catch is that "environment and reality" today are changing at a faster rate than Maltz could have envisioned. To develop a success-type personality today means "leading" your self-image, anticipating what skills and qualities will be needed for success in the year 2000 and beyond.

This chapter is about those skills and qualities and how you can acquire them. You'll learn:

- the seven elements that add up to Maltz's "picture of success."
- how each of these elements contributes to success.
- tips and techniques for acquiring each of these elements and shaping your self-image into a personality geared for success.

"I have found that an easy-to-remember picture of the successful personality is contained in the letters of the word 'Success' itself," Maltz wrote. His picture consisted of the following elements:

S-ense of direction
U-nderstanding
C-ourage
C-harity
E-steem
S-elf-confidence
S-elf acceptance

Let's take a look at each of these elements in turn, see how it contributes to success and discover how you can get it.

⊞ Sense of Direction: Charting a Path for a Lifetime

By now you know all about the importance of goals. A sense of direction means *always* having some goal to look forward to, some problem to solve, some new experience to master. "Develop a 'nostalgia for the future,'" Maltz wrote. "When you're not goal-striving, not looking forward, you're not really 'living.'"

The problem with Maltz's advice today is that there are so *many* futures to choose from that there's a danger of getting lost in the maze of choices. Remember how easy it used to be to choose a pair of athletic shoes? You could have any kind of sole you wanted as long as it was rubber, any kind of upper as long as it was canvas, and any color as long as it was white. Today there are so many options that selection itself becomes a problem. Psychologists have noted the approach-avoidance conflict—shoppers are so intimidated by the abundance of choices that they turn away without buying anything at all.

How does this apply to the *important* decisions in your life? There is a hazard that your goals can be fragmented by the abundance of choices. Success today requires a sense of direction that enables you to steer a path among all these choices to find the ones that are right for you. A sense of direction actually amounts to a "sense of several directions."

Prepare for Several Career Changes

For starters, consider your careers—and note the plural. It used to be the rule that a "career" meant one's life's work. This is no longer the case. According to business experts, tomorrow's worker may expect to have three or four careers during the course of a lifetime. New technologies and new economic realities are creating new careers and making old ones obsolete. Ever wonder what happened to all the blacksmiths and harness makers when the automobile replaced horsedrawn traffic?

It's been widely reported that the United States is moving from a manufacturing economy to a service economy. There's been a general perception that this trend is "a bad thing," an indication of economic decline. In fact, it's neither a positive nor a negative development, just a signpost of change. Its effect will be negative only on people who are ill-prepared. (At least some of those blacksmiths and harness makers became production-line workers, auto mechanics or petroleum-refinery workers.) According to *Workforce 2000*, a report issued in 1987 by the U.S. Department of Labor, your sense of direction regarding your career will have to take these facts into account:

- New jobs will require much higher skill levels than today's jobs. "Very few new jobs will be created for those who cannot read, follow directions, and use mathematics."

- By the year 2000 more than 60 percent of all women over the age of 16 will be in the workforce. This trend will lead to increased demand for employer-provided child care, "flex time" and work at home.

- Adaptability and willingness to learn will be required of older workers.

- The typical workplace in the early years of the next century will employ fewer people, and more people will be employed part time.

- Education and skills training will need to be accelerated to aid in the formation of "human capital."

- There will be a trend toward less equal distribution of wages: more high-earning jobs and more low-earning jobs, with fewer in the middle.

Approach Learning as a Life-Long Process

As the world of work comes increasingly to require adaptability and reeducation, people are taking up the challenge. In 1992 seventeen million Americans were enrolled in college courses full or part time, and fewer than six million of them were in the traditional college age bracket. The availability of evening classes, child care, and financial aid for those who require it are encouraging more and more adults to return to school, including millions who have never attended college before. "This dramatic shift," reports education writer Louis Freedberg, "...has come about as women enter the workplace in vast numbers, displaced workers try to upgrade their skills and baby boomers switch careers in unprecedented numbers." Many adults returning to school find (somewhat to their surprise) that maturity has given them the self-discipline they may have lacked in their youth. "If you can parent your kids, nurture your partner, and orchestrate a family's day-to-day tasks," writes Pam Mendelsohn in *Happier By Degrees*, "you'll probably find college a piece of cake." Typical of people who have sharpened their sense of direction by returning to school are:

- a top food-service salesperson and college dropout who entered an evening program to earn the B.A. required for a management position.
- a 31-year-old single mother with a high-school diploma who enrolled in a business college for training as a legal secretary
- a self-confessed "high-school goof-off" tired of working at low-end jobs who enrolled in a community college, intending to transfer to a university program once he got his grades up.
- a mid-level manager and mother of three completing an M.B.A. on-the-job through satellite and on-line computer instruction.
- a 48-year-old software consultant who took a writing class in a university extention program and subsequently won awards for his fiction.
- a welfare recipient with three children and less than $1,000 in the bank who received a full financial-aid package to the college of her choice simply by filling out a few forms.
- a 50-year-old homemaker who entered graduate school nearly 30 years after her graduation from college.

Adjust to Changes in Your Family Life

The concept of the family is undergoing radical transformation. The very word "family" has the census bureau baffled. The California Task Force on self-esteem dealt with this transformation by defining *family* as "the set of two or more persons within which the individual receives his or her essential care and support." Insecurity and indecisiveness when your family situation is changing can undermine the feelings that lead to success. You may need to adjust your goals while keeping your self-esteem high under any of these situations:

- a "traditional" family: man as breadwinner, woman as homemaker
- a dual-career family
- a dual-career family in which the wife's income is substantially greater than her husband's
- a single-parent household
- a couple, both previously married, whose children include "his, hers and theirs"
- a divorced woman raising her ex-husband's child from a previous marriage
- a retired couple or single grandparent raising their grandchildren
- two single women with children sharing living space to save expenses

Women: Balancing Lives, Rearranging Priorities

Our time offers a special challenge to a woman's sense of direction. She's caught in a classic double bind, trying to maintain the homemaking tradition imparted to her by her mother while simultaneously striving for success in the business world. Her old tapes tell her never to leave home until every dish is done and put away, to have a kitchen floor clean enough to eat off, always to "be there" for her family and to wear clean underwear in case she's in an accident. Meanwhile her "new tapes" have her climbing the corporate ladder, working out eight days a week, baking her own 12-grain bread every day, guiding her 2.3 gifted children through their enlightened private schools and being the most exciting female since Cleopatra. Did I say double bind? I meant multiple bind! In the 1970s we used to call this attempt to cope with fragmentation the "superwoman syndrome." The term may be passé, but the reality isn't. Although a woman may know intellectually that she can't possibly do it all, any time she achieves success in one arena she's feeling like a failure in another. Is it any wonder that she has trouble maintaining her sense of direction? Her self-image can't help but be negatively affected—her poor horse has its hooves splayed out every which way! Based on the stories I hear from the women attending my seminars, I've concluded that this fragmented sense of direction is the number one cause of stress among American women today. If you're a woman trying to keep your balance while pursuing several goals at once, you can probably relate to examples like these:

- Lois, 36, divorced; working full time and spending three evenings a week trying to complete her B.A. while trying to keep up with the responsibilities of raising a seven-year-old son
- Jolene, 27, single, trying to maintain her relationship with her boyfriend while working in the employee-relations department of a bank and being the sole care provider for her widowed, diabetic mother
- Carla 31, separated from her husband and recovering from her third miscarriage, working 60 hours a week at two jobs and trying to squeeze in counseling with her husband
- Trina, 44, married, trying to be a mom to three active children while working as a traveling sales rep for a clothing manufacturer

Prescription: Find Your Compass Heading for Success

Consider your initial efforts in goal striving as a good start, a trial run on a course of lifetime achievement. You can develop a sense of direction that will lead to lifelong success by observing these pointers:

1. *Be aware.* Your mind is like a parachute: it only works when it's open. Be alert to choices that are consistent with your goals and develop your action plan accordingly. Use your creative imagination and other right-brain states for insight into directions you might take. Be aware

of changes in your environment and within yourself that might affect your goals. Keep apprised of social and educational institutions, counseling services, libraries, computer bulletin boards and other resources that can help you avoid "information overload," steer a path through the maze of choices and choose the directions in which you want to go.

2. *Be opportunity-focused.* Be prepared to move in new directions as change requires. Firm up your action plan by checking into opportunities for continuing education. Use the techniques described in this book to keep you confident that you can decisively embrace whatever changes may come your way.

3. *Strive for one-percent changes instead of 100-percent changes.* If you try to improve your success by one hundred percent overnight, you'll end up frustrated. Instead, try to improve by one percent in a hundred different ways. Take your checkbook to your dental appointment and balance it while you wait to be called. Carry your to-do list with you and seize a bit of time to complete one simple project. Do your Exercycling while waiting to transfer your laundry from washer to dryer. Buy a lot of birthday cards at once; stamp and address them and file them in your tickler file under the appropriate month and date. Make a list of the one-percent improvements you can make and *acknowledge* yourself whenever you accomplish one.

4. *Learn to manage change so that it doesn't manage you.* In *The Age Of Unreason*, Charles Handy noted that people used to see change as a long continuous line. It was predictable, and therefore it could be planned for. In the future, however, change is likely to be discontinuous and to reveal no pattern. Be prepared for this inevitability. Don't simply drift along; have a backup plan. If you've learned how to "fake it till you make it," you're one step ahead of the game.

Understanding: The Art of Two-Way Communication

Do you remember the old children's game of "gossip" or "telephone"? You sat in a circle. Someone whispered a phrase to the person on her right. He then repeated what he heard to the person on his right, and so on around the circle. By the time the message got back to the person who originated it, it was hopelessly garbled, and everyone dissolved in a giggling fit.

Great fun, wasn't it? The trouble is that communication between adults too often resembles a game of telephone. The message sent is not always the message received. "Most of our failures in human relations," Maltz wrote, "are due to 'misunderstandings.'... We should remember [that] no one reacts to 'things as they are,' but to his own mental images."

The precise conveying and receiving of information is becoming more elusive every year. Fax machines, electronic mail, answering machines, fiber optics, and other technologies have served to speed communication at the expense of understanding. Remember, only about seven percent of communication is verbal. The rest of the message is conveyed through tone quality and body language. In our "information age," as human contact becomes less and less a factor in communication the potential for misunderstanding mounts.

Strive for Mutual Understanding

How about those situations in which communication *is* verbal and direct? In the workplace, the tendency as we head into the 21st century is away from management from above and toward self-managed teams. This trend increases the burden on us to understand each other. In the traditional workplace the old adage applies: "When your boss says 'Jump,' you say 'How high?'" If his message is ambiguous, you have only one individual's ambiguity to interpret. But when you're a member of a self-managed team, the path to success must meander through a great deal of mutual understanding. If Mona sounds abrasive when she's presenting her ideas, Bob may take it as a personal affront—not for reasons that have anything to do with Mona or her message but because her tone pushes his buttons. If Bob makes an offhand reference to some woman as a "girl," Mona may decide right then and there that he's a sexist pig and refuse to consider his message at all. Ed takes offense at Carl's irritability, Jim interprets Carol's failure to make eye contact as a sign of insincerity, Lana observes two co-workers breaking off their conversation as she walks into a room and concludes they were gossiping about her. There are a hundred ways in which failure to understand can turn a self-managed team into a self-sabotaging team.

And what about that other "self-managed team" in your life—your family? "My wife/husband doesn't understand me" has been a familiar refrain since Adam and Eve were tossed out of the garden, but now Deborah Tannen informs us (in *You Just Don't Understand*) that men and women have substantially different communication styles. What seems to be a clear message to one sex can mean something radically different to the other. In today's typical family-on-the-run, success in our personal relationships can depend on taking time to make sure we have understood spouse and children and fully conveyed our message.

Develop Respect for Diversity

According to *Workforce 2000*, only 15 percent of the new entrants to the American job market between 1987 and 2000 were expected to be white males. In 1960, few Americans had the occasion to relate with people of other races or sexes on a basis of equality, either socially or professionally. In today's "salad bowl" culture, respect for diversity is an essential prerequisite for success. Often a poor self-image lies at the root of cultural oppression—pride in race can be the last refuge of someone who subconsciously feels he or she has nothing else to be proud of. But while relatively few of us are out-and-out racists, diversity can often interfere with understanding. Failure to understand may take the form of stereotyping ("Of course Ilana Chiu is hard to get to know; she's Chinese—equals INSCRUTABLE") or a perception of stereotyping ("Why did he start talking to me about Michael Jordan? Because I'm African American, he assumes I care about basketball?—equals RACIST"). But it may just as often come as a result of differences in perception. A white OB-GYN was speaking about prenatal care to an audience of expectant mothers, most of whom were immigrants from Central America. She sought to defuse any uneasiness or mistrust they might be feeling by opening her talk with a self-deprecating joke. Wrong move—in their culture, people tend to react to this type of humor with embarrassment. The doctor spent the rest of the meeting trying to win back her audience's respect. A man from South Carolina was transferred by his company to its Los Angeles office. He couldn't understand why his female colleagues reacted negatively to his compliments on their appearance and other acts of "courtly gallantry" until someone took him aside and told him that in Los Angeles such behavior was considered sexist. Success today often depends on having the awareness to prevent such misunderstandings from occurring. Understand and respect these "cultural buttons," and you'll be less likely to push them.

Prescription: Promote Success Through Creative Listening

"Adopt the motto, 'It doesn't matter who's right but what's right,'" Maltz advised. Remember that an automatic guidance system works by using data from negative feedback to correct its course. Raise your level of understanding and your success potential by following these suggestions:

1. *Show respect.* "The primary way we show respect to others," observed the California Task Force, "is to step out of the state of anxious self-concern long enough to give others our attention—to listen, to understand, to care." Try to hear and appreciate what the other person is saying instead of reacting to the way it makes you feel. You'll be surprised at how much more information you receive if you actually listen instead of just thinking, "He's wrong." Actively try to understand the other person's point of view. Don't assume that she's "stupid" or "contrary" or "insensitive" or "just doing it to annoy me." She may be thinking the same thing about you.

2. *Separate fact from opinion.* All too often we create misunderstanding by adding our opinion to fact and being unable to tell them apart. The problem arises in our subconscious mind, that plodding old horse that reacts to our opinions just as if they were facts. "Elaine's memo sounded terse" is a fact. "She must be really ticked off at me" is an

243

opinion. "*Who does she think she is?*" is a reaction—and not one that's conducive to success.

3. *Be honest with yourself.* Be willing to admit your mistakes. Denial, rationalization, and blame-casting may make you feel better, but they will never lead to success. Take the bad news about yourself along with the good—your new self-image can handle it. Just sow SEEDS and go forward.

4. *Learn to share information.* Contribute to the other person's success by maximizing *his* chance of understanding *you.* Don't hoard essential information. It may give you a transient feeling of power, but it does not contribute to the understanding that leads to success.

⊞ Courage: A Prerequisite for Creating Change

"The illiterate of the future," Alvin Toffler tells us, "are not those who can't read and write but those that cannot learn, unlearn, and re-learn." To learn, to grow, to move forward from patterns that have become comfortable and secure requires courage—the willingness to take risks, to make decisions, to take the action needed to translate goals and desires into realities.

Most of us live according to the rule "the evil we know is better than the evil we don't know." Change can be terrifying; old habits can be comforting even when we acknowledge that we want to change. We stay stuck in dull, dead-end jobs because they provide security. We seek out relationships for their familiarity and comfort value, not recognizing the pattern we're in but concluding after each unhappy experience that "men (or women) are all alike." We fail to confront an abusive person because we fear that a change in the nature of the relationship might be worse than the pain of the abuse.

We do not develop a success-type personality by standing still. The California Task Force concluded that we can grow, solve problems, and discover the potential within ourselves only by "[d]eveloping the courage to explore new thoughts, behavior, and possibilities, to take appropriate risks, and to venture out across 'safe boundaries.'"

In *Megatrends 2000* Naisbitt and Aburdene conjectured, "The great unifying theme at the conclusion of the 20th century is the triumph of the individual.... It is an individual who creates a work of art, embraces a political philosophy, bets a life's savings on a new business, inspires a colleague or family member to succeed, emigrates to a new country, has a transcendent spiritual experience.... Individuals today can leverage change far more effectively than most institutions."

Acknowledge Your Small Acts of Courage

Courage does not have to mean being a hero in a moment of crisis. It can mean acting boldly in the "little things," such as pursuing your goals when faced with opposition from without and within. It can mean being willing to make mistakes and risk ridicule. It can mean consciously choosing new behavior. It can mean "leveraging change."

A woman with a high-school education and few job skills, married for eight years to an abusive husband, takes the kids and moves to a halfway house for battered women, determined to create a new life for herself and her family. A man whose children are grown gives up a successful law practice to pursue an old dream of becoming a cabaret pianist. An employee chooses to confront her boss when she recognizes that he is pursuing a policy that compromises the integrity of the company and the safety of the workers. A manager, recognizing that his policy of "my way or the highway" has led to a stifling of creativity and low morale, makes a personal apology to his employees and pledges a new policy of openness and respect.

These are all courageous acts.

Prescription: Dare to Take Risks

"Be willing to make a few mistakes, to suffer a little pain to get what you want," Maltz wrote. "Don't sell yourself short." Expanding on his advice, here are some tips for developing the sort of courage that leads to success:

1. *Assess your "courage quotient."* Review your goals. Identify areas that will involve taking risks. Assess ways that you can combine your commitment to your goals with the courage necessary to follow through. Instead of settling on an image of yourself as a stand-patter, visualize and focus on times in the past when you achieved success by taking risks. You've never taken a risk in your life, you say? What about that decision to have a baby even when you knew you were likely to be laid off your job? What about the time you tried out for the high-school play? These were decisions that took *courage.* Write down some practical ways in which you can use the techniques you've learned in this book to expand your capacity for taking risks.

2. *Recognize that fear is often an illusion.* By now you're wise to the ways your subconscious mind can convince you that what you're imagining must be true. Often we respond fearfully to unknown situations simply because we *imagine* that they pose risks. Not every molehill is a mountain; not every small challenge is a life-or-death situation. That's why I find it useful to think of FEAR as an acronym—for False Evidence Appearing Real. The horse whinneys, tosses its head and paws at the ground. The rider needs to recognize that the occasion calls for problem-solving, not panic.

3. *Learn to respond decisively to crises.* Nothing can more effectively make you feel courageous than knowing you've mastered crisis situations in the past. One way to maximize your chances of performing well under pressure is to "practice without pressure" in the theater of your imagination, the same way you learn any new habit. Maltz compared this procedure to a fire drill, by which people learn emergency escape routes by practicing when there is no fire. If your horse learns to follow a path out of the woods when all is safe, it is far more likely to find that path when the woods are on fire. And once you've known the feeling of success that comes from a courageous response, you will be far more willing to take risks in the future.

⊞ Charity: Another Word for Respect

"Successful personalities have some interest in and regard for other people," Maltz wrote. "They have a respect for other's problems and needs. They respect the dignity of the human personality and deal with other people as if they were human beings, rather than as pawns in their own game. They recognize that every person is a child of God and is a unique individuality [who] deserves some dignity and respect."

The California Task Force echoed Maltz in its assertion that "Every human being deserves to be recognized as a unique and valuable individual. To see and appreciate the contribution each of us makes to other people and the world, we need to acknowledge [that e]very one of us has unique gifts...and each of us matters.... The importance of accepting and appreciating people as they are cannot be exaggerated. This includes accepting each person's feelings, thought, body, mind, and spirit. It also includes appreciating people's individual and cultural differences. We must make sure that we do not require others to deny or disown their real selves to earn our approval or love."

Further Your Own Success by Furthering Others'

Developing such an attitude is a necessary consequence of enhancing your self-image—and vice-versa. Your feelings about yourself are inextricably bound up with your feelings about others. If you don't respect your own worth and importance, you're going to find it difficult to acknowledge anyone else's. And if you frequently find yourself judging and condemning others for their opinions, attitudes and "errors," it's probably a sign that you don't think much of your own worthiness either. The old Quaker who remarked to his wife, "All the world is queer except for thee and me, and sometimes I think thee is a little queer" may have talked himself into American folklore, but chances are he led a lonely, unsatisfying life. Acknowledging other people's "real selves" is a sign of a positive self-image—and a key to a success-type personality.

Which attitude do you think is more likely to further your own success—"She's probably after my job—why should I help her do hers?" or "If I give her some advice, we'll all get along better"?

—"What a screw-up he is!" or "We all make mistakes"?

—"That is the most disagreeable person I've ever met! I wouldn't lend him a shovel to dig his own grave!" or "He's sure in a lousy mood. I know what it's like to go around feeling negative about everything."

—"She's lazy!" or "I wonder what it would take to motivate her"?

—"She's got her head buried in the past!" or "Her attitudes and values are different than mine"?

—"He's *weird!*" or "His attitudes and values are different than mine"?

—"Who am I, Mother Teresa? I've got to take care of *me!*" or "'If I am for myself alone, what am I'"?

Even the nature of individualism today is moving away from "enlightened self-interest" and toward a more altruistic, world-wide view that can only be described as charitable. According to the authors of *Megatrends 2000,* "The individualism of the future is not an 'every man for himself' type of individualism, gratifying one's desires for their own sake and to hell with everyone else. It is an ethical philosophy that elevates the individual to the global level; we are all responsible for preserving the environment, preventing nuclear warfare, eliminating poverty. Individualism, however, *does* recognize that that individual energy matters." Make sure that your formula for success includes allowing your "individual energy" to make a positive difference in the world.

Prescription: Recognize That "Every You Is an I"

As with all else in Psycho-Cybernetics, building charity into your personality is a matter of habit. Here are some ideas for developing such habits:

1. *Respect individuality.* Any time you find yourself reacting negatively to another person, remind yourself that he or she is a unique individual—a "child of God," whether you consider that idea in a literal or a humanistic sense. Make a habit of CANCELing your negative feelings about others the same as you do negative feelings about yourself. Consider that the attitudes and behavior you're reacting to are probably a result of someone's poor self-image—and think of how far *you've* had to come.

2. *Consider the other person's feelings, needs and point of view.* Whether your guiding principle is "You cannot know another man until you have walked a mile in his moccasins" or "Do unto others as you would have them do unto you," show your regard for the innate worth of others. "A true appreciation of the worth of others will lead us...to deeds through which we treat others with dignity and respect," the California Task Force reported. "We do not discover our own worth by comparing ourselves to other people.... All of us have equal value as human beings."

3. *Get involved.* "In addition to your purely personal goals," Maltz suggested, "have at least one impersonal goal—or "cause" which you can identify yourself with...not out of a sense of duty, but because you *want* to." Find and commit yourself to a program for helping others—feeding the homeless, protecting the environment, volunteering at a hospice for people with AIDS, anything that requires you to give of yourself. Throwing some unwanted clothing in a box for the Salvation Army to pick up doesn't count.

⊞ Esteem: The Keystone of Success

"Of all the traps and pitfalls in life," Maltz wrote, "self-*dis*esteem is the deadliest, and the hardest to overcome; for it is a pit designed and dug by our own hands, summed up in the phrase, 'It's no use—I can't do it.'"

We've been examining self-esteem throughout this book, and by now you're aware of its fundamental importance. Having a low opinion of yourself is not "modesty"—it's self-destruction. Holding your uniqueness in high regard is not "egotism"—it's a necessary precondition to happiness and success.

In fact we've been so persistent about emphasizing self-esteem that it's a good idea at this point to acknowledge that it's not "the" answer to every human need. If you think of "feeling good about yourself" as a prescription that's going to solve all the problems of the universe, of course you're going to be disappointed. Self-esteem alone is not going to get you a better job, lead to romance, induce you to lose 40 pounds, help your children get better grades, improve the productivity of your company, end crime, poverty and oppression or get your brother-in-law to stop borrowing money. The crucial thing to remember is that *without* self-esteem, the *potential* for achieving these goals as individuals and as a society just isn't there. Self-esteem is not a universal solution. It just may be a universal foundation for a multitude of solutions.

Prescription: Make Psycho-Cybernetics a Permanent Part of Your Life

And how do you achieve self-esteem? You've probably guessed this one: follow the principles and techniques of Psycho-Cybernetics! Stay on top of them by frequently reviewing the key points in this book. Maintain your awareness of your worth and importance by observing these practices diligently:

1. Make CRAFT a part of your daily life whenever you discover "pockets" of poor self-esteem that are keeping you from achieving a success-type personality.
2. Sow SEEDS whenever you discover that you're allowing yourself to evaluate a situation in a way that negatively impacts your self-esteem.

⊞ Self-Confidence: Keeping That Goal Within Reach

Some years ago I was working with autistic children whose behavior was self-destructive. We would reward them with fruit or other small tokens every time they mimicked any positive behavior we were demonstrating. If we could get a headbanger, for example, to stop for even ten seconds, we rewarded him.

Psychologists call this procedure "shaping," or "successful approximation to the goal." Sometimes we more-or-less normal adults could benefit from such shaping. Belief in yourself as a confident, competent human being is the cornerstone of success. Yet as you know, many of our experiences serve to undermine our self-confidence. Too often we tend to forget our successes and dwell on our failures. Keep negative thoughts from undermining your faith in your abilities by keeping your goals in front of you. Any small step you take toward your goal helps shape your self-confidence and point you toward success. Be clear, focused, dedicated and committed. Adopt a "Why not me?" attitude to replace such old childhood tapes as "Who do you think you are?" and "Don't get too big for your britches." Give yourself a mental pat on the back every time you risk something new. As Maltz put it, "*It doesn't matter* how many times you have failed in the past. What matters is the successful attempt, which should be remembered, reinforced, and dwelt upon."

Prescription: Remember Yourself as Successful

The art of self-confidence begins with clear images of success. Use your goals and your past successes as guideposts to future success by observing these principles:

1. *Let imagined success become real success.* The subconscious mind—all together now—cannot tell the difference between a real experience and one that is vividly imagined. By painting a vivid picture of success in your mind, you practice recognizing and gaining what you want. Focus on your goal. *Be patient:* trust that the link between your conscious and subconscious minds will bring about your desired outcome. Be open to receiving gifts from unexpected sources— "manna from heaven."

2. *Learn from your disappointments.* Everybody fails sometimes. The important thing to remember is that the success-type personality doggedly refuses to acknowledge failure. Learn to see failure as a

stepping stone to success, an indication that you're trying something new and different. Consider each mistake as a guidepost to approaching the situation differently next time.

3. *Focus on your past successes.* Every time you hear yourself berating yourself for failure, remember a time you were successful. It's all too easy to forget the goals you've achieved in the past. And when you fail to appreciate your successes, it's all too easy to dwell on your failures. "Self-confidence comes out of a balance for striving for new achievements with ongoing recognition of your existing strengths," Terry Paulson advises us. "...The trouble with goal-setting and achievement as the only source of self-confidence is that you never arrive.... Our victories are easily forgotten; the skills we use in achieving them we easily take for granted.... We possess them, but we no longer experience them.... [W]e no longer count them as significant. Don't get complacent about your successes, but don't discount them, either. Continue to set new goals that allow you to grow, but take time regularly to...catch the things that make you effective."

4. *Let success build on success.* "Confidence is built on an experience of success," Maltz wrote. "...It is literally true that success breeds success. Even a small success can be used as a stepping stone to a greater one." When I began my career as a speaker, my first payment for a presentation came in the form of reimbursement for gasoline. It came to $12.72, and I *still* see it as an important step. I drove home that day thinking, "Well, I got paid, didn't I? Now I'm really a professional speaker!"

5. *Watch out for crabs.* Beware of people who try to undermine your self-confidence by ridiculing your efforts. In most cases these are people who lack self-confidence themselves. They see no possibility of building themselves up, so they try to maintain parity with you by keeping you down. In his book *The Power To Create*, Philip Aaron called such people "crabs in a barrel.... As soon as one tries to climb out, the others reach up and pull it back down." There are a few crabs in every barrel. Make sure they don't pull *you* down.

6. *Be open to your true feelings.* Knowing and expressing who you are can go a long way toward making you feel confident. "Being open, telling the truth, and being authentic enrich our being in the world," the California Task Force observed. "We can share our positive feelings

of love, attraction, joy, relief and excitement as well as sharing our anger, hurt, pain, sadness, grief, and fear. By honoring our true feelings, we can be in harmony with what we say, how we feel, and how we act."

⊞ Self-Acceptance: Acknowledging Your Worth

The cornerstone of happiness is accepting yourself as a worthy human being. "The most miserable and tortured people in the world," Maltz wrote, "are those who are continually straining and striving to convince themselves and others that they are something other than what they basically are. And there is no relief or satisfaction like that that comes when one finally gives up the shams and pretenses and is willing to be himself."

It can be the greatest challenge to accept ourselves in a nonjudgmental manner. "God grant me the serenity to accept the things I cannot change, the courage to change the things I can and the wisdom to know the difference," Reinhold Niebuhr said, and his advice has been adopted as a watchword by any number of self-help programs. The trouble, as we've been emphasizing, lies in the wisdom part of the formula. Our subconscious mind "accepts," serenely or otherwise, everything our conscious mind tells it is so. Instead of accepting our mistakes and using them as stepping stones to success, we tend to internalize and define ourselves by our mistakes. Is this wisdom?

Self-acceptance does not mean striving to be someone we're not or becoming "serene" about failure. "Accepting ourselves does not discount the need for change and growth," the California Task Force maintained. "Just the opposite: it is the first step we take when we want to change. We can decide to do something differently only after we accept who we are, where we are, and that we are capable of change.... The point is not to become acceptable or worthy, but to acknowledge the worthiness that already exists. Our feelings are part of this, and accepting them builds our self-esteem: 'I accept my feelings, and I accept myself.' In turn, this lets us accept more responsibility in our lives: 'I know

I feel this way, and I can choose how to behave. I don't have to blame anybody else.'"

It's the difference between the person who says "Life stinks" and the person who says "I appreciate exactly what my present reality is, but that doesn't mean I'll settle for it forever." It's the difference between the unskilled single mother who thinks "I'm the most abject, worthless person on this earth" and sinks into substance abuse and dependency, and the unskilled single mother who thinks "Today is as grim as it gets, but I have it in my power to create a different tomorrow."

Prescription: Know What It Means to Be Human

Success through self-acceptance, according to Maltz, "means accepting and coming to terms with ourselves now, just as we are, with all our faults, weaknesses, shortcomings, errors as well as our assets and strengths.... We must learn to recognize our mistakes and shortcomings before we can correct them." To help bring about this recognition, follow these guidelines:

1. *Appreciate your creative power.* Creative expression, whatever form it may take, enhances our feeling of individuality and personal worth. It gives us the power to say realistically, "I'm not doomed to this present condition. I'm a human being, which means I can find a creative way to (earn more money, establish better relations with my spouse, resolve this conflict with Rita at the office)." Learn to acknowledge and cultivate your own creative power, whether it expresses itself through painting a picture, developing a marketing campaign, planning a special day with your children, facilitating harmony between feuding co-workers or rearranging the storage space in your kitchen. "We are all creative workers," Maltz taught us.

2. *Appreciate your body.* The California Task Force reflected that, "To be ashamed of our bodies or to refuse to accept them takes away from our wholeness as human beings, just as much as if we were ashamed of our spirits or our minds." I first became aware of how closely self-acceptance is tied in with appreciation of our physical bodies when working with obese people in a medical fasting program. One of the hardest tasks I had as a psychotherapist was helping these

people to appreciate their worthiness. Value and respect your senses, your physical capabilities, your health, and your sexuality. You'll find that an appreciation of your physical nature is an important component of self-esteem and the enjoyment of life.

3. *Appreciate your spirituality.* You're not *just* a mind and a body—you're a creature of spirit. Many people associate spirituality with religion, but the idea is broader than that. It's the way you experience yourself in relationship with everything outside you, and as such it ties in directly with your self-image. When you're in touch with your spiritual side, your subconscious and conscious minds are synchronized in appreciation of your essential worthiness. Your horse can't be mired in the swamp while your rider is focused on the mountaintop. Whether or not you're grounded in traditional religious belief, whether your approach is through prayer, meditation, an appreciation of nature or by any other path, cultivating your spirituality is a key to appreciating your value as a human being.

4. *Challenge negative self-thoughts rigorously.* Be constantly aware of false, negative beliefs about yourself that erode self-acceptance. By now you're well aware of the power false beliefs have over your attitudes and behavior when they're embedded in your subconscious mind. Use CRAFT regularly to cast out those negative thoughts that undermine your success.

5. *Develop "character ethics."* We all give lip service to "traditional values," but how many of us consider what values are really "traditional," let alone how they may contribute to success? In *The Seven Habits Of Highly Effective People,* Stephen Covey discusses the shift away from the "psychological ethics" (do your own thing, grab all the success you can, etc.) which emerged in our culture during the 20th century, back to the "character ethics" (self-restraint, moderation, etc.) of our country's founders. As a young man Benjamin Franklin wrote a list of thirteen "key virtues" he wished to develop in himself and concentrated on one per week, running through the list four times each year until they had become habits. Talk about "Fake it till you make it"! Franklin's "key virtues" represent a blueprint of values developed in 18th-century New England and Pennsylvania (industry, justice, temperance, sincerity, humility, etc.) but the general principle they express is that those who cannot control their negative tendencies will

inevitably be controlled *by* them. By making a habit of "character ethics," you can develop the inner strength necessary for success.

▦ Drawing Your Own Picture of Success

"Our...goals are like orchards: the more energy we put into them, the more they bear fruit," the California Task Force observed. "We need goals that are appropriate and attainable... Setting our own goals reflects our self-esteem: 'I want to grow in my own direction, and I am capable of making competent and responsible progress as I learn.' It is important to know that we are not on earth to live up to someone else's expectations."

And that is as an appropriate definition of success as you could want: "to grow in my own direction, and to make competent and responsible progress as I learn." Think about the directions you want to grow in. Consider each of the seven elements of SUCCESS in the context of your own goals. Be open to your thoughts and feelings. Consider which of these qualities you already possess and which you'll need to acquire to keep moving along your own path to success.

Targeting on Ideas

- A "success-type personality" will empower you to set and achieve worthwhile goals throughout your lifetime.
- You can take specific measures to acquire the elements of a success-type personality: sense of direction, understanding, courage, charity, esteem, self-confidence and self-acceptance.

SET YOUR OWN TARGETS

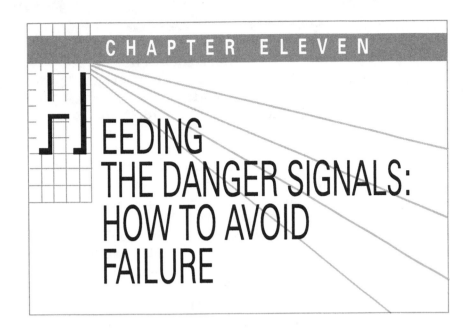

CHAPTER ELEVEN

HEEDING THE DANGER SIGNALS: HOW TO AVOID FAILURE

No one is immune to...negative feelings and attitudes.... The important thing is to recognize them for what they are, and take positive action to correct course.

—*Maxwell Maltz,* Psycho-Cybernetics *(1960)*

Learned helplessness could be cured by showing the subject his own actions would now work [and] by teaching the subject to think differently about what caused him to fail. It could be prevented if, before the experience with helplessness occurred, the subject learned that his actions made a difference.

—*Martin E. P. Seligman, Ph.D.,* Learned Optimism *(1991)*

259

The new job was going to be a snap, Frederika figured. She was 36 years old and had just been promoted to a managerial position at Hayden Electronics. She'd started out four years ago on the assembly line and quickly made shop foreman. Now she would be supervising the new foreman as well as seven assemblers. Frederika had no engineering background and only a few college credits, but her boss Phil assured her that this was no problem. "There's no one better qualified for this position than you," he assured her, "and Noah [*his* boss] agrees with me 100 percent." All but one of her staff were men, but this was no problem either. Frederika had learned to relate to them during her years on the line, and she was comfortable with their gruff, outspoken way with one another. At once she developed her own plan to meet a goal of accelerated productivity. "Okay, listen up, you guys," she told them, "Here's the deal—Phil and Noah are sold on the team approach, so the team approach is what we'll give 'em. I know it's not exactly S.O.P. around here, but if you just grin and bear it you'll all get used to it. Okay? Okay! Let's go!"

From the start nothing seemed to go right. Her people seemed unresponsive and cool to her efforts. They nudged each other and rolled their eyes during her pep talks. "I guess they can't accept a woman as boss," she told herself resentfully. Phil gave her a folder of articles on management that he urged her to read, and he suggested she take a seminar on supervision skills for new managers. "What is he telling me—I'm not doing my job?" she said to herself. "Didn't he and Noah tell me I was qualified? I'm doing it by the book. I've implemented the new plan, and I'm taking responsibility to make sure everyone follows through. What's Phil's problem? He must feel threatened—he's afraid I'm going to show him up." When Ruth, the other woman in the department, suggested that she might be coming on a little strong, Frederika's reply was, "Look, thanks for your advice, but I know what I'm doing, okay? I know these guys; you've got to club 'em hard to get their attention." Ruth had been her frequent lunchtime companion, but now whenever Frederika suggested they eat together she seemed to have other plans. "They're jealous,"

Frederika decided. "It's nothing but plain old jealousy. Guess it comes with the territory." When Ruth announced that she was leaving for another job, Frederika wished her well and promptly hired a replacement.

After three months Frederika was called into Phil's office for her first performance review. On the plus side, he told her, she was prompt and efficient at filing reports, the plan she had initiated looked like a winner, and she had successfully hired and trained Ruth's replacement. On the minus side, she hadn't discussed with Phil the articles he'd given her, nor had she enrolled in the seminar he recommended. More of a problem were her people skills: Ruth had left, Phil informed her, because she felt Frederika talked down to her; and several of the other assemblers had complained that she was pushing the idea of teamwork down their throats. As a result morale and productivity had declined, and Noah had expressed "disappointment."

Phil shook Frederika's hand and told her he had faith in her abilities and would be happy to work with her in her problem areas. Nevertheless Frederika was angry. Why had they all turned against her? Ruth had never said anything to *her* about "talking down." None of the workers had ever complained to *her* about her managerial style. Hadn't she pursued the team approach at Phil's request? Why was it her fault that they resisted it?

Old tapes were whirring in Frederika's subconscious mind: "You're an impostor.... You don't have the smarts to be a manager.... They're all going to find out.... Nobody likes a person who talks down to them.... *Know your place*." Despite Phil's reassurances, Frederika began to fear for her job. She couldn't issue an instruction without worrying how the workers were taking it. She couldn't make a decision without wondering whether Phil and Noah would approve. She found herself feeling resentful—of Phil, Noah and the men who worked for her but also of her mother who had been unable to teach her any workplace survival skills, of "the system" that made things so difficult for women in supervisory positions, of people who made demands on her time. She dreaded going to work, but away from the job she felt bored and restless, wandering her apartment from room to room looking for "something to do." There was no goal, no matter how small, that seemed worth pursuing. Nothing in her life seemed to bring her enjoyment any more. She began to feel self-conscious whenever she was among people. She began "eating out of control" and soon could no longer fit into her clothes.

Frederika is a classic illustration of what Maxwell Maltz called the *failure mechanism*. She's a not-too-extreme example of what can happen when your automatic guidance system fails to respond correctively to negative events. She made a few mistakes, as we all do; but instead of letting feedback guide her back on course, she veered so wildly *off* course that she lost sight of her goal. It was only after she learned to recognize her negative responses as danger signals that she was able to respond to feedback in a positive way, deactivate her failure mechanism and achieve success.

"Steam boilers have pressure gauges that show when the pressure is reaching the danger point," Maltz wrote. "By recognizing the potential danger, corrective action can be taken....The failure-type personality also has its [danger signals]. We need to be able to recognize these failure symptoms in ourselves so that we can do something about them.... We need to recognize them as "undesirables," as things which we do not want, and most important of all to convince ourselves deeply and sincerely that these things do not bring happiness."

This chapter is about those danger signals and how you can use them to correct your own course. You'll learn:

- the seven warning signals that comprise the "failure mechanism."
- how to recognize when each of these signals is negatively impacting your self-image and deflecting progress toward your goal.
- how to use feedback to point you back on course toward success.

Just as Maltz used an acronym to enumerate the personality elements that lead to success, he used a similar acronym to illustrate the failure mechanism:

F-rustration
A-ggressiveness
I-nsecurity
L-oneliness
U-ncertainty
R-esentment
E-mptiness

As with the famous "seven warning signals of cancer," these negative attitudes and behavior patterns do not *necessarily* indicate a problem. By paying attention to them, we can act to keep a problem from developing. "We can cure these failure symptoms," Maltz wrote, "...by understanding—by being able to "see" that they do not work.... And when we can see the truth, then the same instinctive forces which caused us to adopt them in the first place, will work in our behalf in eradicating them." Let's see how each of these elements serves as a warning of failure and what steps you can take to avoid them.

Frustration: The First "Red Flag"

Frustration isn't necessarily a bad thing. It's a reminder that there's a goal you're not reaching or a desire that can't be immediately satisfied—and that's good. Without the essential tension of frustration we'd have little motivation to pursue our goals and desires. "A man's reach should exceed his grasp, or what's a heaven for?" It was frustration that led you to seek change in your life. It was frustration that led you to pick up this book.

Frustration makes your goals *less* likely to be attained only when you fail to respond to it as a warning signal. In Frederika's case, it led her to conclude that her subordinates and her boss were jealous of her success. Instead of using the workers' resistance, Ruth's coolness and Phil's suggestions as guideposts for course correction, she chose to throw ownership of the problem onto them. Eventually her sense of futility led to a loss of self-esteem.

Frustration may result from several sources. You may be striving for perfection instead of realistic results. A negative self-image may keep you habitually thinking that you're not worthy of success. Your subconscious mind may be playing an old childhood tape that tells you "someone" will take care of your needs. Of course as an adult your rider recognizes that there's no "Mommy," no Santa Claus or fairy godmother who's going to come along and meet your goals for you. But what path is your horse following when you expect that "something will turn up," when you blame "the system" for not solving your problems, when you find yourself on the "pity pot"?

Your Frustration Index: A Questionnaire

The first step toward eradicating frustration is to recognize when you're experiencing it. Answer the assessment questions below. Then note the ones to which you answered "yes" and let the corresponding reminders guide you toward corrective action.

ASSESSMENT	CORRECTIVE ACTION
Do you frequently awaken with an urgent feeling that there are things you *have* to do today? ❏ yes ❏ no	Recognize that there are few things in life that you *have* to do. There are many things that you may *choose* to do. Use your daily and weekly to-do lists to prove to yourself that you almost always have a choice and that you are indeed prioritizing and making choices.
Do you find yourself fulfilling obligations grudgingly? ❏ yes ❏ no	Upgrade your obligations to choices. You don't *have* to spend Thanksgiving with Aunt Lucretia and Uncle Adolf. You *choose* to do so in order to accommodate your spouse. It's a trade-off.
Do you often feel that nothing you do seems to make a difference? ❏ yes ❏ no	Again, use a realistic to-do list as you tackle any project. Check off items as you complete them as a reminder that you *are* getting things done.

ASSESSMENT	CORRECTIVE ACTION
Do you feel that you have "lost heart" regarding pursuit of your goals? ❑ yes ❑ no	Use the SMART method to reevaluate your goal. It might just be it needs some adjustment to get you moving again. *Specifically* determine what you can do to feel better about the project—*e.g.,* call a friend; brainstorm with a co-worker. Take the *measure* of your progress so far. Evaluate what you've done to "get off the dime"—even if it's only been to get a good night's sleep and take a fresher look. Write an *action plan* for completing the task. Build in some incremental rewards to give yourself as you complete successive phases of the project. Take a *realistic* look at your goal. You may need to make some adjustments. Remind yourself that although your enthusiasm has waned, the project is still doable and you're only taking a breather to reassess. Assure yourself that your goal is still *timely.* Rekindle your enthusiasm by estimating how soon you'll be seeing the light at the end of the tunnel.
Do you often have a feeling of "damned if I do, damned if I don't" about your endeavors? ❑ yes ❑ no	Remember that you're just one person. If *any* course will result in frustration, remind yourself that you're pursuing the best course possible *at this time.* Avoid berating yourself for a decision that turned out less than perfectly. Acknowledge that if you had chosen the other way you'd be berating yourself for a different reason. A good motto to remember is, "I did the best I could with what I had at the time."

ASSESSMENT	CORRECTIVE ACTION
Do you find yourself unduly blocked or delayed in pursuit of your goals? ❑ yes ❑ no	Give yourself permission to check your frustration level periodically. Instead of *reacting* to events that seem to be blocking or delaying your goals, make a conscious decision to *act* on them. Grandma was right: there *is* no use crying over spilled milk. Instead of feeling frustrated about the way things have gone in the past, take some action that will have a positive impact on the future.
Do you often tell yourself "I'm not even getting *close* to being caught up"? ❑ yes ❑ no	Remind yourself that you may indeed never catch up but you're doing what's realistically possible.
Do you often feel you are "just spinning your wheels"? ❑ yes ❑ no	"Spinning your wheels" can be a sign that you're in sensory overload—you're trying to accomplish everything at once. Try to take five minutes every hour as a frustration barometer. *Stop, look* and *listen,* just as you did when you were six years old and learning to cross the street by yourself. *Stop* feeling anxious. *Look* at what you're trying to acomplish and evaluate it realistically. *Listen* to your body—is your stomach in a knot, are your fists clenched, are you holding your breath? Take a quick break from your activities to relax and reevaluate.
Do you often feel that people are tugging you in different directions? ❑ yes ❑ no	Give yourself permission to say NO appropriately. It isn't possible to please everyone all the time. Tell people you'll be glad to help them later, but right now your priorities just don't allow for it. Make a point of building bridges to people you turn down—take them to lunch, bring them flowers from your yard—but don't let yourself be frustrated by an unwillingness to say no.

ASSESSMENT	CORRECTIVE ACTION
Has it been more than a few days since your last full-bellied, gut-shaking laugh? ☐ yes ☐ no	Get yourself some laughs. Spend time with a person who makes you laugh, read a humorous book, rent a funny video (or even a silly one), spend an evening at a comedy club.

Aggressiveness: A Consequence of Frustration

"Excessive and misdirected aggression," Maltz wrote, "follows frustration as night follows day." A manager is frustrated in getting her workers to implement a plan; she reacts by calling them stupid and lazy. A worker is refused a raise by his boss; he goes home and yells at his kids. A community is frustrated by poverty and injustice; they loot stores and trash police cars. Such acts may relieve frustration on a short-term basis, but they are clearly counterproductive. Some people will respond to your aggressive behavior by lashing out in kind. Others will sabotage your efforts in more subtle ways. Still others, like Frederika's co-worker Ruth, will withdraw. In the long run aggressiveness does not alleviate frustration, it only increases it.

The secret for avoiding failure lies in changing aggressiveness into assertiveness. Both are strategies for going after what you want, but there the similarity ends. The aggressive personality uses such tactics as yelling, blame-casting, badgering and bullying to go after what he wants with no regard for anyone else. The assertive personality uses a win-win strategy, persuading others that they all want the same thing and allowing them to walk away with their dignity intact. The aggressive personality can only raise her self-esteem relative to others by tearing theirs down. The assertive personality succeeds by raising the self-esteem of the people around her and, by extention, her own.

AGGRESSIVE STANCE	ASSERTIVE STANCE
"Listen up, you guys—we're going to pull together as a team."	"We've got a great opportunity to try something new here, and upper management is in full support."
"She's *your* mother, not mine. Just get dressed and stop grumping at me!"	"I know she's difficult at times, but she's getting older, and we'll both feel better if we stop by."
"I only have two hands! Can't you do anything for yourself?"	"I'm very busy, so please understand that I can't help you right now."
"Why do I bother to do a good job—nobody here notices anyway!"	"Let's make a pact to reinforce each other to keep our morale up."
"What's the matter—you got mashed potatoes for brains?"	"I don't think you understood what I was asking for. Let me explain."

How to Change Aggressive Behavior to Assertive Behavior

Anyone can tell the difference between assertiveness and aggressiveness—as long as its someone else's behavior. When it's our own, we often have trouble telling them apart. We ignore feedback unless it takes the form of a punch in the nose. Use these questions to help you recognize whether your strategy for getting what you want from others tends to be aggressive.

1. *Pay attention to your body language.* Do you get your point across by thrusting your finger at the other person or placing your hands on your hips? Do you drum your fingers on the desk when someone else is speaking? Do you notice yourself squinting or rolling your eyes, pursing your lips or frowning when listening to others present their ideas?

2. *Pay attention to your voice.* Do you tend to talk louder than usual when trying to wrest compliance from someone else? Do you choose words

that sound like a critical parent ("You should have known better")? Do you affect a tone that can be interpreted as condescending? Is there a sense of demanding rather than requesting? If you were on the receiving end of your communication, would you take offense?

3. *Pay attention to other people's body language and facial expressions.* Do they draw back from you, raise their eyebrows, or display other signs of offense or intimidation?

4. *Pay attention to your words.* Are you attacking the person instead of the problem? Are you finding fault instead of finding solutions?

If your answers to these questions tend to be "yes," you may be setting yourself up for failure. A pat on the back is only a few vertebrae removed from a kick in the behind, but that short distance can mean the difference between success and failure. Follow these strategies to remain assertive instead of aggressive:

1. *Control your anger.* Even if you're fighting mad, practice releasing your fists, unhinging your jaw and relaxing your facial muscles. Lower your voice and keep some distance between you.

2. *Correct your talk.* If you catch yourself being aggressive, back off and try a different approach: "Sorry, Hank, I don't like the way that sounded. Let me try again." If you suspect after the fact that you were perceived as aggressive, go back and check it out. If guilty, apologize at once.

3. *Use alternatives to aggressive talk.* Say what you mean and mean what you say, but in a nonoffensive manner. Ask yourself at all times whether you would feel comfortable being spoken to in such a manner. Would you feel motivated to go along with the other person's request, or would you be thinking "What a jerk"? Instead of "my way or the highway," try the *fog technique:* "I see your point and I respect your point of view. I'd like to suggest an alternative plan." Another useful strategy is the *broken record,* which we discussed in an earlier chapter: "I know you'd rather let Jack handle this project, but I'm convinced you're better suited for it." Be *hard* on issues but *soft* on people. Instead of "Doug, that's a stupid idea," try "Doug, I don't think that idea will work; let me explain why."

4. *Allow others to disagree.* Let them be vehement if they want to—you have the right to be assertive, and so do they. *Don't* let sleeping dogs lie. If there is unresolved conflict, be willing to do your part in acknowledging at least part ownership of the problem. Focus on solutions to problems instead of hanging someone out to dry: "Okay, we both agree that this could have been handled better. I was indeed late in getting the data to you, and that was glitch number one. I think if you had confronted me about it directly instead of writing a note to Jill, we could have resolved it sooner. Let's both try to be more accountable in the future."

5. *Be sincere. You* can spot a phony a mile away. Give the other person credit for perception too. If you don't *mean* it, don't *say* it.

⊞ Insecurity: When You Keep Hitting Those Curbs

Insecurity results from a feeling of inadequacy, a sense that you are not meeting others' expectations or your own. It can lead to failure because it presents the wrong target for your automatic mechanism. Instead of focusing on a goal, you're watching the curb.

"Not meeting expectations" is a function of your chosen end result. Remember when I asked you to write down your life's most important goal? Remember I warned you not to write "I want to be happy"? If "happiness" is your goal (or "wealth" or "competence" or any other undefined ideal), you're thinking in terms of absolute perfection, and you'll never measure up. But if you're making progress toward a SMART goal, you're *going* to feel happy; you're going to feel *secure* in your awareness that you're moving toward a tangible result.

Your false beliefs can lead you to set unrealistic standards. You feel that you need to attain your goal *right now* or you'll prove yourself incapable of attaining it. "If I can't implement this new team plan, I'm not cut out to be a manager." "If he/she doesn't love me, my life is over." "If I don't get that job, I'll be working in this dead-end position forever."

See how the elements of failure can reinforce each other? When you're frustrated your aggressive behavior, "coming on too strong," can lead to rejection by others. Then you're in for another session with the old negative self-tapes, another round of self-punishment and recrimination, another confirmation that things are never going to be right.

How to Knit Your Own Security Blanket

"Security is mostly a superstition," wrote Helen Keller. "It does not exist in nature.... Life is either a daring adventure or nothing." Recognizing and canceling your feelings of insecurity as they arise will short-circuit the failure mechanism before it can draw you too far off course. Use the left side of the table below as a guide for recognizing your own "insecurity statements." Form the habit of defeating insecurity by repeating the appropriate goal-oriented "secure response" on the right side. Use the last two spaces on each side of the table to write in your own personal "insecurity statements" and the goal-oriented responses you'll use to counter them.

INSECURITY STATEMENT	SECURE RESPONSE
"What if...?"	"So what if...?"
"Suppose...?"	"Suppose what? I don't know anything for sure. Why expect the worst?"
"If only I had..."	"Next time, I'll..."
"If only I hadn't..."	"From now on, I'll..."
"I wonder what might have happened if I'd..."	"I'll never know for sure by agonizing over it. Maybe there's someone I can talk with. Meanwhile I'll continue to do my best."

INSECURITY STATEMENT	SECURE RESPONSE
"I probably did it all wrong."	"If I did, I'll just learn from the feedback and do it right next time.
"They must think I'm an idiot."	"There's no point in blaming myself; I just didn't know. Next time I will."
"If only I had known..."	"I'll choose differently next time this situation comes up."

Loneliness: "Lack of 'Oneness'"

"He who is able to love himself is able to love others also," wrote theologian Paul Tillich; "he who has learned to overcome self-contempt has overcome his contempt for others." The feeling of extreme loneliness, of being cut off from others and unable to accept human contact, is a sure sign that you're cut off from yourself as well. This feeling of isolation, of "lack of 'oneness,'" as Maltz called it, is a sure sign that your failure mechanism is in operation.

Please note: there is nothing wrong with being *alone*. There is nothing symptomatic of failure about *wanting* to be alone or enjoying being alone. You can enjoy your quiet time, read a good book, putter around in the garden, clean out a closet, devote yourself to a creative project or go fishing. When you're *lonely*, you're putting all your energy into feeling sorry for yourself.

"Loneliness," Maltz wrote, "is a way of self-protection. Lines of communication with others—and especially any emotional ties—are cut down. It is a way to protect our idealized self against exposure, hurt, humiliation." This is exactly what happened to Frederika when she allowed her performance review to make her feel insecure about her job. Unwilling to face the possibility that her perception of events did not correspond with reality, she retreated into isolation and despair.

Loneliness—Another Habit You Can Break

How can you tell the difference between loneliness and "being alone"? When you're alone, you feel content. You're productive. Even when you're missing a loved one, you experience a certain "aliveness" in your longing. When you're experiencing the extreme loneliness that is a signpost of failure, you tend to have feelings like these:

- "Poor me!"
- "I'm cut off from everyone."
- "Nobody cares!"
- "Nobody calls me any more!"
- "I have nothing to do!"
- "I'd call Sarah, but she'd probably tell me she's busy."
- "Paul was so evasive when I talked to him—I bet he's having a party this weekend, and he didn't invite me!"
- "I'm so boring nobody wants my company!"

Of course what you really mean is that you're bored with your own company. "This type of loneliness," Maltz wrote, "...is a loneliness from your real self.... The lonely person often sets up a vicious cycle. Because of his feeling of alienation from self, human contacts are not very satisfying, and he becomes a social recluse. In doing so, he cuts himself off from the pathways to finding himself, which is to lose oneself in...activities with other people. Doing things with other people [helps us] become interested in something other than maintaining our own shams and pretenses."

"Lack of oneness," in other words, is simply another negative habit that you can break. Listen to your self-feedback. If you find yourself thinking thoughts like those listed above, take them as a warning. *Force* yourself to be with people. This is another situation in which you have to "act as if"—in this case, "as if" you weren't lonely. Nothing cures loneliness as surely as getting involved. Join an interest group or a team. Go on a hike with your local Sierra Club chapter, take a class in boat building or Chinese cooking, join

273

a bowling league, a bridge club or a book-discussion group, volunteer for work with a charity or social-action organization—just *do something*. It'll help keep you out of the doldrums, and it'll put you back on track for success.

⊞ Uncertainty: When You Put Yourself on the Sideline

"I am not judged by the number of times I fail but by the number of times I succeed," Tom Hopkins reminds us, "and the number of times I succeed is in direct proportion to the number of times I can fail and keep on trying."

Uncertainty is a strategy your horse adopts as a means of avoiding mistakes. It knows it can't get on the wrong path if it never leaves the barn. It's a losing strategy because it inhibits the risk taking, decision making and action that are essential to goal attainment. This is what happened to Frederika when Phil's criticism left her worrying about her every decision. She was so afraid of doing something wrong that she became afraid to do anything at all. Risk taking by definition implies a chance you won't succeed. But if you give in to uncertainty, you're guaranteed not to succeed. "It is in the nature of things that we progress by acting, making mistakes, and correcting course," Maltz wrote. "...You cannot correct your course if you are standing still. You cannot change or correct 'nothing.'"

Uncertainty most often translates itself into procrastination. You put off making a decision or acting on one you've already made. Sometimes you may find yourself using the rationalization, "I'm just waiting for all the evidence to come in." If that's your attitude, recognize that "all the evidence" will *never* be in. You'll always be waiting for that one more item.

Unwillingness to take risks is not the only warning sign of uncertainty. Some people cover it up by taking risks all the time and blaming others when they fail. "This type of person makes decisions," Maltz wrote, "—but he makes them hastily, prematurely and is well-known for going off half-cocked. Making decisions offers him no problem at all. He is perfect. It is impossible for him to be wrong.... He is able to maintain this fiction when his decisions backfire, simply by convincing himself it was someone else's fault." Of course sooner or later such a person is going to run out of scapegoats. Everyone else will see through his fantasy, even if he doesn't. He'll continue on along the path to failure, putting the blame everyplace but where it belongs.

Change Uncertainty into Action

You don't have to be right every time to be a success. If you're right more than half the time, you're beating the odds. If you're wrong zero times out of zero, you haven't made any mistakes—but your score is zero nonetheless. Consider indecisiveness as a warning signal; then take corrective action:

1. *Don't be afraid to make mistakes.* It's important to act decisively when you find yourself inhibited by uncertainty. *Expect* that course corrections will be necessary. Be aware of junctures in your action plan where you can stop, backtrack and change direction.

2. *Challenge procrastination with decisive action.* Review and implement the techniques for overcoming procrastination introduced in chapter 8. Remember that it's not necessary to have all the evidence before you commit yourself. Sometimes it takes a leap of faith. Reassure yourself that you're willing to live with the results—good, bad or indifferent. Then jump in. Remember that "tomorrow is another day" doesn't cut it in today's world. If you don't take that action, someone else will.

3. *Pay attention to feedback.* If you're covering up uncertainty by making a lot of hasty and ill-considered decisions, you'll receive plenty of warning signals. Avoid this path by watching for feedback from others. Do people resist acting on your ideas? Do they walk away shaking their heads and muttering under their breath? If so, approach them and ask whether they feel you've been unfair in handing out blame. Self-feedback is often the most effective feedback. Make a note each time you find yourself rationalizing failure by determining it's someone else's fault. Acknowledge your own mistakes and the uncertainty that

led to them. Put yourself back on course by focusing on decisions you've made that *have* produced successful results.

⊞ Resentment: Anger Gone Rotten

Of all the robbers of personal happiness I've encountered in my professional career, resentment is the worst. Resentment is anger gone rotten. The word literally means *re-feeling*—to keep re-animating that toxic sentiment over and over as if you were Frankenstein and it was your own personal monster.

"When the failure-type personality looks for a scapegoat," Maltz wrote, "...he often blames society, 'the system,' life, the 'breaks.' He resents the success and happiness of others because it is proof to him that life is shortchanging him.... Resentment is an attempt to make our own failure palatable by explaining it in terms of unfair treatment, injustice. But, as a salve for failure, resentment is a cure that is worse than the disease. It is a deadly poison to the spirit, makes happiness impossible, uses up tremendous energy which could go into accomplishment.... [It is] also a 'way' of making us feel important. Many people get a perverse satisfaction from feeling "wronged." The victim of injustice...is morally superior to those who caused the injustice."

When resentment becomes a part of your personality, it becomes like any other habit. Your horse isn't comfortable unless it can feel like a victim. Whenever something goes wrong, it looks around for someone to blame. It *needs* to feel that it's been wronged. And how do you think such a habit affects your self-image? What kind of goals can you achieve if your automatic mechanism is following a program that says I'M A VICTIM? You're letting someone else control your life.

Who is your "someone else"? Whom do you resent—your father, your mother, your ex-wife, your boss, your next-door neighbor? Your sister who was more popular than you? Your friend who always seems to catch the breaks you miss? Anyone who makes more money than you? Anyone whose marriage seems happier than yours? Does your resentment make you feel any better? Of course not. It's like an infected wound that never heals. Do you think Frederika felt any better about her situation by blaming Phil, the workers or "the system"? Frederika began to solve her problems only when she stopped handing out blame for her failure and came to recognize her blame-casting as a *warning* that she was failing. By overcoming her resentments, by recognizing that her actions in the present could do nothing to change the past, she was able to place herself back on the path to success.

Practice Forgiveness—The Antidote to Resentment

The good news is that resentment, like any habit, can be broken. "When we let go of resentment toward ourselves and others," the California Task Force on self-esteem reported, "we are able to live constructively in the present. Forgiving releases us from the burden of hostility that eats away at our energy and self-esteem. Accepting forgiveness from others likewise allows us to move on with our lives."

On the surface forgiveness may appear to be a way of "wimping out" on your problems. You may have very good reasons for your resentment. It's very possible that you *have* been victimized—by an abusive parent, an exploitative boss, poverty, injustice, the self-inflicted burden of alcoholism or drug abuse. I'm not suggesting that you *forget* these incidents or the pain they caused. With anything short of a lobotomy you're not going to forget! But resentment keeps your horse hobbled. Feeling like a victim provides it with an excuse for never leaving the corral. Through forgiveness—accepting that the incident happened, you can't change it and it's time to move beyond it—you'll break the habit of seeing yourself as a victim. And breaking that habit is *essential* if you want to find your path to success. Watch out for thoughts like these that indicate a resentment of someone else:

- "After all I've done for her..."
- "I've given you the best years of my life, and this is the thanks I get?"
- "He's been taking what's rightfully mine all his life!"

- "One of these days she's going to come to *me* for help. I'm looking forward to the satisfaction of shutting the door in her face!"
- "They're all jealous of my success!" (Frederika)

...And these, which indicate a resentment of yourself:

- "How could I have been so stupid?"
- "I'd be rich now, if I'd had the guts to go in on that deal with Harry ten years ago."
- "Am I *ever* going to learn to keep my big mouth shut?"
- "I let him walk all over me...*again!*"
- "I had a chance to be a manager, and I blew it." (Frederika)

Every time you catch yourself thinking such thoughts, put yourself back on course by sowing SEEDS. Consciously *choose* to evaluate the situation in a different light: "I'm feeling sorry for myself because our relationship seems so one-sided. Maybe I'd better readjust my thinking." "It's too bad I didn't think I could afford to invest in Harry's scheme." Change your emotions to fit your new evaluation. Then *do* something to restore your self-esteem: release your resentment by forgiving yourself and others.

Once Frederika was able to view her situation as neutral and acknowledge ownership of the problem—"I came on too strong with the workers; I refused Phil's advice"—her emotions underwent a shift from resentment to understanding. "Of course the guys were resisting my leadership," she told herself. "This is uncharted territory for them, and I came on like a cavalry charge. I can get a positive response about this team approach if I talk to them as one human being to another. As for Phil, he was sincerely trying to help, not putting me down."

Then Frederika *did* something about the situation: she read the articles Phil had given her and signed up for the seminar he'd recommended. Most importantly, she took the step of forgiving the workers for their resistance and forgiving herself for her inappropriate behavior. She consciously told herself, "I've been punishing myself, but that's okay—it's over. They *were* resisting my leadership, but starting tomorrow I'm going to try a different approach."

Emptiness: When Nothing Seems Worthwhile

Every American schoolchild of an earlier generation used to learn Edward A. Robinson's "Richard Cory," a poem about a much-envied "man who has everything" who commits suicide. The moral of Richard's story was plain to any 13-year-old: you can have all the material success people dream about and still end up feeling that life isn't worth living. It is this profound sense of emptiness that is the last and most destructive symptom of the failure mechanism.

This feeling goes deeper than the loneliness we examined earlier. It is a sense of loss of self, a void we just can't seem to fill. In some cases, like Frederika's, we may feel literally, physically *empty* and seek to fill the void with food. The feeling has nothing to do with a lack of "success" as we usually consider it. "A person who has the capacity to enjoy still alive within him finds enjoyment in many ordinary and simple things in life," Maltz wrote. "He also enjoys whatever [material] success he has achieved. [But] the person in whom the capacity to enjoy is dead can find enjoyment in nothing. No goal is worth working for. Life is a terrible bore. Nothing is worthwhile."

Think of the successful young people who inhabited our media consciousness during much of the 1980s—the "yuppies," if that word can stand being dragged out one more time. Here were a group of individuals, at least so far as they conformed to stereotype, whose lives were furnished with all the symbols of success—health, money, sexual attractiveness, the right cars, the right neighborhoods, the right schools for their children, the trendiest restaurants, the spiritual fads explored one after another in an endless search for fulfillment, the frantic scramble to stay one step ahead of boredom.

This is success? This is emptiness. This is working toward someone else's goals. For all your rider may think they're your own, your horse knows better. This is the type of "success" that literally gives success a bad name: "the bitch-goddess," in William James's famous phrase.

"Emptiness," Maltz wrote, "is a symptom that you are not living creatively.... It is the person who has no purpose of his own who pessimistically concludes, 'Life has no purpose.' It is the person who has no goal worth working for who concludes 'Life is not worthwhile.'... The individual who is *actively engaged* in a struggle, or in striving toward an important goal, does not come up with pessimistic philosophies concerning the meaninglessness or the futility of life."

Emptiness, in short, is another symptom of a poor self-image. It can be a justification for a lack of personal fulfillment ("I'm a zero; there's no possibility for joy in my life; why go to the trouble, we're all going to go when the ozone layer disappears anyway"). It can be a feeling brought about by the hollowness of success that's not consistent with genuine personal goals ("I feel rotten; I don't deserve this; if they only knew what a fraud I am; life isn't worth living; I think I'll go out and buy a new BMW"). In either case, it's a sign that your automatic mechanism has no target to aim for.

How to Get That Feeling of Fulfillment

It all comes back to goals. It's easy to feel overwhelmed when you first sit down to think about goals, especially when you haven't yet freed up your servomechanism through creative imagination. Some years ago I took a class called Success Plus given by Terry Cole Whittaker. She used *Psycho-Cybernetics* as a text and introduced the subject of goals by asking us what possibilities were open to us. What was the range of things we could do that might be *fun*—with no commitment, pledge or action plan to worry about?

If you find yourself in a state of despair and need a "jump start" to begin thinking about goals, use this approach to find something that catches your fancy. Try some of the following ideas to channel linear, left-brain, what's-the-use thinking into creative, right-brain, this-sounds-like-a-kick thinking. They can jar your servomechanism into remembering that life does have its rewarding moments. No matter how trivial these moments may seem, they can give you the power to fill the emptiness within.

1. If you had 24 hours all to yourself, what would you do? You have a month's salary to spend and you are not accountable to anyone for your time.

2. Now expand your fantasy: you have an entire week to spend as you desire and three months' salary to splurge on what you will. Where would you go? Would you be alone or with someone else? Plan your week in detail.

3. Give yourself a fun job title—Tsar of Shipping and Receiving, Empress of WordPerfect—and spend a work day functioning under that title.

4. Design your ideal career. Map out your duties, office surroundings and particulars.

5. Design your ideal environment: if you could surround yourself with art and artifacts, what kind would they be?

6. Focus on memories of fulfillment. Recall the last time you lost yourself in a project. How did it feel (*e.g.,* warm, exciting, "like time stood still")? Remember a time in childhood when you mastered something fulfilling—learned to swim, beat your older brother in a foot race, understood long division, baked chocolate cookies without burning them. Recall a recent moment, even a fleeting one, when you felt fulfilled— seeing a fluffy white cloud float by, cleaning out the attic, listening to a favorite piece of music, cuddling with your dog, seeing the smile on a child's face.

⊞ Use Negative Feedback the Right Way

Deactivating the failure mechanism and getting yourself back on a course to success is simply a matter of recognizing these seven signs for what they are and what they aren't. They *are* warning signals that must be heeded if you want to avoid failure. They are *not* indications that you *have* failed. A detour sign on the highway doesn't mean you're a bad driver. It *is* a signal to change direction— an indication that you're likely to have an accident if you continue on your present course. There's no need to be continually watching the road for detour signs. If you do, you're almost certain to hit one. Instead, you simply note the warning and correct your course.

So it is with frustration, aggressiveness and the other signals that warn you when you're off course. If you focus on these negatives, you're likely to run right smack into them. If, however, you use them as guideposts for your internal guidance system, you'll remain targeted on success. This was what Frederika did after she evaluated her initial responses. Instead of allowing the elements of failure to become habits, she took corrective action:

WARNING SIGN	NON-CORRECTIVE ACTION	CORRECTIVE ACTION
frustration: workers don't respond to her leadership	Blamed it on jealousy"	Learns management techniques: reads articles, attends seminar
aggressiveness: workers react negatively to management style	Showed no respect for workers	Builds bridges to workers: apologizes, accepts their input
insecurity: worried about boss's disapproval	Became "overly anxious to please"	Accepts boss's advice on negative aspects of performance, "keeps on doing her job" on the positives
loneliness: feels cut off from people	Felt sorry for herself	Has dinner with other "rookie managers" she met at seminar to discuss common concerns

WARNING SIGN	NONCORRECTIVE ACTION	CORRECTIVE ACTION
uncertainty: doubts her decisions	Avoided risks	Challenges indecision, focuses on effectiveness of past decisions
resentment: blames boss, mother, "system"	Felt justified for failure	Uses SEEDS to reevaluate situation and move past resentment
emptiness: feels apathetic, "It's not worth the effort."	Lost interest in work	Revitalizes enthusiasm for goal, leading to fulfillment

By correcting your course every time you're confronted with one of the elements of failure, you develop the habit of sensitivity to these danger signals. By learning this habit, you avoid developing a "failure-type personality." By avoiding failure, you can't help but achieve success!

Targeting on Ideas

- The seven warning signals of failure are: frustration, aggressiveness, insecurity, loneliness, uncertainty, resentment, and emptiness.
- Your automatic mechanism reaches its goals by responding to these signals not as indications of failure but as guideposts to corrective action.

ET
YOUR OWN
TARGETS

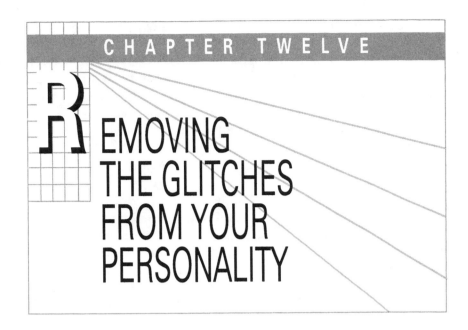

CHAPTER TWELVE

REMOVING THE GLITCHES FROM YOUR PERSONALITY

When a person has adequate self-esteem, little slights offer no threat at all—they are simply "passed over" and ignored. Even deeper emotional wounds are likely to heal faster and cleaner, with no festering sores to poison life and spoil happiness.

—*Maxwell Maltz,* Psycho-Cybernetics *(1960)*

Attractive, fun-loving, divorced mother of two, 37, can't believe all the good men are taken. Love dancing, bicycling, Brazilian food, *Star Trek,* and cozy romantic evenings. No smokers or walking wounded, please.

—*Anonymous, urban weekly newspaper (1992)*

Some of the images in our language are particularly apt. Maxwell Maltz compared our responses to emotional injuries with the scar tissue that forms over physical wounds. "[N]ature protects against further pain and injury by forming...a protective shell," he wrote. "We...do very much the same thing whenever we receive an emotional injury.... We form...'scars' for self-protection. We are apt to become hardened of heart, callous toward the world, and to withdraw within a protective shell."

The woman who requested "No walking wounded" knew all about such scars. We can well imagine the experiences that might have led her to include such a plaintive phrase in her personals ad. We can invent a history of her relationships that probably wouldn't be far from the truth. Let's start with her ex-husband Tom: bright, charming, her ideal match until she began to recognize his evasiveness, his inability to share feelings, his unwillingness to commit himself to anything—a job, their relationship, even a consistent story about where he was last Friday night. She wasn't surprised when he left her for another woman, only angry about the time she'd wasted trying to get him to change. Then there was Dick, the self-made businessman with a glamorous lifestyle who made her feel giddy with his energy—and who reacted to any slight as if it were a declaration of war. She was embarrassed by his abusiveness toward a waiter who had mistotaled their bill; she feared for her safety whenever another driver cut him off on the highway. He was indifferent to her children, and if the truth be known he was no great lover either, though he did his best to convince her that this was her fault. She cut him loose after he raged at her ten-year-old for allegedly cheating at Monopoly. Finally she met Harry—confident and successful in his work life, crazy about her kids and a wonderful lover—who turned into an insecure toddler whenever she raised any question about any aspect of their relationship. When she began to pull back from him, he started on a cycle of pressuring her for commitment, apologizing, making up to her through her children and pleading for another chance. When she finally broke off their relationship, he threatened to kill himself.

Emotional scars, indeed! They're pretty dismaying when we see them on someone else's personality, aren't they? But now let's turn the mirror around. Consider these scars from the point of view of the walking wounded themselves. "These people have been...injured by someone in the past," Maltz wrote. "To guard against future injury *from that source* they form a spiritual callus.... This scar tissue, however, not only 'protects' them from the individual that hurt them—it 'protects' them against all other human beings. An emotional wall is built [that] cuts us off from all other human beings, and from our real selves."

Your automatic mechanism is programmed to target on goals, but sometimes a wound you've received can cause a flaw to develop in your program. When your internal guidance system encounters one of these glitches, it stops dead in its path. The results are frustration, aggressiveness, all those elements of failure we discussed in the last chapter. The experience of being ridiculed by a parent may make you hostile toward bosses and other authority figures. The cruelty of schoolmates long ago may cause you to lash out in anger at any slighting remark, real or imagined. Taken advantage of by a trusted associate in your youth, you may have adopted "Never trust anybody" as your watchword. When you consider your own "emotional scar tissue," as Maltz called it, you feel more understanding than when you look at the wounds of any Tom, Dick or Harry.

This chapter is about those personality glitches and what you can do to get rid of them. You'll learn:

- how to detect the glitches caused by emotional wounds that may be negatively impacting your personality.
- techniques for removing the glitches from your personality.
- five ways to build immunity against emotional wounds.
- how to free your personality from inhibition by responding appropriately to negative feedback.

⊞ Emotional Scars: How They Cut You Off from Living

Emotional scars can be as visible as physical scars. You see them in people like Johanna, a one-time neighbor of mine. Johanna, a phone-company employee, was 32 years old but looked 52. She had marked frown lines on her forehead and at the corners of her mouth, and there was not a hint of sparkle in her eyes. I would see her trudging home every evening, her body bent in the shape of a question mark and a sour expression on her face. As a teenager Johanna had been 60 pounds overweight. Her peers had made fun of her in the typically insensitive manner of adolescents, but far worse for her self-esteem was the abuse she took from her mother. She berated Johanna for her weight in front of others and took to calling her "Bubbles," the name of a hippopotamus in the local zoo. These psychic wounds had left Johanna with a scarred personality. Though she had long ago dieted away her excess poundage, in her subconscious mind she still had an ungainly body. She hid herself from people and was easily embarrassed by comments about weight—anybody's weight. Often when she heard people laughing, she was sure they were laughing at her. Any association with "bubbles," such as a bathtub full of sudsy water or a glass of champagne, sent her into depression.

Just in case you're thinking that a person so deeply wounded in spirit can't be a material success, consider Duke. He was a 45-year-old attorney who owned his own business and pulled down $350,000 a year. His work was his life. In court Duke was a tiger, much admired in the legal community for his incisiveness in presenting a case to a judge and his charm in winning over a jury. In his office he was a considerate boss who always got the best out of his workers. But people who saw him on the street sometimes looked the other way. His face was a mask of anger, and he walked with an intensity that suggested that he was looking for a fight. A closer look would have revealed a dangerously unhealthy man, a potbellied chainsmoker with pallid skin, no body tone and a tremor in his hands. He spent his evenings and weekends at home in his huge dark house, watching television and snorting cocaine. Duke had grown up the only child of alcoholic parents. While he was not subjected to deliberate abuse like Johanna, neither was he shown any model for intimacy. Feelings were often acted out by his parents, but they were never discussed. By age 14 Duke had become a lightning rod for the unvoiced tensions between them. Often when they were drinking he was forced into the role of taking care of *them*. By the time he reached adulthood, Duke had developed a glitch in his programming. His early relationships with women were over before they could begin. Duke would say or do something that would drive the woman away, or he would "just let the relationship die." By age 30 he had stopped trying. By 45 he had come to despise women and to look cynically on other people's relationships. His only sexual encounters were with prostitutes and always involved huge quantities of cocaine.

Anyone knowing Johanna or Duke might say, "There goes one of the walking wounded." But what about you? Is there an old wound that you're still responding to with emotional withdrawal, insecurity, loneliness, defensiveness, aggressiveness... downright *nastiness*? Because you have worn the scars so long, you may not recognize them as such. But often the source of unhappiness, bitterness or chronic depression may be a single experience or circumstance. It might have happened years ago, but it's been inhibiting you ever since.

You were rejected by a lover. Your rider sent your horse the message "Any wo/man is going to reject me" so many times that eventually your horse knew no other path

You were the smallest kid in your class in a tough school. Today you're a success, but you're still taking revenge on those bullies who stole your lunch money. You react with resentment, sometimes with rage, any time a salesperson comes on too strong, any time someone solicits you for a charitable contribution, any time you think someone is "trying to take what's yours."

For fifteen years you shared a room with your older sister. She criticized your taste in everything from boys to clothes to music. It's been a long time now, and your sister probably never knew how much she hurt you, but just last week you went into a screaming rage at your boyfriend when he said, "You know, those windows would look a lot better with curtains instead of Levolours."

Your father used to call you "sissy boy" when he got drunk. Your wife has expressed embarrassment about your "ridiculous macho swagger" in front of company. You lost your last job because you couldn't avoid picking a fight whenever someone made a remark that you inferred as a slur on your masculinity.

You're a member of an ethnic minority. You've been stung so often by racism that you've come to anticipate it every time you have to deal with the majority culture. You try to put on a cool front, but any time you look at a white face you see a white hood. It's a particularly self-sabotaging habit at job interviews. You look at the person across the desk, and you feel so resentful that before you even begin to speak the score is one to nothing, his favor.

When you were a college freshman you were the victim of date rape. No one had ever heard of "date rape" then. You were raised in a strict religious family, and you convinced yourself that the incident was your fault. Now your rider knows better, but your horse is still hanging its head in shame. You've never been able to achieve orgasm, and a healthy, loving relationship with a man seems a goal beyond reach.

⊞ Recognizing Your Glitches

"Emotional scars, " Maltz wrote, "...lead to the development of a scarred, marred self-image; the picture of a person not liked nor accepted by other human beings;...of a person who can't get along well in the world."

Such scars are more easily identified than your false beliefs. If you face the world with such a profoundly negative attitude, chances are you already know it. You just may have trouble recognizing it for what it is: a *habit* formed by your reaction to an emotional wound. Your rider has been telling your horse, "Don't even leave the stable; you'll only get whipped for your trouble."

But just in case you think your negative perception constitutes a "realistic" image of your life, use these questions as a quick diagnostic test.

1. Do you often find yourself unable to return smiles or to make eye contact?

2. Does nonsexual touching make you feel uncomfortable?

3. Do you tend to be on your guard and overly protective of your feelings? Do you tell yourself, "If I let this person know my real thoughts and feelings, s/he's going to think I'm terrible"?

4. In sexual situations, do you tend to find yourself focusing on concern about how your partner will evaluate your performance?

5. Are you frequently self-conscious about not knowing the "right" thing to do, think or feel in a personal interaction?

6. Do you tend to regard other people in an adversarial context, as people who are "out to take something from you"?

If your answer to any of these questions is "yes," you may have a glitch inhibiting your personality. Try to identify its source by engaging your right brain for creative insight. Try the desktop-covered-with-butcher-paper technique. Relax yourself. Write down whatever thoughts come to you, regardless of sequence, concerning the situation that produces your negative response. It probably won't take much digging to recognize your emotional wound.

Body Images Can Affect Your Personality

Often, as with Johanna, a personality glitch reveals itself through your images of your body. You'll remember that Maltz came to his ideas about the self-image based on his experiences as a plastic surgeon. Patients he had successfully treated continued to think of themselves as ugly if they held a negative image of themselves. A study published in 1990 by another plastic surgeon, Dr. Milton T. Edgerman, underscores Maltz's intuitive conclusion. Edgerman based his report on long-term observations of 100 "psychologically disturbed" patients. "We have found that many such patients can experience relief from their profound sense of deformity if provided with *combined* surgical and psychological therapy," he and his colleages reported. In one case a woman complained that her nose had been "made larger" by rhinoplastic reduction surgery (a 'nose job'), "[a]lthough pictures show evidence to the contrary.... In retrospect, it appears that the [surgical] team failed to clarify preoperatively the patient's motivational pattern for surgery. She now states that *she had expected to erase the 'emotional scars' of an early childhood trauma.*" (Emphasis mine.)

Just as your mind conditions your feelings about your body, so your body images condition your mind. Your perceptions of your body are intimately intertwined with your perceptions of your self. Your most fundamental sense of yourself is as a body. You probably first recognized yourself in a mirror at the age of two. From then on your self-image was shaped and molded to a great extent by the way you were led to feel about your body by your parents, other caregivers, and such disparate social influences as TV commercials and religion. For various reasons women tend to be more sensitive to body images than men, but men are hardly immune. While women suffer from eating disorders and seek cosmetic surgery more frequently, it's the guys whose self-image is threatened by shortness of stature and receding hairlines. For every woman self-conscious about how her breasts compare to *Playboy* standards, there's a man stealing furtive glances at other men at urinals and worrying how his penis measures up. Whether male or female we seek to raise our self-esteem by altering our body image through clothes, cosmetics, jewelry and personal fitness. Both genders experience anxiety about sexual performance. Both experience the developmental changes in our body images associated with the aging process. And we all are susceptible to having our information-processing and goal-striving systems conditioned by our body images.

Johanna's personality had been scarred by her perception of her body. Her low self-esteem led her to experience "phantom fat." When she made some self-disparaging remark about her weight to me over the back fence one day, I had to comment that she didn't appear at all overweight—not then. "Yeah, but look at all this loose skin," she said. "I look like my mother." Indeed, I'd met her mother once and found myself looking at an older Johanna look-alike—the same creased forehead and turned-down mouth, the same bitterness in the eyes. Johanna's image of herself was the one her mother had chosen, and her automatic mechanism sought to reconfirm that image exactly.

How about you? Consider that your personality may have been conditioned by an image you hold of your body. When I was a consulting psychologist in that obesity program I mentioned earlier, there was a set of questions I would ask to give patients insights into their body image. Answer them now yourself:

1. What is the first thing you notice when you see your face in the mirror?
2. When you see yourself in a full-length mirror, where do your eyes tend to go?
3. What is your overall impression when you see yourself in a photo or video? What seems to stand out?
4. When you get dressed, what do you pay attention to as you put clothing on various parts of your body?
5. Have you ever looked in a trick mirror in an amusement park? What is your reaction—do you laugh, frown or quickly turn away? Why?

Glitches caused by body images can often be addressed by climbing out of the "perfection trap." Note the points of similarity in your answers to these questions. What aspects of your body is your negative image focused on—your weight, your height, your skin, your nose, your musculature? Realistically ask yourself if you know anyone who is "perfect" in that respect—not Hollywood ideals, *real people*. Now think of some aspect of that person's body where *s/he* is flawed and *you* shine. The point is that everyone's body is a trade-off. There are some parts that are fine and others that are not so fine. Keep telling that horse of yours not to expect perfection.

Emotional Wounds Can Lead to Fear of Intimacy

Okay, so that's not your problem. Maybe your body *is* perfect. In any event you don't expend much emotional energy worrying about it. Yet you still sense that you're "cut off from the real world, and from your real self"—as Duke did. "The person with emotional scars," Maltz wrote, "not only has a self-image of an unwanted, unliked and incapable person, he also has an image of the world...as a hostile place. His primary relationship with the world is one of hostility, and his dealings with other people are not based upon giving and accepting, cooperating, working with, enjoying with, but upon concepts of overcoming, combating and protecting from. He can neither be charitable towards others nor towards himself. Frustration, aggression, and loneliness are the price he pays."

Sounds like Duke all over, doesn't it? In the combative, adversarial world of the legal profession, he was a king. But in the personal realm, he was a slave to the psychic wound he had received from his alcoholic parents. For Duke, intimacy was something to be expressed through wounding remarks. It was something associated with substance abuse and dependence. Any woman who was interested in him must be wanting to trap him in such a relationship and therefore was an object of contempt and fear. He could avoid the frustration of such encounters by making himself as unappealing as possible in his personality and his appearance. With his cocaine and cigarette abuse, he had chosen (as Johanna did) to imitate his parents.

Johanna saw the world as a hostile place because of the pain caused by her mother's emotional abuse and lack of caring. Duke saw the world as a hostile place because he had never had personal closeness modeled for him. One had been *deprived* of positive reinforcement in intimacy; the other had *disclaimed* the results of intimacy. How about you? If you tend to regard the world in an adversarial context, chances are you're bearing the scar of an old emotional wound—a personality glitch that prevents you from pursuing or perhaps even perceiving worthwhile goals.

Fortunately there are ways of healing your emotional wounds. As you've probably guessed, getting the glitches out of your personal programming is simply a matter of your rider retraining your horse.

How to Free Your Personality from Glitches

That day I was chatting with Johanna over the back fence, she was talking morosely about "feeling so fat." I suggested that she take a body-toning class at the local YWCA. "I'm too tired after work to do all that jumping up and down," she said. "Besides, my mother tells me I'll never get rid of this excess skin, and she ought to know."

"Johanna," I said to her, "mothers aren't always right about everything."

She looked at me as though I had just come down from a mountain with a new revelation. I could almost see a light bulb flash on in her face: *it didn't have to be this way.* Johanna signed up for the body-toning class and began looking into improving herself in other ways. (One of the steps she took was to read *Psycho-Cybernetics* and some of Maxwell Maltz's other books.) As part of a class in personal development, she was asked to lie down on a piece of butcher paper while one of the other women outlined her body. The image was then pinned to the wall. When Johanna was able to see her actual body image instead of the distorted one she carried around in her mind, she broke out in tears. "I had no idea my body was so slim and pretty," she said.

For Johanna, this experience was a "teaching moment." She set out to change her self-image by healing the emotional wound that had scarred her since adolescence. Let's take a look at the steps she followed and how you might adapt them to your own needs:

1. She recognized that her mother's image wasn't the one she wanted to live with. (You can choose *not* to live with the emotional wound.)

2. She immediately took action to challenge the image that was the source of her wound by signing up for the body-toning class. (You can *take action* toward healing your wound instead of choosing to react to it.)

295

3. She consciously told herself after seeing her actual image on paper that the image that had caused her wound was false. (You can begin to erase old tapes by CANCELling them and replacing them with new data.)

4. She continued with a self-generated fitness program: daily walking, workouts at the "Y" three times a week, and a modeling class. She had no expectation of becoming a professional model, but she wanted to learn to carry herself in a way that was consistent with her new body image. (You can train your conscious mind to eliminate the self-image associated with your emotional wound by consciously and consistently selecting your new image.)

5. She put a mirror on her desk beside her telephone computer. She made a point of looking into it and *smiling* every time she took a call until it had become a habit. (You can "fake it till you make it.")

6. Every time she found herself resenting her mother for the pain she had caused her, she *forgave* her. (You can choose not to bear resentment.)

"Own Up" to Your Glitches

Duke went through a similar process regarding his emotional scars. For him the "teaching moment" came when he was recovering from a five-day cocaine binge. Previously his drug consumption had been a strictly after-hours thing. Because it hadn't negatively affected his professional life, he'd been able to convince himself it wasn't a problem. But for the last few days he'd been incapable of going to work. How much longer could he keep telling his associates that he had the flu? "This is crazy," he said to himself. "I'm committing slow suicide. If I don't figure out a better way to live, I'm going to be dead in five years."

Duke's starting point was several steps behind Johanna's. He hadn't identified his emotional wound or its source, and he had a serious substance-abuse problem to overcome. But the first step was the same for them both: a realization that something was wrong and a determination to find a way to heal themselves. "I'm a smart, successful guy," Duke told himself. "I don't know whether I'm lonely because I'm so miserable or miserable because

I'm so lonely. All I know is that somewhere along the line I started thinking of myself as someone who was incapable of having normal relationships with people."

Duke made the decision to withdraw "cold turkey" from his addiction. For that he needed help. He "didn't believe in therapy" and had cut himself off from friends out of embarrassment about his lifestyle, but he remembered reading an article about an actor, a former cocaine addict who had made a large contribution to Alcoholics Anonymous "for saving my life." Duke didn't know much about AA, and he "knew" he was no alcoholic—he had hardly taken a drink in his life and couldn't stand the taste of the stuff. His *parents* were alcoholics, and he sure wasn't anything like *them!* But if AA wasn't just for people with drinking problems, maybe it would be the place to start.

It is outside the scope and purpose of this book to discuss in any detail the "recovery movement" and the celebrated "twelve-step program" of Alcoholics Anonymous. Certainly it does not represent a universal cure-all for emotional wounds. But for Duke, AA and its adjunct group, Adult Children of Alcoholics (ACOA) provided the environment to begin his healing process. Let's take a look at the steps he followed (not the twelve steps of the program) and see how you might adapt them to your own healing process:

1. By joining the program, he *took action* in the direction of change.

2. By participating in ACOA meetings, he learned about the dynamics of alcoholic families and *came to an awareness* about his parents, the wound their emotional distance had caused him, and how drugs had helped to sever him from his feelings about himself.

3. By openly acknowledging his fear of intimacy and the despair and loneliness it had caused him, he *became aware* of how his emotional wound had affected his self-image and of what steps he needed to take to heal himself.

4. To *break the habit* of loneliness, he took in a roommate.

5. To *break the habit* of cutting himself off from his feelings and withdrawing from intimacy, he reinitiated contact with two trusted friends and

297

asked their permission to openly discuss with them the process he was undergoing.

6. To *break the habit* of thinking contemptuously of women and looking disdainfully on "normal" relationships, he began to practice the five steps of CRAFT process, including daily relaxed visualization and, ultimately, dating for the first time in over fifteen years.

7. To remove his emotional scar, he made a habit of *forgiving* his parents for the pain they had caused him.

Learn to Unleash the Power of Forgiveness

The attitude most people take toward those they blame for the pain, bitterness and humiliation of their emotional wounds is one of revenge. Of course we don't go out and horsewhip our parents, our bosses, our ex-spouses (though I suppose some of us *would*, if we thought we could get away with it). Instead we take revenge in our hearts. We harbor grudges.

It's natural to resent the person who wounded you. The problem is that it runs completely counter to the healing process. Revenge may be sweet, but as an old Chinese proverb says, "Before you start out on the road to revenge, dig two graves." If your goal is to remove the glitches from your personality, resentment won't work. Forgiveness will.

We spoke briefly in the last chapter about forgiveness as an antidote to the poison of resentment. Maltz compared it to a scalpel with which you can "give yourself an emotional face lift."

"Old emotional scars cannot be doctored or medicated," Maltz wrote. "They must be 'cut out,' given up entirely, eradicated. Many people apply various kinds of salve or balm to old emotional wounds, but this simply does not work.... Forgiveness, when it is real and genuine and complete, and forgotten—is the scalpel which can remove the pus from old emotional wounds, heal them, and eliminate scar tissue.... Therapeutic forgiveness cuts out, eradicates, cancels, makes the wound as if it had never been.... The only difficulty is to secure your own willingness to give up and do without your sense of condemnation—your willingness to cancel out the debt, with no mental reservations."

It is crucial to take that step of cancelling the debt. Otherwise forgiveness itself becomes a form of revenge. Instead of whacking the person who wronged you with a stick, you get even by flaunting your moral superiority—and your personality glitch remains in place. Every time you catch yourself feeling resentful of the parent who abused you, the spouse who deserted you, the associate who cheated you, consciously forgive the person who inflicted the wound.

Remember: when you bear a grudge, your horse forms the habit of believing that it's a helpless victim. It re-experiences the pain of its whipping every time it pokes its nose outside the stable. It doesn't feel comfortable unless it can *expect* to be whipped. It will never find a path to success as long as it has someone on whom to lay the blame for failure—no matter how justified that blame might be. Each conscious act of forgiveness is a message that it's safe to come out of the barn. As you make a habit of forgiveness, you train your horse away from its inhibition against learning new paths.

When Dale learned that Darryl, her husband of twenty-three years, was having an affair, her first reactions were shock, despair, rage and sorrow. She resolved to hit him with both barrels—order him to move out, tell their friends what a rat he was, find a lawyer and take him for everything she could. As the afternoon wore on, Dale found herself pacing the house rehearsing what she would say, but her stress was so intense she could hold no thought. She went into the backyard and put herself into her mind's "decompression chamber" in an attempt to focus herself.

As Dale sat there among the flowers she and Darryl had planted, feeling her stress diminish, she began to have different thoughts. Did she really want to end her marriage? She was ready to believe Dale had been having affairs all along, but she felt intuitively that this was the first time. He had always been easy and gracious to live with. They had raised two children together. What would be served by confronting him with anger and blame-casting? Did she want to spend the next forseeable part of her life expending her emotional resources on rage, bitterness and anxiety?

Dale acknowledged the release she would experience if she confronted Darryl with forgiveness instead of condemnation. All this she knew and accepted intellectually. But alone in the garden, she was all emotion. She focused on the times she and Darryl had had to get past rough spots in their marriage. She knew and felt that she could choose to confront Darryl without hurling emotional grenades at him but without backing down from her feelings either. It would be easier to free herself from her pain by being open, direct and unvengeful than by choosing resentment and retribution.

When Darryl came home that evening and saw Dale sitting in the garden, he could tell at once by the look on her face that she knew. "I spoke to Margaret today," she said quietly. "She told me all about it." Instead of denying the affair or countering with defensiveness, Darryl apologized and told her how ashamed he was. "I love you, and I don't want our marriage to end," he said. "Can you ever forgive me?"

"I've already forgiven you," she said. "The question is, what are we going to do about it? Will you join me in seeking counseling?"

Now, do you think Dale's story would have had a happy ending if Dale had chosen the path of revenge instead of forgiveness? The question would be relevant whether or not Darryl had admitted to the affair. She might have thrown him out and sued him for divorce. She might have "taken him back" with a sense of power, "forgiving but never forgetting" and reminding him in subtle ways how she had condescended to keep their marriage together. But do you think she could ever have freed herself of the emotional wound caused by Darryl's unfaithfulness if she had followed either of these courses?

You can get even with life, or you can get on with life. It is impossible to do both at the same time.

Forgive Yourself Too

"Not only do we incur emotional wounds from others, most of us inflict them upon ourselves," Maltz wrote. "We beat ourselves over the head with self-condemnation, remorse and regret. We beat ourselves down with self-doubt. We cut ourselves up with excessive guilt."

We condition ourselves to remember our mistakes and forget our successes. It's those old tapes again. In our culture parents have traditionally been taught not to "spoil" their children. Many well-meaning parents would never have dreamed of praising their child for fear of giving him a swelled head. That's why many of us today are uncomfortable with praise. There's almost a superstitious quality about our reluctance to focus on our successes—it's as though we expected God to strike us dead. But that's not the case with our mistakes! Chances are you're still embarrassed about things you said or did or didn't do when you were a child, let alone last week. And if your rider tends to focus only on your mistakes, your horse can only come to define you by your mistakes. Instead of "I fouled up," you tell yourself "I'm a foul-up."

"You make mistakes—mistakes do not make 'you,'" Maltz asserted. *There's nothing you can do about your past mistakes.* Forgive yourself for them—it's the only way to avoid letting them negatively impact your present and your future. Focus instead on your successes. The next time you find yourself kicking yourself for something that happened in the past, say "Cancel!" Immediately replace the memory by focusing on one of your successes. And the next time you catch yourself ducking a compliment, say to yourself, "Wait a second—if she was kind enough to tell me what a good job I did, I should at least be decent enough to return her kindness with an acknowledgment." It makes the other person feel good, and it makes you acknowledge your success. Everyone wins!

Learn from Others' Mistakes—And Your Own

A postscript to Johanna's story: Several months after our back-fence conversation I moved, and it was eleven years before I saw her again. I bumped into her at a shopping mall. She was married, with a delightful six-year-old daughter, and she showed no sign of her earlier wound. She had successfully managed to keep that glitch out of her programming, she told me, by keeping up her body work, by reassuring herself *daily* that she had the right to be happy, by selecting supportive people to be around and by staying away from negative people.

In that latter category was her mother. "I told her how hurt I'd been by the way she ridiculed me," Johanna said. "I told her that I loved her, and I sincerely forgave her, but I told her I would never allow her to hurt me again. She didn't speak to me for seven months after that, and I don't see her much any more. But I'll tell you the *best* thing I did. The day my daughter was born, I looked down as I was nursing her and said to myself, 'I'm not going to repeat my mother's mistakes. I'll be a better role model to you than she ever was to me. I'll *never* ridicule you or do anything to injure your self-esteem.'"

Johanna was absolutely right: choosing not to repeat her mother's mistake was the most significant step she could have taken. Of course it was no coincidence that both Johanna and Duke resembled their parents in attitude and behavior—and no surprise. They were the images of adulthood that they observed as children. Your conscious mind selects such images as models of behavior, and your subconscious mind moves toward them—even though you may tell yourself, "Like my *mother?* I'm not *anything* like my mother." Besides, when you've been living with an emotional wound, there can be an unfortunate tendency to pass it along. If you can't get back at the person who wounded you, you try to dull the pain of the wound by inflicting it on someone else. It's as though we tell ourselves, "*My* father beat *me*—why should my kid get off easy?" "No one ever gave *me* a break when I started out in this business—why should I help *her* along?"

Of course when you consciously realize how destructive such an attitude is—and how it serves to perpetuate your glitches—you can choose *not* to repeat others' mistakes. And once you've consciously made such a decision, it becomes a goal. Your subconscious mind will inevitably agree and come to move toward it. I left the mall that day with every expectation that Johanna's child would grow up far happier than she did.

For Duke a key moment came in an AA meeting when he consciously acknowledged for the first time that he wasn't bound by his mistakes of the past. He recognized that he could learn from his own mistakes instead of wallowing in them. He was already beginning to learn: instead of beating himself up for having "wasted his life," he acknowledged his professional success and his conscious decision to get help. Yes, he had made mistakes in the past. But he had consciously chosen not to add to those mistakes in the future.

Don't let yourself be controlled by your mistakes. They may have wounded you in the past, but you can choose not to let them hurt you in the future. Watch for that moment of creative insight—the "teaching moment" when you acknowledge your power to choose to learn from your mistakes.

Five Techniques for Keeping Your Personality Glitch-Free

When you were a child, there wasn't much you could do to defend yourself against emotional wounds. All you could do was build up scar tissue. But now that you're an adult, there's a great deal you can do to immunize yourself. Beyond freeing yourself from past hurts and removing the personality glitches they caused, you can take steps to guard against future emotional wounds.

Maltz suggested the following three rules for minimizing the chances of absorbing emotional harm:

1. Be too big to feel threatened. "Many people become 'hurt' terribly by tiny pinpricks or what we call social 'slights,'" Maltz wrote. "Everyone knows someone...who is so thin-skinned and 'sensitive' that others must be continually on guard, lest offense be taken at some innocent word or act. It is a well-known...fact that the people who become offended the easiest have the lowest self-esteem.... Even real 'digs' and 'cuts' which inflict a terrible injury to...the person with low self-esteem, do not make a dent in...the person who thinks well of himself."

A strong self-image can be a magic shield against real or imagined thrusts at your emotional well-being. As you work your way through the Psycho-Cybernetics program, you're likely to find that those comments and brush-offs that used to hurt your feelings or send you into a rage now glance right off you. Having a positive, realistic sense of your own worth and importance is the most effective way of dismissing the imaginary emotional threats while you protect yourself against the real ones.

2. Develop a self-reliant attitude. "The person who has little or no self-reliance, who feels emotionally dependent upon others, makes himself most vulnerable to emotional hurts," Maltz maintained. "Every human being wants and needs love and affection. But the creative, self-reliant person also feels a need to *give love*. His emphasis is as much or more on the giving as on the getting. He doesn't expect love to be handed to him on a silver platter. Nor does he have a compulsive need that 'everybody' must love him and approve of him."

Think about it—is it essential that *everyone* thinks you're terrific? Isn't that an unreasonable demand to make of the world? It's an impossible demand—and by making it, you put your self-esteem in other people's hands. You leave yourself open to emotional wounds when their approval is not forthcoming. You're guaranteed to be hurt. Instead, be a person who *gives* approval. Take responsibility for your own emotional needs and support others' through love, acceptance and understanding. "What goes around comes around."

3. Combat emotional wounds with relaxation. Ever pay attention to the circumstances under which your feelings get hurt? Does it ever happen when you're relaxing, enjoying yourself, laughing with friends? Someone makes an insensitive joke or cutting remark; you respond in kind—"Hey, Tompkins, I'm going to ask your wife if *you're* the man you used to be!"—and you laugh over it and forget the whole thing. At worst there may be a moment of embarrassed silence, but does it bother you? Chances are you just think

"What a jerk!" and go back to having a good time. But what happens when you hear such a comment when you're feeling tense, worried, frustrated, angry, depressed or insecure? You're not laughing then. You're wounded.

What does this prove? Only what we talked about at length a while back: we respond not to an event but to the way we feel about an event. Our emotional wounds come not so much from other people's actions but from our own responses. The choice is yours. By diligently practicing the relaxation techniques introduced in this book, by learning to *live* in a state of relaxation, you can practically immunize yourself against emotional wounds.

To Maltz's list I now add my own suggestions:

4. Appreciate yourself as a spiritual being. When you're experiencing your spiritual nature, it's impossible to absorb any emotional injuries. Both your subconscious and conscious minds accept your worthiness. Your horse is veritably prancing in its awareness that you're *entitled* to protection from being wounded by yourself or by others.

Again: it is important not to confuse spirituality with religiosity. Dr. Maltz often reminded his readers that they were "children of God," and if the practice of religion is important to you, you can readily incorporate your spiritual life into your religious life. If religion plays no part in your life, you can develop your spiritual nature through creativity, meditation, enjoyment of nature, any activity that enhances your awareness of yourself in relation to the universe. Plant a garden, play your guitar, find a special place where you can go frequently for a break from the cares and concerns of your life, get involved in some aspect of the effort to save the planet.

Whatever you choose to do, it's important to appreciate yourself as an *expressing entity*. It is the nature of life to express: flowers bloom, birds sing, human beings create. Your spiritual side longs to be creating, to be moving life forward. And when your spirit is creatively engaged, it is practically invulnerable.

There's a saying I learned to appreciate so long ago I don't even remember where I first heard it: "It is the nature of the spirit to give; it is in the nature of the ego to take." If you're actively engaged in expressing your spiritual nature, anything anyone says or does that's potentially injurious to you appears so clearly a product of their own ego that it hardly affects you. "There he goes again, trying to build his self-esteem by tearing mine down," your rider tells your horse. "*I'm* still okay."

5. Give of yourself to others. Many people have found that an excellent way of immunizing themselves against emotional wounds is to give of themselves in a meaningful way. This can't be accomplished simply by writing a check to your favorite charity. You need to do something that shifts your focus away from yourself. By "getting involved" you gain fresh insights into your own life as you enhance the lives of others. Those digs and cuts are less likely to injure your spirit when you develop a new perspective on the scope and range of human injuries.

A participant in one of my seminars told me of the emotional trauma she felt when she discovered the body of her twin sister who had committed suicide. She might have carried the pain of the experience throughout her life if she hadn't gone to a local hospital after the funeral and volunteered to work in any way she could with people who had attempted suicide. She protected herself against being wounded at the same time as she helped others avoid her sister's path.

Volunteering even one day a month can be a great way to guard against emotional pain. Visit a nearby retirement home and find out what you can do to help out. Check out such organizations as Mothers Against Drunk Driving. Offer your services to the pediatric oncology ward of your local hospital, spending time with children who are struggling against cancer. Don't think of it as being a "do-gooder"—think of it as a spiritual vaccine for yourself. That you'll be helping other people as well is a fortunate side effect.

⊞ How to Free Your Personality from Inhibition

Emotional scars are not the only way glitches can form in your personality. It can happen far more innocuously from the way you handle negative feedback.

As you well know by now, your internal guidance system is a feedback-activated mechanism. Negative feedback is the signal that warns you when you're off course. If you respond to it by correcting your course, you remain targeted on your goal. If you respond by overcorrecting, you'll never hit your target. And if you allow yourself to be *controlled* by negative feedback, you come to a dead stop. We call it inhibition.

"'Poor personality' and 'inhibited personality' are one and the same," Maltz wrote. "The person with a 'poor personality' does not express the creative self within. He has restrained it, handcuffed it, locked it up and thrown away the key.... For one reason or another he is afraid to express himself, afraid to be himself, and has locked up himself within an inner prison."

"The symptoms of inhibition are many and varied: shyness, timidity, self-consciousness, hostility, feelings of excessive guilt, insomnia, nervousness, irritability, inability to get along with others. Frustration is characteristic of...the inhibited personality. His real and basic frustration is his failure to 'be himself' and his failure to adequately express himself. But this basic frustration is likely to color and overflow into all that he does."

Respond Positively to Negative Feedback

How you respond to feedback—let's call it "criticism"—from yourself and others determines whether your personality will prosper. If your boss chews you out for a costly mistake, there are a number of responses you can make. You can note where you went wrong and make a point not to repeat your error. You can take a seminar or class if that will help you correct the problem. You can use reflective relearning—"mental practice"—to improve your chances of proceeding correctly next time. All of these are positive responses to negative feedback. But if you allow your boss's criticism to lead to worry and self-punishment, you can become so anxious about the possibility of making a mistake you won't be able to do your job effectively. You anticipate possible mistakes to such a degree that you become frozen by inhibition.

Criticism doesn't have to be direct to result in an inhibited response. It can be implied or even imagined. Say you're at a party. You're talking with a group of people, and everyone seems to be ignoring you. Or, you're talking with one particular person, he looks distracted and excuses himself to refill his plate. You can respond by thinking, "Well, that was obviously the wrong subject to bring up with *this* bunch," or "So much for getting something going with *him*—who else looks interesting here?" But suppose you conclude, "They think I'm dull," or "I sure bored *that* one half to sleep"? The next time someone strikes up a conversation, you might be so self-conscious that you come off stiff and awkward, or you might babble on nervously until *that* person makes a break for the buffet. After a while the criticism you're receiving (or inferring) has inhibited you so much that you spend the rest of the evening examining the ficus plant in the corner.

The same is true of self-criticism. In fact, self-criticism can be even *more* inhibiting because it often takes place on a subconscious level. Your horse is being whipped and tugged in all directions until it doesn't know what path to follow, and your rider doesn't even know it. Suppose you're invited to another party. You feel ambivalent all week about whether you want to go, and you finally decide at the last minute to stay home and watch videos. Your rider is aware only of a certain regretfulness and heaviness of spirit, but your horse is receiving a clear message. Instead of remembering your social successes, it's responding to the way you felt at the last party: *I'm boring. Everyone ignores me. I have my most successful interactions with the potted plants.*

What is the greatest conscious fear of most human beings, as expressed in survey after survey? It's not being mugged or going bankrupt or having their children kidnapped. It's *speaking in front of a group,* by a wide margin. And why is that? Are these people responding to past experiences of being hissed or laughed at? Or does their excessive self-consciousness come from excessive self-criticism?

Fortunately you have the choice of whether to respond to negative feedback with inhibition or corrective action. Here's a table that gives you some guidelines for responding Psycho-Cyberbnetically instead of self-consciously:

SITUATION	FEEDBACK	INHIBITED RESPONSE	PSYCHO-CYBERNETIC RESPONSE
You lose a client	Boss yells at you	"I always mess up!"	"I can learn from this experience."
You're chatting with someone at a party	S/he walks away	"I'm boring!"	"Did I say something offensive? If not, I won't worry about it."
Marital problems	Spouse leaves you	"I'm no good!"	"We both need to change. How can *I* create change?"
Financial worries	Took a bath in the stock market	"My father was right. I'm hopeless with money."	"I'll tighten my belt and get better investment advice."
Problems at work	A pink slip	"I'm a loser!"	"I knew the company was in trouble. Bad luck for me."
Late for dental appointment	Dentist's gone fishing	"I have *no* sense of time! It's been this way since I was ten!"	"I'll commit myself to a goal of becoming responsible about time."

SITUATION	FEEDBACK	INHIBITED RESPONSE	PSYCHO-CYBERNETIC RESPONSE
Went on a beer-and-pizza binge	You've gained ten pounds	"I have no self discipline!"	"I'll join a weight-loss program."

How to Free Your Personality from Inhibition

The corrective action you choose to take in response to negative feedback will depend on you and your situation. It's simply a matter of breaking the habit of inhibition—and at this point you have several habit-breaking tools to choose from. The first thing you need to ask yourself, however, is whether you might be getting a secondary payoff from your inhibited responses. If so, you will need to balance your needs against one another and make a choice.

"How could I possibly expect a payoff from inhibition?" I hear you ask. Consider Maureen, a 26-year-old customer-service representative for a trucking company. Her friends had noticed her shyness in social situations and were always encouraging her to "open up more." Her response was to become self-conscious and even more inhibited to the point where her shyness became embarrassingly apparent. At work her inhibited responses to customers' criticism was a more serious problem. "You've got to be more outgoing," her boss told her. "That's how to get the customers to stick with us. Hang in there. Stay tough."

After one disastrous day on the job, Maureen sat down in a relaxed environment to contemplate why she had formed the habit of inhibiting herself in her personal and professional life. How had she *learned* to respond to negative feedback in this way? She was forced to conclude that she got a secondary payoff from being "shy." It brought her extra attention from her friends and sympathy from angry customers when she fell back into her "helpless little girl" mode. It was a role she had often played with her father. He regarded her as "fragile" because of a rheumatic heart condition she'd had as a child. Now she saw the connection between that experience and the attention she solicited from her friends and her boss.

Maureen recognized that this was an immature way of getting results. She knew that her self-esteem would be enhanced if she could learn to respond to criticism as an adult instead of as a child. She compared the responses she was making to the ones she wished to make:

SITUATION	FEEDBACK	INHIBITED RESPONSE	PSYCHO-CYBERNETIC RESPONSE
Mixing socially with people	Friends encourage her to "loosen up"	Stammers, blushes, withdraws	Breathe deeply, fake it till I make it. "So *what* if I don't click with everyone?"
Dealing with customers	Customer gets angry	Backs down, acts helpless	Practice making eye contact, relaxing, responding assertively

Maureen used daily reflective relearning to visualize herself literally stepping out of her childlike role and into that of a mature woman competent in handling negative feedback in a positive, corrective way. She drew a lovely picture in colored chalk of herself as a shy, fragile child stepping into the figure of herself as a mature woman. She hung it over her desk as a symbolic reminder never again to allow excessive criticism, whether from others or herself, to inhibit her pesonality.

Keep Yourself Inhibition-Free

Keep excessive inhibition from forming a glitch in your personality by learning to respond positively and proactively to criticism. Here are a few tips to follow:

1. Challenge the what-will-the-neighbors-think syndrome. Remember: you were not put into this world to continually please others.

2. Practice CRAFT to free yourself from inhibited responses. CANCEL inappropriate self-criticism. Consider the outward signs of self-consciousness—tense facial muscles, unwillingness to make eye contact, reluctance to speak up, excessive shyness—as habits that you can break. "Act as if" you were free of inhibitions, and in time you will be.

3. Learn from your regrets instead of letting yourself cook in them. Sow SEEDS when you perceive that you've overreacted to negative feedback, whether it came from yourself or from someone else. Check your "sensitivity index" every day. Did you overreact? If so, use your daily relaxation time to visualize a more appropriate response. Did you say exactly how you felt without injuring anyone else? If so, what are you worried about?

⊞ Unlock Your Real Personality

"Everyone has personality locked up within him," Maltz wrote. "When we say that a person 'has a good personality,' what we really mean is that he has freed and released the creative potential within him and is able to express his real self." The bad news is that emotional scars and excessive inhibition can have negative effects on your personality. The good news is that there are steps you can take to liberate yourself from them.

Think of that for a moment. By removing the glitches from your personality, you liberate *your self*. You free the aspect of you that is unique and creative. And once you've brought your real self into the light, all those negative, unattractive images you've been holding of *your self* will simply vanish. "The real self within every person *is* attractive," Maltz wrote. "It *is* magnetic. It [has] a powerful influence upon other people. We have the feeling that we are in touch with something real—and basic—and it does something to us." Let yours do something to you.

Targeting on Ideas

- Glitches can form in your personality as the result of emotional wounds or excessive negative feedback.
- Forgiveness is the key to freeing yourself from the "scar tissue" caused by emotional wounds in the past.
- You can take proactive measures to guard against emotional wounds.
- You can free your personality from inhibition by learning to respond correctively to criticism.

SET YOUR OWN TARGETS

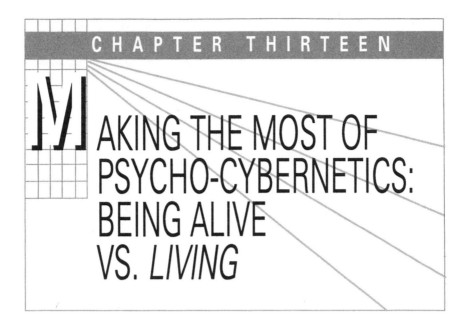

MAKING THE MOST OF PSYCHO-CYBERNETICS: BEING ALIVE VS. *LIVING*

Everyone's real goal...is for more life—more living. Whatever your definition of happiness may be, you will *experience* happiness only as you experience more life. More living means among other things more accomplishment, the attainment of worthwhile goals, more love experienced and given, more health and enjoyment, more happiness for both yourself and others.... [L]et us not limit our acceptance of Life by our own feelings of unworthiness.

—*Maxwell Maltz*, Psycho-Cybernetics *(1960)*

The most exciting breakthroughs of the twenty-first century will occur not because of technology but because of an expanding concept of what it means to be human.

—*John Naisbitt and Patricia Aburdene*, Megatrends 2000 *(1990)*

As I begin this final chapter, the summer Olympic Games are in progress in Barcelona, Spain. I'm not much of a sports fan, but like hundreds of millions of others around the world I've been caught up in the spectacle as presented on TV and described in print. And while taking in the competition and the "human interest" sidebars, I've been struck by the unwitting testimonials given by so many athletes, coaches and commentators to the principles of Psycho-Cybernetics.

At the age of ten, Scott Donie wrote a school paper in which he stated his intention of winning a medal in the Olympic Games. It's a safe bet that Donie, a silver medalist in platform diving in Barcelona, does not need to be convinced of the efficacy of goal setting.

Romanian weightlifting champion Dragomir Ciroslav severely injured himself two months before the 1984 Olympics in Los Angeles when he dropped a 600-pound barbell on his neck. Stuck in a hospital for a month and unable to train, he spent eight hours every day visualizing his workout in minute detail. Ciroslav took home a bronze medal from the L.A. games. Today as coach of his country's weightlifting team, he attributes its success in international competition to the "mental methods" he introduced as a result of his experience.

American gymnast Shannon Miller was not considered a top contender in Barcelona; the leading U.S. challenge to the Eastern European women was expected to come from Kim Zmeskal. But in the end it was Miller who took home the medals while Zmeskal finished back in the pack. The key to young Shannon's performace was summed up by a commentator as she stood awaiting her turn on the balance beam. "Look at her," the announcer said. "She's completely relaxed."

U.S. Table Tennis champion Sean O'Neill "practiced" at the United States Olympic Training Center in Colorado Springs by sitting in a special chair watching a video of his best games while listening to the taped voice of a sports psychologist. According to an article by Paul Shepherd, O'Neill was subsequently "able to relive the positive environment of the...chair and visualize a flawless performance. During the year O'Neill is spending...to prepare for his Olympic qualifying trials, he wakes up every morning...and writes his goal: 'I am a member of the 1992 Olympic team.' Over and over, he writes the words until he believes them—and makes the team. 'If I had to say one thing that surprises most people about table tennis, it would be the amount of preparation I do. I spend one to one and a half hours a day just on mental training—visualization, relaxation, goal setting, and listening to tapes.'"

You too now have the power to become a champion. Armed with the tools of Psycho-Cybernetics, you can choose your event and "go for the gold." And there's nothing that limits you to a single "event." You can be a winner in your career, your love life, your family relationships, your creative endeavors, your spiritual development. All that's necessary to get and keep "that winning feeling" is the healthy and realistic self-image that makes success possible.

"Once you give it a definite goal to achieve, you can depend upon [your] automatic mechanism to take you to that goal," Maltz wrote. "...But to accomplish this...you must think of the end result *in terms of a present possibility*.... "[I]f we keep our positive goal in mind, and picture it to ourselves so vividly as to make it 'real,' and think of it in terms of an accomplished fact, we will...experience...self-confidence, courage, and the faith that the outcome will be desirable. We cannot consciously peek into our creative mechanism.... But we can determine its present 'set' by our feelings. When it is 'set for success,' we experience that 'winning feeling.'"

By now you're an expert on accessing those feelings that lead to success. This final chapter is about maintaining those feelings throughout your life—about making *life itself* your primary, overarching goal. It's a collection of information, observations, exercises and assorted odds and ends, a summary and tying together of ideas about using this book as a springboard, a starting block, a vaulting pole to more energy, more creativity, greater happiness—literally *more life*. You'll learn:

- how a healthy self-image can actually add to your longevity.
- how to tap the energies that let you take charge of your own life.

- how to access and maintain feelings that keep your self-esteem high.
- steps you can take to transcend negative experiences and make happiness a habit.

How a Healthy Self-Image Can Add Years to Your Life

In this book you've seen numerous examples of what you can achieve when your self-esteem is high. You've seen how a positive self-image:

- lets you set a high set point for success and keep it in focus.
- turns you into a problem solver instead of a problem saver.
- keeps stress under control so that it doesn't become distress.
- allows you to "over-believe"—Maltz's term for focusing on goals even when the "facts" as you see them may not justify your pursuit of them.
- aids you in achieving the relaxation necessary for physical health.
- assists you in releasing your spirit and your enthusiasm for life.
- enables you to persevere even when circumstances are difficult.
- helps you to use a crisis as an opportunity, not a defeat.
- shows you the way to keep yourself pointed in a positive direction.

Let me now add what may be the single most important function of your self-image: *it can actually help you live longer.*

"If we think of man as a goal-striver," Maltz wrote, "we can think of...Life Force as the propelling fuel or energy which drives him forward toward his goal.... I believe that we establish [life force] by looking forward to the future with joy and anticipation, when we expect to enjoy tomorrow, and above all, when we have something important (to us) to do and somewhere to go....

"I believe that life is adaptive; that life is not just an end in itself, but a means to an end.... [I]s it not unreasonable to assume that if we place ourselves in the sort of goal-situation where more life is needed, that we will receive more life?"

"Life force" is one of those ideas that's difficult to define, but everyone knows what it is. We all know people who are alive only in a biological sense. They're breathing, but they're not *living*. They're no longer participating in life or growing in spirit. Whatever it is that's "killed" them, a single emotional blow or a series of disappointments, their life force has gone out. They've lost the fundamental goal of all living things—to keep and extend life. And while such individuals may physically linger on for years before we bury them, a person who is spiritually and emotionally dead at age 45 is far less likely to live to a ripe old age than a person who continues to discover and pursue new goals, new experiences, new areas of growth.

A Positive Self-Image Equals Longevity

"In many ways...putting the brakes on mental aging may depend on a positive and aroused response to the challenges presented by the world around us," wrote Kathy Keeton in her book *Longevity*. "The same is true, apparently, of our attitudes toward ourselves and others."

In Maltz's day the link between "life force" and longevity was largely a matter of folk wisdom. In recent years the direct relationship between a positive self-image and a longer and healthier life span has been confirmed by study after study. For example: the sense of empowerment you feel when you take charge of your life may actually contribute to the extention of your life. A study of seniors in a Connecticut nursing home by psychologist Judith Rodin compared the health, attitudes and life expectancy of two groups of residents. One group was given a degree of decision-making control over their activities, the other's needs were entirely taken care of by the staff. The payoff for the "take-charge" group in observable activeness, mental alertness, reduced need for medication and lower death rate indicated that the feeling of "being in control," of having a sense of purpose, is "of central importance in influencing psychological and physical health, and perhaps even longevity."

We've talked about excessive shyness as a symptom of low self-esteem. Now a study by psychologist Jerome Kagan indicates that "shyness" can actually be hazardous to your health. It tends to be associated with such danger signals as accelerated heart rates, muscle tension, and high levels of stress hormones.

A four-decade study led by George E. Valliant of the Dartmouth Medical School indicated that those who had the most pessimistic view of life while in their twenties tended to be more likely to die or suffer from serious illnesses in their forties or fifties.

Remember our discussion of charity as an element of the success-type personality? A study by psychologist Larry Scherwitz indicates that the more people tend to talk about themselves, the more susceptible they are to heart disease and death by heart attack. (He used the number of times his subjects used the words "I" "me" and "my" in taped conversations as his criterion.) Scherwitz's conclusion? "Listen with regard when others talk. Give your time and energy to others; let others have their way; do things for reasons other than furthering your own needs. Develop an attitude of love, because love erases the imaginary boundaries between self, others, and the world."

How to Use Psycho-Cybernetics for Longer Life

Before you start writing your will—relax. None of this data is meant to scare you, only to get you thinking about the way you may be living. A poor self-image and the symptoms that go along with it—living according to someone else's goals, a tendency to withdraw from human interaction, excessive stress, a pessimistic outlook, self-preoccupation—they're all *habits,* and as such they're all reversible. They're emotional habits that can shorten life, just as smoking, poor diet and lack of exercise are physical habits that can shorten life.

Think about it. By developing a joy and enthusiasm for life, you create a need for more life. By cultivating a "nostalgia for the future," you can actually expand your future. You can regenerate your life force and possibly add years to your life *no matter how old you presently are.* You can do it by:

- refusing to set limitations on yourself.
- creating a *need* for more life through goal setting.

- doing away with the sense of futility that can lead to stress.

- replacing the false pride and self-preoccupation that come from low self-esteem with the genuine appreciation of yourself that comes from a positive personal attitude.

- choosing to treat yourself with the respect and dignity you deserve.

Becoming the Master Planner of Your Life

When Arthur signed up for the seminar on "life planning," he was looking for advice on long-range financial management. What he got was a renewal of his life. Arthur, 36, lived in central Florida, where he worked for for a metal-stamping company. He had started there fresh out of college and worked his way up to a senior management position. He had been married eleven years and had two children. His wife Clare worked at home part time in telemarketing and made a modest salary, but he often found himself feeling envious of the time she was able to spend with the kids while he was off being Mr. Power Lunch.

For Arthur the key moment of the seminar came when he was asked to take a sheet of paper, fold it lengthwise and list on either side the pros and cons of his job. To his amazement he found he had listed three times as many cons as pros. The only things he liked about his work were the money, the challenge of managing people, and the occasional perks—two free trips to Hawaii in fifteen years. Among the cons: not enough time to spend with his family, not enough time for recreation, too much stress, putting on weight (those power lunches), indifference to the metal-stamping business, frequent boredom and depression—the list went almost to the bottom of the page.

Arthur went home thinking seriously about making a career change. What, where, when and how to do it? He considered his longest-running interests, all of which went back to his childhood—baseball, stamp collecting and scuba diving. Sigh. Scuba was by far his greatest passion, but he hadn't been diving in six years, not since his second son was born.

But if you're going to create your ideal job, there's no better place to start than your passion. Arthur considered what transferable skills he had. Well, his people-managing skills would be useful across the board. He had learned to be time-conscious and well organized, and these qualities too would help him in any field.

Next step: how did one make money in scuba diving? Arthur considered becoming an instructor, working as a manager in a large scuba shop or investing in his own small one. He talked to several diving instructors and shop owners to get a feel for the business. By this time his wife had caught his enthusiasm. To get a better idea of the commercial possibilities of scuba diving, they rejoined the diving club they had belonged to when they were first married. They discovered that there was a growing need for dive shops in Canada, particularly in Nova Scotia and New Brunswick. Arthur had spent the first nine years of his life in Toronto; he held dual U.S.–Canadian citizenship, so this was a real possibility. The move would mean serious changes in income and lifestyle, but by now Arthur recognized that he was feeling more enthusiasm than he had in years. The more he and Clare explored the idea, the more excited they became. He could manage the shop, instruct summer tourists, and spend the winter months teaching beginners at a local pool. Clare would be a whiz on the phone and at keeping the books. She could also supplement the family income by giving piano lessons in their home. In fact there would be a greater demand in New Brunswick than in Florida, where there were fewer young families and more retirees.

To keep this story short: four years after Arthur attended that seminar, he and Clare owned two scuba shops and were doing splendidly. They had successfully made the transition to new jobs, cold weather and a foreign culture. For Arthur the key to his success was his enthusiasm, his joy in what he was doing. Instead of following the "group plan" for success—get a job, move up, play the game, collect your perks—he was thriving on his own.

Find Your Own Best Self

When you choose to become the master planner of your life, you create what psychologist Charles Garfield calls *vertical longevity:*

"the art of living as fully as possible during each moment of chronological life." It's important to find the things that are most meaningful to you—to create your ideal job, to immerse yourself in a creative project, to find an emotionally fulfilling way to improve your finances, to live in a way that is spiritually satisfying to you; to take command, to grow, to *express*. You may be thinking that you don't have Arthur's options, but you don't need them. It wasn't his options that were crucial to his success, it was his passion. Explore your own options. Investigate your own passion. Brainstorm, identify your transferable skills, join interest groups to find informal avenues of entry, uncover ways that you can take control of your life. Start by considering these questions and exercises:

1. What is the *most exciting thing* I have ever done in my life?

2. What experiences of the past five years have I found emotionally stimulating?

3. What were the common elements in these experiences (*e.g.:* change, physical challenge, creative thinking, working with people)?

4. Pinpoint why these events were exciting for you (*e.g.:* allowed you freedom, gave you spiritual fulfillment, gave you the opportunity to travel). Make a list of your reasons.

5. Use your list as a starting point to brainstorm with selected friends, colleagues and loved ones. Identify ways in which you create similar experiences and challenges in a different arena.

6. Brainstorm these ideas with yourself. Let your right brain make its contribution. Use a large sheet of butcher paper and let any ideas emerge—no matter how strange or impractical they may seem.

7. Make a point of going over each day's activities and asking yourself, "What was the *best part* of my day? What made it so?" Circle these key events.

8. After seven days, make a list of the events you circled. Choose the one that was the best part of your week. Note any recurring themes. This becomes your treasure map for finding more of what you really like to do.

9. Once you've identified your focal points for taking control of your life, translate them into goals. Review the SMART plan in chapter 7 and begin the process of establishing your "best self" as a set point.

How to Keep Your Servomechanism Well-Tuned

Change can be a challenge at any point in your life. You may be riding a wave of self-esteem when some event sets the old I-can't tapes whirring. New situations pop up, new people bend the direction of your life, you have an unexpected interaction with a "problem person" from your past. Suddenly your goal is clouded by self-doubt. Negative thoughts shift you this way and that. You find relaxation difficult; you react to criticism as if it were a bullet; you get discouraged about the process you were feeling so pleased about.

Please note: *This will happen.* Because a servomechanism can only work by correcting its course, there'll be times you'll find yours alarmingly off course. The secret is to avoid developing a bleak outlook when this happens. Instead of giving up, be aware of the danger signals your internal guidance system is sending you and take action that will keep it operating smoothly.

Elsbeth was a dancer, age 29, who thought she had her self-esteem problem licked. During her career she'd had to overcome a great deal of anxiety deriving from old childhood tapes—a father who'd criticized her as "lazy" for her devotion to the arts instead of a "real" career, and a boarding-school dorm mother who had frequently chided her for "not keeping up with the group." Now she was in New York, the big time, with a prestigious dance-repertory theater, and she was ready to turn around and go back to Allentown. She was tense and irritable in rehearsal, discouraged and lonely in her reflective moments. The choreographer was snapping at her for "not listening," for "not putting in enough rehearsal time," for "making everyone stop and begin again." She was not only angry, she was embarrassed in front of the rest of the company.

Elsbeth had attended one of my seminars, and she remembered the "SEEDS-backwards" procedure. Perhaps there was a way in which she was *choosing* a negative outcome that she could easily reverse.

Her *self-esteem* had certainly taken a nosedive in the two months since her move to New York. All her old self-doubts had come marching back in like the mouse army in *The Nutcracker*. What was she *doing* wrong? Nothing: she *was* listening to the choreographer; she *was* rehearsing diligently. That was not her problem. The routines weren't that difficult, yet she couldn't seem to master them. What *emotions* could she clearly identify? Embarrassment, confusion, bewilderment, anger, resentment and frustration to name a few. Were these feelings resulting from actual circumstances or from her *evaluation* of them?

Just what was her evaluation? Elsbeth sat down with a notepad and pen and made a list of the thoughts that were preoccupying her:

- Did I make the right move in coming to New York?
- The choreographer is breathing down my neck.
- The producer is going to think she made the wrong move in hiring me.
- The rest of the troupe is so familiar with these moves. I'll never catch on, let alone catch up with them.

Here was Elsbeth's key to understanding. The *situation* was that she had moved to New York and joined a new dance company—period. Her negative emotions had arisen from the way she had *chosen* to evaluate her decision—not from the decision itself, certainly not from the choreographer or from any objective assessment of her talent as a dancer.

Now that Elsbeth had a handle on her sudden loss of self-esteem, she was ready to do something about it. She practiced saying "Cancel!" whenever she was consciously aware of her self-doubting thoughts. She made a point of spending fifteen minutes every day in relaxed visualization, seeing herself performing the dance steps with the rest of the company and feeling the emotional well-being that came from the choreographer's approval.

Of course her subconscious mind responded to these imagined rehearsals as if they were actual experiences. Back in the studio, Elsbeth found herself relaxing into the rhythm of the dances. Within two weeks she had not only caught on and caught up, she had fully accepted herself as a member of the company. She was pleased with herself for having uncovered the hidden cause of her frustration and even more pleased that she had been able to reverse its effects.

Practice Perceiving Yourself as a Success

Use the "SEEDS-backwards" procedure whenever you find yourself doubting your capabilities, whenever your spiritual energy is at a low ebb, whenever you need a booster shot for your self-image:

1. Self-esteem. Sit down and write a description of yourself as you would be with an adequate, healthy measure of self-esteem. Take some time to relax and picture the "ideal you." Write down exactly how you would look and feel and what you would do with a fully positive self-image. Consider how you could go about formulating a fake-it-till-you-make-it attitude:

- Smile more often.
- Maintain good posture: keep your head up and your shoulders squared.
- Assume that others like you.
- Pretend you're having a great day. Focus on saying only positive things. If anyone asks how you are, tell them "Top form, thank you!" (Yes, I'm telling you to be a Pollyanna, or at least to act like one!)

2. Do. If you're having trouble maintaining self-esteem, determine what action you can take to restore it:

When you receive criticism (including self-criticism), use rational thinking to ask yourself whether it's valid. If so, take corrective action. If not, forget about it. Just keep moving toward your goal.

- When your buttons get pushed, delay your response. Ask yourself how many emotional dollars it's worth spending on the situation.
- When an obstacle is blocking your path to your goal, ask yourself what action you can take to circumvent it. Then *do* it!
- When others doubt you, remind yourself that their doubt is *their* problem, not yours.
- When discouraged, relax. Use your right brain to find a creative solution.
- When depressed, remind yourself "This too shall pass." Use the theater of your imagination to remember the good times and the feelings they produced.

3. Emotions. Remember to think of emotion as *energy* in *motion*. Take an inventory of the ways in which you're moving *your* energy. Are you moving toward your goal or away from it? If your emotions are preventing you from taking positive action, stop, relax, and shift your focus:

- If you feel angry, focus on allowing your body to relax. Your mind cannot be under stress unless your body is under stress.
- If you feel discouraged, re-evaluate your goals, but don't fail to focus on the successes you've already gained.
- If you feel frustrated, take a moment and shift your awareness to other alternatives. Take a moment to define just what the feeling is. Then ask yourself what alternate approaches you can take. Sometimes a mental checklist of your options is a great help.
- If you feel resentful, remember that resentment is only anger gone rotten. Deal with it immediately: forgiveness is the only remedy.
- If you feel lonely, ask yourself what you can do to help someone else.

4. Evaluation. Are your negative feelings the result of something that's happened or only of the way you're perceiving it? Step back from the situation and focus on the way you're reacting. Consciously ask yourself the following questions:

- Have I thoroughly checked out my assumptions? Is this the only interpretation I can put on the situation?

- Where did I *get* this interpretation? Are there any old tapes I can identify?
- *Why* do I think this way about it? What might I be reading between the lines?
- Did I really *listen* to the feedback, or am I just reacting to it?

5. Situation. Ultimately life is *not* a stacked deck. It deals out situations to us all in a completely random way. Learn to view each situation as a random deal—even if you feel you've been getting more than your share of deuces and not enough face cards. Even when the situation seems unfair or cruel, remember that "life" isn't cheating you:

- Remind yourself that the situation could have happened to anyone.
- Remind yourself that *you* determine whether or not to let your buttons be pushed.
- Remind yourself that you're *reacting* to the situation. Ask yourself at once what you can do to *act* upon it. Immediately begin responding to the situation in a problem-solving, course-correcting way.

Don't Let Negative Thoughts Erode Your Self-Esteem

No matter how diligently positive you are in your responses to feedback, there will be times when negative thoughts intrude. They may creep in as you go about your daily activity, or they may burst in as you awaken in the middle of the night: "I'm such a jerk. Who am I fooling with this self-image garbage? Just me, good old Chump Number One. Everyone else can see how worthless I am!"

The trick is to deal with such thoughts before they erode your self esteem. Don't dwell on them to the point where your horse starts interpreting them as instructions. As Maltz put it, "[I]f there is one simple secret to the operation of your unconscious creative mechanism, it is this: call up, capture, evoke the *feeling of success.* When you feel successful and self-confident, you will act successfully. When the feeling is strong, you can literally do no wrong. The [feeling] itself does not *cause* you to operate successfully.... [I]t is more in the nature of a sign or symptom that we are geared for success."

When your automatic mechanism goes into a tailspin, put it back on course by making yourself aware of your negative feelings. Then consciously select positive feelings to eliminate the negative ones:

1. Make a point of *listening* to your internal dialog. Turn off all distractions and tune in to yourself. Become consciously aware of the things you're saying to yourself. Think about how you'd react if someone else said such things about you. Adjust for mood swings by choosing three different times each day to listen to your self-talk. For example: during your morning shower, just after lunch and while getting ready for bed.

2. Keep a journal or diary for a week or two. Record your self-talks—the exact words as well as the flavor of what you're saying. Note the direction in which you're pointing your horse.

3. Now you know what to listen for. When those negative tapes start to roll, say "Cancel!" State positive messages at once to replace the negative ones.

4. By now you know the drill: make a few three-by-five inch affirmation cards to remind your automatic mechanism of whatever you wish to reinforce. Place them on your desk, your bathroom mirror and in other strategic locations.

5. Relax and focus on the progress you've made. Think of how far you've come, of the triumphs you've enjoyed on your path to your goal. You've spent six weeks on reflective relearning. You're no longer faking it—you've made it! There's nothing wrong with you. You simply need to give your servomechanism a tune-up, a front-end alignment. Don't even *think* of scrapping it!

Don't React to Imaginary Failure

Then there are those times you're so preoccupied with the possibility of failing that you manage to fool yourself into believing you *have* failed. These are the times, Maltz said, when you "worry about possible unfavorable results, accompanied by feelings of anxiety, inadequacy, or perhaps humiliation[.] For all practical purposes we experience the very same emotions in advance, that would be appropriate if we had already failed. We picture failure to ourselves, not vaguely or in general terms—but vividly and in great detail. We repeat the failure images over and over again to ourselves. We go back in memory and drag up memory images of past failures."

Remember—the subconscious mind can't tell the difference between a real experience and one that is vividly imagined. When you find yourself dwelling on failure, worrying about failure or thinking of yourself *as* a failure, ask yourself these questions and take the appropriate corrective steps:

1. Am I concerned with the here and now or with future fears and conflicts? If it's something that *might* happen down the road, I'll face up to it when the time comes. There's no point in worrying about it now.

2. Am I playing the "what if?" game? If so, "So, what if...?"

3. What do I stand to gain by worrying? Is it getting me closer or farther away from my desired goal? If farther, what's the use of worrying?

4. Is this imagined, projected, worst-case-scenario fear? If so, CANCEL. I'll relax and focus on my successes.

How to Make Happiness a Habit

"Don't worry—be happy!" is more than just the message of a catchy popular tune. It's actually a prescription for success and longer life. Psychologist Martin E. P. Seligman has made a career-long study of what he calls the "explanatory style" of optimists and pessimists. "The defining characteristics of pessimists," he wrote in his book *Learned Optimism*, "is that they tend to believe bad events will last a long time, will undermine everything they do, and are their own fault. The optimists, who are confronted with the same hard knocks of this world, think about misfortune in the opposite way. They tend to believe defeat is just a temporary setback, that its causes are confined to this one case. [They] believe defeat is not their fault: Circumstances, bad luck, or other people brought it about. Such people are unfazed by defeat. Confronted by a bad situation, they perceive it as a challenge and try harder....

"Literally hundreds of studies show that pessimists give up more easily and get depressed more often. These experiments also show that optimists do much better in school and college, at work and on the playing field.... Their health is unusually good. They age well, much freer than most of us from the usual physical ills of middle age. Evidence suggests they may even live longer.... The good news is that pessimists can learn the skills of optimism and permanently improve the quality of their lives."

Maxwell Maltz had reached the same conclusion more than 30 years earlier. "Happiness is a mental habit which can be cultivated and developed," he wrote. "...No one, other than a saint, can be 100 percent happy all the time.... But we can, by taking thought, and making a simple decision, be happy and think pleasant thoughts a large share of the time, regarding that multitude of little events and circumstances of daily living which now makes us unhappy. To a large extent we react to petty annoyances, frustrations, and the like with grumpiness, dissatisfaction, resentment and irritability, purely out of habit. We have *practiced* reacting that way so long, it has become habitual."

Don't Wait to Be Happy

How do you acquire and cultivate the habit of happiness? When we were first exploring goal setting, we looked at the way people play the when-is-life-going-to-get-better game. They use "magical thinking" to tell themselves that life will be better just as soon as they pass the next milestone—gaining the freedom of their first car, attaining adulthood, finding their true love and so on. If that's your approach to happiness, it's almost certain that it will continue to elude you. Happiness doesn't operate on a schedule. If you're waiting for the "right time" to be happy, chances are you'll wait forever.

Instead, recognize that you'll find the path to your goal much smoother if you consciously *choose* happiness. Don't be one of those people who puts happiness on hold. There is only one right time to make your move to happiness: *now*. You can make happiness a habit in the same way you make any other attitude and behavior a habit—through conscious, repeated practice until it has become a subconscious act. You can realistically expect optimism to be your usual state (allowing for occasional bumps in the road) if you diligently observe the following tips:

1. When negative thoughts and feelings creep in, deal with them Psycho-Cybernetically. Don't let your evaluation put a negative spin on events. CANCEL pessimistic thoughts about situations you are powerless to change at the present moment. Regardless of what outrages the day throws at you, react as rationally and unstressfully as possible.

2. Give happiness your best shot. Always be open to the smallest possibility of it. Focus on the feeling you get from enjoying a special meal, watching a sunset, completing a long-term project, having a favorite old movie pop up on late-night cable, seeing a 1920s biplane swoop down low over your neighborhood, getting a special present when it isn't your birthday. You know the moments that work for you. Try to keep the feeling they give you in your consciousness as much as you can.

3. Practice *being* happy. This is an "act-as-if" exercise. Tell yourself and others that you are generally a happy person. Rehearse your smile often. Practice giving thanks daily, hourly, for the dozens of small happinesses that come your way each day—waking up this morning, for instance.

4. Go out of your way to make small daily contributions to others' happiness. If you see someone struggling with packages, offer to help. If you see someone staring at a map and looking confused, ask her if she needs directions. Openly acknowledge when someone else makes a contribution to *your* happiness. Remember the old saw, "happiness is contagious"? It works!

5. Think of a person whose presence in your life has stimulated your spirit, added to your sense of self-worth and truly strengthened your life force. Take some time to focus on this person, whether parent, grandparent, friend or teacher, and acknowledge his or her contribution to your happiness.

6. Practice being less critical of other people's faults, failings and mistakes. Put the best possible interpretation on their actions and you'll avoid the emotions that negate happiness.

7. Strive for a one percent/one hundred percent ratio. Instead of trying to be one hundred percent happier, make yourself one percent happier in a hundred different ways.

8. If you can stand reading it one more time, "fake it till you make it." Act as though your self-image is exactly the way you want it to be, as though the success you desire has already been achieved.

Just Don't Expect to Be Happy Every Minute

Many people are chronically unhappy because their rate of expectancy is unrealistic. An optimist recognizes that happiness is a relative quantity, a range on a continuum, a now-you-see-it, now-you-don't proposition. Don't delude yourself that you can ward off unhappiness in all situations all the time. There's no such thing as lasting and eternal happiness on this earth.

"Who ever said life was fair?" your old tapes may tell you. The point to recognize is that life isn't unfair either. Life is *fragile*. We're all subject to its slings and arrows. The important thing is to learn to accept them without thinking of them as permanent conditions of your life, without convincing yourself they'll destroy you, without blaming yourself or resenting others. When you learn to do that, you'll have caught the happiness habit.

⊞ Find Your Flow: Becoming a Champion

"[H]appiness is not something that happens," observes psychologist Mihaly Csikszentmihalyi (pronounced CHIK-seh-mee-HIGH). "...It does not depend on outside events, but, rather, on how we interpret them. Happiness, in fact, is a condition that must be prepared for, cultivated, and defended privately by each person. People who learn to control inner experience will be able to determine the quality of their lives, which is as close as any of us can come to being happy...."

"[W]e have all experienced times when, instead of being buffetted by anonymous forces, we do feel in control of our actions, masters of our own fate. On the rare occasions that it happens, we feel a sense of exhilaration, a deep sense of enjoyment that is long cherished and that becomes a landmark in memory for what life should be like."

Csikszentmihalyi uses the word *flow* to define this "optimal experience." He interviewed hundreds of subjects around the world, from artists to assembly-line workers to homemakers to athletes to chess masters to motorcycle enthusiasts, in an attempt to understand what leads people to experience flow. For most of his subjects there came a transcendent moment when "a person's body or mind is stretched to its limits in a voluntary effort to accomplish something worthwhile.... When all a person's relevant skills are needed to cope with the challenges of a situation, that person's attention is absorbed completely by the activity.... As a result, one of the most universal and distinctive features of optimal experience takes place: people become so involved in what they are doing that the activity becomes almost spontaneous, almost automatic; they stop being aware of themselves as separate from the actions they are performing." As Olympic athlete Sean O'Neill describes it, "I seem to have all the time I want to think through every option, like my mind is a CD player searching the entire disk for the right song."

Once you've known such a peak experience even once, you've acquired a valuable tool for determining the quality of your life. By recalling those moments when achievement was effortless, when you were at the pinnacle of accomplishment, you establish a comparative norm, "a landmark in memory for what life should be like." Your horse can weather those times when it's mired in a thicket or struggling to learn new paths if your rider can remind it that it once won the Kentucky Derby.

Just don't expect to induce flow through "will" or any other left-brain process. It occurs naturally and spontaneously from a state of relaxed concentration when you are engaged in passionate pursuit of a goal, when your pleasure in striving and achivement becomes so great that you approach it almost as a game. You *can* attempt to pinpoint the circumstances under which it happens to you. Think about the circumstances that might awaken in you this feeling of effortless achievement, of being at the pinnacle of accomplishment.

When have you felt that time was standing still?

When have you suddenly awakened to the realization that you have solved a difficult problem?

What activities let you become "lost in thought" as you perform them?

What projects have been so absorbing to you that you've worked on them without any awareness of time passing?

When have you had the feeling that you were absolutely the best in the world at what you were doing at that moment—the gold-medal winner?

Take some time to think about these questions. There's nothing like the experience of flow to lift your self-image into a state from which nothing can pull you down. There's nothing like having known it, even once, to make you pursue with enthusiasm the goal of "more life in your life."

Enthusiasm. The word literally means "to experience God within." Isn't that a feeling worth working for?

With all the amazing tools being developed to probe the deep structure and functioning of the human brain, techniques such as PET scans and magnetic resonance imaging, it may only be a matter of time before science comes to understand how flow is triggered. Until then, keep your right brain limber. Keep your goals imprinted vividly in your consciousness through visualization; keep enhancing your ability to achieve relaxation as you pursue them. Keep up your enthusiasm. Your happiness, your success, your life force itself will all be enhanced.

"What Can I Do as a Working Mother...?"

Often I'm approached at seminars by women who say to me, *"You've* been a working mother—how do you work a job all day and then come home and be Supermom? Where do you get the time and energy?"

Answer: from your own life force. It's when you're most active that it tends to be stronger—especially for women. A long-range study by Cornell University sociologists tracked a group of women from 1956 through the late '80s and compared the lifespans of those who had juggled parenthood, careers, and community activities in their youth with those who had stayed home with the kids. The results indicated that the working mothers typically lived much longer than the stay-at-homes.

I believe you can achieve flow through the passionate pursuit of parenting, and when that happens it can be the most satisfying of all ways to experience it. The secret may lie in that tired old phrase "quality time": you can't be actively engaged as a parent all the time, so it's important to create those times when you're focused on your children. Here are some ways to do it:

1. Spend at least ten minutes daily alone with each child. During those ten minutes, give her your undivided attention. Don't ask a lot of so-how-was-school-today questions. Just let her ramble. Your job is to listen.

2. Create small projects based on activities that you and your child(ren) both enjoy. Make a point of spending time *alone* with each child at least once a month doing what he likes to do best with you—whether it's baking cookies, playing on the swings in the park, throwing a ball around or just sitting and reading. If it's an interest you can share with other parents and children, so much the better.

3. Let your child(ren) see the *real* you—not an artificially exuberant copy or a depressed and dejected husk. Avoid too much *protection* as well as too much *projection*. It's fair and appropriate to say, "Yes, I've had a tough day. Everyone has them from time to time."

4. Model the happiness habit. Never blame anyone else for your frustrations or disappointments. Never express the idea that any personal setback, yours, theirs or anyone's, is an indication of inadequacy or a permament situation. Let them know that life simply deals out cards. Sometimes we get good ones and sometimes we don't, but it's how we play them that counts.

5. It's never too early for children to learn to coordinate left- and right-brain problem-solving techniques. Teach them how to use relaxation

and guided visualization. Sit down with them and help them develop action plans for their own goal setting.

"...Or Half of a Dual-Career Couple?"

With or without children, being part of a dual-career couple presents a challenge to anyone trying to keep his life force strong and her relationship working. The unavoidable conflicts and unsatisfying compromises can lead to discouragement and frustration, interfere with personal and spiritual growth and put a crimp in the dynamics of the relationship. Your goals as individuals often seem at odds with your goals as a couple. When that happens, increase your chances of achieving flow in your relationship by observing these guidelines:

1. Tell each other truthfully which chores or projects you would prefer to do. Maturely negotiate who'll do what: "I'll do the shopping if you paint the kitchen cabinets; you hate vacuuming so I'll take care of that if you'll give the dog a bath."

2. Allow your partner the private time that he or she requests. We all need these times, and excessive togetherness can become as much of a problem as the ships-passing-in-the-night routine.

3. Plan on an evening just for the two of you every two weeks. It needn't be a fancy or "romantic" activity. As long as it's a pleasant reason for being together, it keeps your respective servomechanisms focused on enjoyment of your time together. Having dinner out works. Sitting down to plan a trip works. Paying bills does *not* work.

4. Plan family occasions judiciously. Be fair and equitable about the time you spend with your respective relatives. Don't insist that you always go to *your* mother's house on Thanksgiving just because "her feelings will be hurt if we don't." If there's friction between your partner's sister and your cousin Charlotte, resist the temptation to take care of all your family obligations at once by inviting them to the same function. It might be better for your relationship if you kept them separate.

5. Are you psychic? Good; didn't think so. Then don't *assume* you know what's going on in your partner's head. Let him tell you.

"...Or a Single Parent?"

This situation is far more common for women than for men, but whatever gender you are it can present serious obstacles to keeping your life force strong. There's just so much to do and so little time to do it in that it's easy to let discouragement and loneliness seep in. And then likely as not you feel guilty for "thinking of yourself"; for "letting your children down."

Just be careful you don't let yourself down. If you're a single mom or dad, all the guidelines listed above for the working parent apply to you. In addition, to keep your optimism up make sure you observe these "seven D's":

1. *Demand*—a strong word, but a necessary measure. Demand quiet times alone for yourself and see that you get them.
2. *Design* times together for shared activities with each child.
3. *Delegate* certain age-appropriate "do-able" tasks to each child.
4. *Diligently* keep track of each child's follow-through on tasks and create a consistent, motivational reward structure. *Example:* beds made by 7:45 every morning for a week is worth a trip to the pizza parlor on Saturday.
5. *Dates* must not be undermined. Whether it's a "date-date" or just an evening with a friend, let your child(ren) know that this is a part of your life, as important to you as their friends are to them.
6. *Decisiveness* is absolutely essential for the single parent. There's no such thing as "wait till your father gets home" if Father is living in St. Paul with his new wife. Make your decisions as quickly as possible and follow through at once. You can always re-decide if necessary.
7. *Direction*—as in sense of. Let your child(ren) know what your goals are. Give them a sense of where you're going and how it will affect where *they're* going. Keep apprised of their goals too. Get an idea of how their sense of direction is. Balance time talking about your goals with letting them talk about theirs.

"...Or Getting Older?"

It's never to late to be concerned about keeping your life force strong.

"[P]erhaps to a larger degree than we ever realized," Kathy Keeton observes, "getting old is all in the mind—or, to be accurate, in that most vital of all organs, the brain." Since the 1960s psychologists have been studying the power of the mind to influence the health and lifespan of elderly people. Again and again the data have shown that a positive attitude, goals to pursue, above all else the desire for health and longer life have contributed to increased vigor, reduced hospitalization...more years.

So, in addition to the usual caveats about diet and exercise, I'd make the following suggestions to our aging population:

1. Be a joiner. Get involved in groups, participate in activities, make a contribution to your community. Your arthritis won't bother you any more when you're on the go than when you're on the sofa.

2. Keep up your mental gymnastics. Take a seniors' trip to an archeological dig, do crossword puzzles—do whatever you can to exercise those connections between your brain cells.

3. You've worked hard all your life, and now for a change your time is largely your own. Keep it that way. Babysit for your grandchildren only when you want to. Don't let your children's requests become a burden. You've already had your turn.

4. Plan a new "career"—either vocational or avocational—and throw yourself into it. Join organizations that are devoted to your interests for brainstorming and interaction. Now's the time to immerse yourself in those creative projects you never seemed to have time for when you were younger. The ancient Roman statesman Cato learned Greek at the age of 80. Anna Mary Robertson ("Grandma") Moses took up painting at the age of 76. Norman Maclean, after a career as a university English professor, published his first work of fiction, the award-winning *A River Runs Through It*, at 75.

5. Keep your love life active. I'm not talking about your sex life (though that too is important, if medically possible) but the "caring and cuddling" aspects of love. Surround yourself with people you care about. Volunteer to read to kids at the children's ward of a hospital. Don't allow love to pass out of your life, whatever age you may happen to be. As you grow in your own self-esteem, do what you can to help others grow in theirs.

The Magic Word Is: *Infundibulum*

"I believe that there is ONE LIFE, one ultimate source, [that] has many channels of expression and manifests itself in many forms," Maxwell Maltz wrote. "If we are to "Get More Living out of Life,' we should not limit the channels through which Life may come to us. We must accept it, whether it comes in the form of science, religion, psychology, or what not."

In reflecting on these interconncected channels through which we achieve self-fulfillment, I found myself thinking about one of the wisest people I know, Archbishop Warren Watters of the Free Church of Antioch. He was 101 years old when I last saw him, in his home in Santa Barbara, California; still mentally alert, still playing the piano and singing in his strong baritone voice. He had known and worked with Maxwell Maltz, and he showed great interest when I mentioned that I was writing this book. He asked if he could help me by answering any questions about his own formula for happiness, for empowering people to find their own best self. The archibishop's life has been devoted to helping people find their spiritual path, and I was delighted by his offer. "I know this is very simplistic and naive," I said, "but how do you think I can best impart to my readers how to achieve the happiness habit?"

He smiled and took my hands. "My dear, lovely woman," he said, "let me give you a word. Words are precious gifts. The word is *infundibulum*."

I said: "What?"

"*Infundibulum*," he repeated robustly.

"Okay, you got me," I admitted. "What does it mean?"

The archbishop insisted that I get one of his many dictionaries from his library shelf and read the definition aloud to him.

infundibulum 1: the hollow conical process of gray matter to which the pituitary body is continuous with the brain **2:** funnel

"'Funnel'?" I said, gazing at him. "*Funnel* is the secret of happiness?"

"Yes, that's it," he said, smiling. By now I knew he was really enjoying playing with me—obviously *he* was happy.

I asked him if he could elaborate. "Every day I meditate on happiness," he said. "I see the great universe funneling through the top of my head and throughout my being. Here, in my mental-emotional-spiritual infundibulum, I let it all pass through me, and I accept everyone and everything as being in its right and proper place. My infundibulum allows me to funnel the spiritual into the material until they blend into one. When it's working, I am able to *think with my heart* and *hear with my head*."

On this last word I leave you with the challenge to reformulate your life—to find your own intrinsic worth and greatness, your right and proper place in the great universe.

Targeting on Ideas

- The way you feel about yourself can have an impact on your longevity.
- Strengthen your life force by taking control of your life.
- To keep your internal guidance system well tuned and your life force strong, take steps to make happiness a habit.

SET
YOUR OWN
TARGETS

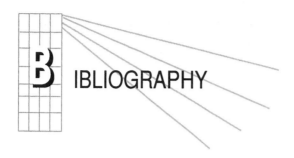

BIBLIOGRAPHY

A selection of non-technical books on self-image psychology and other subjects relating to Psycho-Cybernetics:

Benson, Herbert, and Miriam Z. Klipper, *The Relaxation Response.* New York: William Morrow and Company, 1975.

Borysenko, Joan, and Larry Rothstein, *Mending the Body, Mending the Mind.* Reading, MA: Addison Wesley, 1987.

Branden, Nathaniel, *Honoring the Self.* New York: Dell Books, 1988.

California Task Force to Promote Self-Esteem and Personal and Social Responsibility, *Toward a State of Esteem.* Sacramento: California Department of Education, 1990.

Cousins, Norman, *Anatomy of an Illness.* New York: W. W. Norton, 1979.

Covey, Stephen, *The Seven Habits of Highly Effective People.* New York: Simon and Schuster, 1990.

Csikszentmihalyi, Mihaly, *Flow: The Psychology of Optimal Experience.* New York: Harper and Row, 1990.

Dyer, Wayne, *The Sky's the Limit*. New York: Simon and Schuster, 1980.

Handy, Charles, *The Age of Unreason*. London: Business Books, 1989

Johnson, William B., *Workforce 2000*. Indianapolis: Hudson Institute, 1987.

Keeton, Kathy, *Longevity*. New York: Penguin USA, 1991.

Maltz, Maxwell, *The Magic Power of Self-Image Psychology*. Englewood Cliffs, NJ: Prentice-Hall, 1964.

_____, *Psycho-Cybernetic Principles for Creative Living*. New York: Pocket Books, 1974.

_____, *Psycho-Cybernetics*. Englewood Cliffs, NJ: Prentice-Hall, 1960.

Mendelsohn, Pam, *Happier By Degrees*. Berkeley, CA: Ten Speed Press, 1986.

Miller, Alice, *For Your Own Good*. New York: Farrar, Straus and Giroux, 1983.

Miller, Tom, *The Unfair Advantage*. Manlius, NY: The Unfair Advantage Corporation, 1986.

Naisbitt, John, and Patricia Aburdene, *Megatrends 2000*. New York: William Morrow and Company, 1990.

Ostrander, Sheila, Lynn Schroeder and Nancy Ostrander, *SuperLearning*. New York: Dell Books, 1979.

Paulson, Terry L., *They Shoot Managers, Don't They?* Santa Monica, CA: Lee Canter and Associates, 1988

Pelletier, Kenneth R., *Mind as Healer, Mind as Slayer*. New York: Dell Books, 1977.

Satir, Virginia, *Peoplemaking*. Palo Alto, CA: Science and Behavior Books, 1972.

Seligman, Martin E. P., *Learned Optimism*. New York: Alfred A. Knopf, 1990.

Siegel, Bernie, *Love, Medicine and Miracles*. New York: Harper and Row, 1986.

Simonton, O. Carl, Stephanie Matthews-Simonton and James Creighton, *Getting Well Again*. Los Angeles: J.P. Tarcher, 1978.

Springer, Sally P., and Georg Deutsch, *Left Brain, Right Brain*. San Francisco: W.H. Freeman, 1985.

Steinem, Gloria, *Revolution From Within: A Book of Self-Esteem*. Boston: Little, Brown and Company, 1992.

Tannen, Deborah, *You Just Don't Understand*. New York: William Morrow and Company, 1990

Wonder, Jacquelyn, and Priscilla Donovan, *Whole-Brain Thinking*. New York: William Morrow and Company, 1984.

Wurman, Richard, *Information Anxiety*. New York: Doubleday, 1989.

Zdenek, Marilee, *The Right-Brain Experience*. New York: McGraw-Hill, Inc., 1983.

Ziglar, Zig, *See You at the Top*. Gretna, LA: Pelican Publishing Company, 1974.

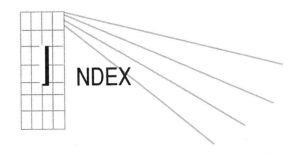

INDEX

C

Career
  career advancement example, use of
      psycho-cybernetics for, 219-224
  career change, example of, 321-322
  sense of direction about, 236
Change, resistance to, 91
Character ethics, development of, 255
Charity work, benefits of, 306
Children
  creating quality time for, 336-337
  and parental self-esteem, 90-91
Ciroslav, Dragomir, 316
Communication
  creative listening, 243-244
  mutual understanding in, 241-242
  and success-type personality, 240-244
Compliance principle, meaning of, 28-29
Conscious mind
  elimination principle, 29-31
  selection principle, 29-31
Courage
  and change, 244-245
  development of, 246
  examples of, 245
  and success-type personality, 244-246
Cousins, Norman, 140
Covey, Stephen, 255
Creativity
  acknowledgment of creative powers,
    254
  and relaxation, 100-101
  and stress, 99-100
Crisis, and decisive action, 246
Criticism. *See* Negative feedback
Csikszentmihalyi, Mihaly, 333-334

D

Daydreaming
  and goal setting, 164
  stress control, 139
Depression, 34-36
  cause of, 34-35
  exercises for, 35-36
Destructive instinct, 3-4, 10
Donie, Scott, 316
Donovan, Priscilla, 117
Dreams
  and goal setting, 164
  as stress control, 140

Dual-career family, creating flow in, 337
Dyer, Wayne, 41

E

Edgerman, Dr. Milton, 291
Einstein, Albert, 96
Elderly, guidelines for, 339-340
Elimination principle, 45
  meaning of, 29-31
Emotional scars, 14
  effects of, 288-290
  examples of, 286-287, 289
  and fear of intimacy, 294
  healing of, 295-306
    forgiveness, 298-301
    learning from mistakes, 301-303
    owning up to problems, 296-298
    stress control method, 144-147
    teaching moments, 295, 296
  identification of, 290-291
  minimizing present harm
    giving of oneself, 306
    relaxation, 304-305
    self-reliant attitude, 304
    spirituality, 305-306
    strong self-image, 303-304
Emotions, guidelines for positive action,
  327
Emptiness, 279-281
  corrective action for, 280-281
  meaning of, 279-280
Enthusiasm, meaning of, 335
Escalante, Jaime, 7
Exercise, for stress control, 137-138

F

Failure
  fear of, 186-187
  imaginary failure, 329-330
Failure mechanism, 13
  correction of, 281-283
  examples of, 23-24, 259-262
  signs of
    aggressiveness, 267-270
    emptiness, 279-281
    frustration, 263-266
    insecurity, 270-272
    loneliness, 272-274
    resentment, 276-279

V

Valliant, George E., 320
Vertical longevity, 322-323
Visualization
  for creating new self-image, 60-61
  for depression, 35-36
  for reprogramming, 26-27
  steps in, 60-61, 63-64, 213
  for stress control, 125-128
  for success, 47-49, 58-60, 316

W

Wells, M.G., 209
Wiener, Norbert, 4

Willpower, 51, 53
Wishful thinking, trap of, 155-156
Women
  creating quality time with children,
    336-337
  multiple goals of, 239
  superwoman syndrome, 238-239
Wonder, Jacquelyn, 117
Workplace, relaxation exercises, 117
Writer's block, 99-100

Z

Zdenek, Marilee, 108
Zen breathing, for relaxation, 107-108
Ziglar, Zig, 151
Zmeskal, Kim, 316